ALSO BY JAMES GOODMAN

Stories of Scottsboro

Blackout

But Where Is the Lamb?

But Where Is the Lamb?

IMAGINING THE STORY OF

ABRAHAM AND ISAAC

JAMES GOODMAN

Schocken Books, New York

All rights reserved. Published in the United States by Schocken Books, a division of Random House, Inc., New York, and in Canada by Random House of Canada Limited, Toronto.

Schocken Books and colophon are registered trademarks of Random House, Inc.

Owing to limitations of space, permissions acknowledgments appear on pages 305–306.

Library of Congress Cataloging-in-Publication Data
Goodman, James E.
     But where is the lamb? Imagining the story of Abraham and Isaac / James E. Goodman.
          p. cm.
Includes index.
ISBN 978-0-8052-4253-9
   1. Isaac (Biblical patriarch)—Sacrifice.   2. Abraham (Biblical patriarch).   3. Bible. O.T. Genesis XXII, 1–19—Criticism, interpretation, etc.   I. Title.

BS1238.S24G66 2013
222'.1106—dc23   2012048124

www.schockenbooks.com

Jacket design by Pablo Delcán

Printed in the United States of America

First Edition

9 8 7 6 5 4 3 2 1

TO MY FATHER AND TO MY MOTHER,

WHOM I LOVE

And it happened after these things that God tested Abraham. And He said to him, "Abraham!" and he said, "Here I am." And He said, "Take, pray, your son, your only one, whom you love, Isaac, and go forth to the land of Moriah and offer him up as a burnt offering on one of the mountains which I shall say to you." And Abraham rose early in the morning and saddled his donkey and took his two lads with him, and Isaac his son, and he split wood for the offering, and rose and went to the place that God had said to him. On the third day Abraham raised his eyes and saw the place from afar. And Abraham said to his lads, "Sit you here with the donkey and let me and the lad walk ahead and let us worship and return to you." And Abraham took the wood for the offering and put it on Isaac his son and he took in his hand the fire and the cleaver, and the two of them went together. And Isaac said to Abraham his father, "Father!" and he said, "Here I am, my son." And he said, "Here is the fire and the wood but where is the sheep for the offering?" And Abraham said, "God will see to the sheep for the offering, my son." And the two of them went together. And they came to the place that God had said to him, and Abraham built there an altar and laid out the wood and bound Isaac his son and placed him on the altar on top of the wood. And Abraham reached out his hand and took the cleaver to slaughter his son. And the LORD's messenger called out to him from the heavens and said, "Abraham, Abraham!" and he said, "Here I am." And he said, "Do not reach out your hand against the lad, and do nothing to him, for now I know that you fear God and you have not held back your son, your only one, from Me." And Abraham raised his eyes and saw and, look, a ram was caught in the thicket by its horns, and Abraham went and took the ram and offered him up as a burnt offering instead of his son. And Abraham called the name of that

place YHWH-Yireh, as is said to this day, "On the mount of the
15 LORD there is sight." And the LORD's messenger called out to Abra-
16 ham once again from the heavens, and He said, "By My own Self
I swear, declares the LORD, that because you have done this thing
17 and have not held back your son, your only one, I will greatly bless
you and will greatly multiply your seed, as the stars in the heavens
and as the sand on the shore of the sea, and your seed shall take
18 hold of its enemies' gate. And all the nations of the earth will be
blessed through your seed because you have listened to my voice."
19 And Abraham returned to his lads, and they rose and went together
to Beersheba, and Abraham dwelled in Beersheba.

— Genesis 22:1–19

But Where Is the Lamb?

I

~~~~

I didn't think he'd do it.

I really didn't think he would.

I thought he'd say, whoa, hold on, wait a minute. We made a deal, remember, the land, the blessing, the nation, the descendants as numerous as the sands on the shore and the stars in the sky. You said: through Isaac you'd make my name great. I have kept my word. Don't you go back on yours.

He might not have put it precisely that way. He tended to say what he had to say more succinctly. But you know what I mean.

I didn't think he'd do it, certainly not without asking when, where, how, or why. Why should I sacrifice my son? I readily concede that he answered God's initial call without a moment's hesitation. That was undoubtedly among the reasons that he was so special to him. But I can't help thinking that he came to regret that he hadn't taken some time to consider what he was getting himself into. From then on, almost everything he said to God took the form of a question: a question about God's promise of greatness, a question about offspring and inheritance, a question about land, a question about the likelihood that a child could be born to a hundred-year-old man and his ninety-year-old wife, a question (in the form of a wish) about Ishmael, and most memorable of all a barrage of questions, pointed questions, no matter how humbly couched, about the innocent and the guilty of Sodom and Gomorrah.

So you can imagine my surprise when God asked Abraham to take Isaac to the land of Moriah and offer him up as a burnt offering, and Abraham didn't say a word. Not one word. One question after twenty-five years of questions is all it would have taken. He and God could have talked, and God could have explained what he was up to.

And remember: This is the guy God chose to show the world his way. To do what was just and right. Was Abraham always sure what God's way was? Of course not. Was he always sure that God's way was the right way? Not likely. Did he make mistakes? He did. For instance: he never should have given his wife, Sarah, to another man. Did he always learn from them? Who does? Several years later, he did it again. Did he have days he wished he could do over? Sure. That's literature. That's life. Who doesn't, including God? Remember when he promised not to destroy the innocent along with the guilty of Sodom, to forgive the city of sin for the sake of the good? Not long after, God's angels visited Abraham's nephew, Lot, and the citizenry of Sodom went after them, to a *man*. God reduced the place to cinder and ash, somehow neglecting to include the city's women and children in his calculation.

Still, on his worst day, I didn't think Abraham would do it, not without saying a word. At the very least I thought he'd stall for time, say, hey, wait, wait, give me a few minutes, and I'll get back to you, I simply need to talk it over with the boy's mother. Or, I thought, that in the hours between God's command and bedtime, or bedtime and morning, Sarah would have read God's command on her husband's face. Anyone who has followed the travail of the two of them since they left Ur for Canaan would know that that would have been the end of the matter right then and there.

But he didn't say a word. Not to God. Not to Sarah. Not to anyone. Instead, he rose up early the next morning, saddled his donkey, called for two servants and Isaac, his son. He split the wood and headed out. God led him on and on, made the journey three days, giving him plenty of time to think about it, to change his mind, to figure a way out. I thought one of his servants might catch on, and perhaps he did too. Abraham stopped—when he saw the place from afar—and said, you two stay here, with the donkeys. We'll be back after we go up and pray.

That left Isaac. Whether or not he knew it, he asked exactly the right question in exactly the right way. But Abraham reached deep, and somehow found a way to answer. And for all the awe that readers have expressed at his composure, the simple truth is that all Abraham had to do was not fall apart. Isaac was just a boy, thrilled to be on a special errand all alone with his father. He was not about to parse his father's words for hidden meanings.

Right up to the last moment, I thought, I hoped, I may even have prayed, that Abraham would protest: I can't do it, I can't. I obey you as I obeyed my own father, Terah, but Isaac: he is my son.

But he didn't.

And so God, through a messenger, had to stop him himself: "Do not reach out your hand against the lad, and do nothing to him, for now I know that you fear God and you have not held back your son, your only one, from me."

I was stunned. It was not at all what I had anticipated. I had no illusions about God, not after Adam and Eve, Cain and Abel, the Great Flood, and the Tower of Babel. (I have never been persuaded that the citizens of that apparently peaceful place, working together and getting along, had done anything wrong.) Nor confidence that I could predict his behavior or fathom what he was thinking. Still, I harbored a sneaking suspicion that it was not what God had anticipated either. But what could he do? He tried to make the best of a difficult situation, adjust on the fly, cut his losses and Abraham's too. Look forward. Move on. Try not to let one bad day spoil the rewards of a good long life. Sometimes events take unexpected turns, even when you are thought to have everything under control.

And what could I do? I was just a reader who thought the story had come out wrong. And a son, like Isaac, who had to try to make sense of and peace with a difficult father. And a Jew, like any Jew who gives any thought to Jewish experience, past or present, who had to decide what to make of, and do with, an enormous inheritance, an inheritance that includes nearly three thousand of years of history, literature, ritual, and law. And a father, another difficult father, who had to figure out what part or parts of that inheritance I wanted to try to pass on to my sons. And a skeptic, by nature and nurture resistant to things we believe simply because (it is said) they have always been believed, things we do simply because they've always been done. And a historian, uncomfortable with the idea that the way things are is the only way they could possibly be. And, as if that weren't enough, a lover of stories, driven to show and share the power and beauty of stories, sometimes even terrible stories. And to do that showing and sharing at a most inopportune time, a time (like so many times) when not a day goes by when someone somewhere doesn't commit some horrible atrocity in the name of the God of Abraham and Isaac, in the name of their scripture or revelation, making it all the more challenging to convey my appreciation for those stories and their history, or even to answer those who see nothing but the dark side, the undeniable dark side, of their long lives.

Happily, I was also a writer, and every writer knows that sometimes a character gets away from you, surprises you, takes on a life of his or her own, even when you think you have a handle on him, even when you appear to be pulling all the strings. Sometimes an entire story gets away from you. It is an occupational hazard, all the more (if you'll pardon a mixed metaphor and then bear with me for a few pages of speculation) when you are called in, as I imagine the author of the story of the near sacrifice was called in, like a relief pitcher, late in the game, without an outline, or even clear signals from the catcher, to finish someone else's story.

So you see, I was a reader, a son, a Jew, a father, a skeptic, a historian, a lover of stories, and a writer. I had no choice, or little choice. Tradition virtually compelled me to write the story of Abraham and Isaac.

~~~~~

2

He was a writer. Of that I am sure.

The rest I am left to imagine. Everyone is.

Here goes:

He was a writer. Some readers have called him a "dictator," by which they (at least the sympathetic ones) mean "one who dictates." Remember, his was still largely an oral culture. The point is that he did what writers do: he made things out of words: put them down, moved them around, added some, took others away, decided which ones had to go and which should stay.

He was, however, no ordinary writer.

To begin with, he was not driven to publish. Precious little of his work has seen the light of day. For every word he published, there were thousands, perhaps tens of thousands, he just discarded, or filed away. Believe me when I tell you that most of what has been attributed to him was the work of others.

What he did publish he published under other people's names, or no one's name at all. Today he would be called a ghostwriter, though he did it for love, not money. He worked behind the scenes—I picture him at a small table in a small room, a bare bright room with big windows looking out on the universe—helping writers who, for one reason or another, were unable to help themselves. In the spirit of the biblical scholars, I will call him G.

Now, obviously G couldn't help every writer in need. For one thing, he wasn't interested in every writer's project. What writer would be? I know historians who don't read fiction, let alone write it. They can't understand why anyone would waste their time reading stories that aren't true. I know poets who read only poetry. I know fiction writers who think "nonfiction" is the Latin word for "memoir." No other form of experience-based prose ever penetrates their literary airspace. G was partial to short stories, family history, and brief lives. When he was young, he dabbled in poetry. He steered clear, despite ample opportunity and plenty of evidence he'd be good at it, of the law.

Even if he had been interested, he would not have had the time. The portrait of an artist in Exodus, dictating from the mountaintop, is magnificently drawn. And it makes me, for one, green with envy, for I know that there are writers out there who, despite every kind of distraction (on Sinai there were pillars of fire and clouds of smoke and enough thunder to make the earth tremble, and between thunder cracks the deafening blast of trumpets), work in white heat, without sleep, at breakneck speed, and (with apparent ease) somehow manage to get it right the first time.

But G was not one of them. Words did not come easy to him. Not the kinds of words that ended up on stone, clay tablets, animal hides, and papyrus. Or even the words read on special occasions in the public square. He could talk up a storm. But there is a big difference between speaking words and writing them. Spoken sentences don't have to be grammatical. They don't even have to be sentences, and they don't have to come in any particular order or lead neatly and logically from one place to another. The truth is that he could, and often did, go around in circles for long periods of time before the people he was speaking to even noticed. And even when they did notice, most didn't mind, because they were busy and his rambling on and on freed them to do other things with their time.

And if, as he talked, he saw them stiffen, frown, wince, shake, groan, glare, or just stare at him without the slightest glimmer of interest, sympathy, or comprehension, he could revise on the fly.

And if he got a word, phrase, sentence, or even an entire passage that was not quite right, or even completely wrong, he hadn't scratched his sentiments or self into stone or a copper scroll that was going to outlive him by thousands of years. They were gone, like the breath that delivered them. And all he had to do was take another breath and try again, with different words or a different tone, or from a different point of view.

Written words are another matter. You know what I am talking about if you have ever tried to spend a day, let alone one day after another, trying to make sentences meant to be read, trying to find just the right word, out of all the words out there, and put them in just the right order. To say enough without saying too much, to leave room for readers to breathe and wander without leaving them lost or bewildered, wondering what's happening and what it means. Everywhere but his writing table everything was so clear. Words came to him in well-turned phrases, which attached themselves to others to make paragraphs with winning beginnings, middles, and ends. But the moment he tried to put them down, they scattered, or came at him so fast he could not possibly keep pace. In the end, they rarely looked as nice, or sounded as sweet, on the page as they first sounded in his head. Hours passed, and every good line seemed like a miracle.

Oh, you write beautifully, he'd hear people say. As if writing beautifully were like being beautiful, or tall, something you are by birth, not something you have to work at. And he'd think: You have never seen a line I've written before I've revised it fifty times. You don't see a page or even a paragraph that hasn't taken dozens of different forms. And those are just the words you see. You can't imagine and don't want to know how many complete sentences, pages, chapters, you will never see, earlier versions in which the voice was wrong or the perspective was wrong or the language or imagery or sound of the words was wrong—or, and this may be the most painful of all, something was wrong he could hear or feel but not name.

It was hard work, and there was no shortage of writers in need. He had to be choosy. But there were some projects that had his name written all over them, and the story of Abraham was one of them.

I don't have a clue who asked him for help, just a hunch what they asked for. A writer or several writers, perhaps a whole team of writers, had written a history, or saga, about a man, his family, and a God. The God approached the man, born Abram, out of the blue, and offered him a deal. Follow me, walk in my way, do what I say, and I'll take care of you. Good care. Really good care. Not just you, but your children, and your children's children, my blessing, a great nation.

Think of it as an insurance policy, full life, plus annuity, fully transferable not just to a few designated beneficiaries but to all of his descendants, through the ages. The first premium was migration. Abram paid it, no questions asked, and almost immediately he discovered that, as always, there was fine print, and in the fine print, gaps in the coverage. The first was famine. Abram left Canaan for Egypt, where, worried about his well-being despite all those promises, he told his wife, Sarah, to say she was his sister, in the hope that Pharaoh would take her and spare his life. Pharaoh did, and God had to bail them out, but that wasn't the last of Abram's troubles. He had to deal with quarrelsome shepherds, warring kings, and his well-meaning but ne'er-do-well nephew, Lot. He had to deal with his and Sarah's difficulty getting pregnant, with the conflict between Sarah and Sarah's maidservant Hagar after he (at Sarah's suggestion) conceived a child with Hagar, with sin in Sodom, with several harrowing misunderstandings with Abimelech, king of Gerar, and with more trouble between Sarah and Hagar after his and Sarah's son Isaac was born. Along the way there were additional premiums, or demands, most notably a name change, from Abram to Abraham, and circumcision at ninety-nine.

Don't let me give you the wrong impression. There were good days, many good days, glorious days. Imagine how Abraham must have felt on his way out of Egypt, escaping from his first close encounter with the Egyptians, not just with his life and his wife, but with a generous portion of Pharaoh's livestock, silver, and gold. Or on his way back to Hebron after rescuing Lot from the alliance of kings who had overrun the cities of the plain. Or as he quizzed God about his plans to destroy those same cities and God seemed to understand what he was saying about justice.

But those bright moments could be short-lived. I think often of the morning, just a few days after that conversation with God, when Abraham stood on the very same spot, a hillside above Sodom, and got a good look at the fate of those who crossed him. Smoke rose from the ashes as if from a kiln.

Inevitably he had questions: When God promises greatness, Abraham asks how. When God promises land, he asks how he would know it was his. When God promises Isaac, Abraham laughs (though it is Sarah's laugh, a little later, that most people remember) and then asks about Ishmael. Inevitably there were misunderstandings. One does not get to know and understand a brand-new God in a day. There were days of doubt and perhaps even regret. Covenant regret. All the more when that God, at once demanding and mercurial, assumes he is completely in charge.

And though we don't know what God was thinking, it would not be wholly unnatural if over time Abraham's doubts became self-fulfilling, generating doubts in God. What was I thinking? Is this guy the real thing? I've got a lot riding on this. Is this another dead end? He is generous. He is magnanimous. He is a magnificent host and a skilled diplomat. When conflict or even the possibility of it arises with his nephew, with neighboring landowners, with powerful political figures, he shrewdly trades land and wealth and even water wells for good feeling and peace. Most important, he does everything that I ask. On the other hand, there is no end to his questions.

This goes on for many years, but it can't go on forever. The man and his wife are getting old and it doesn't take a prophet to figure out that there is a lot of history to come between the end of their lives and the realization of God's promises. One descendant might have been delivered quickly, though he wasn't. But nation building takes generations, and it was time to move on. And the author did move on. After Sarah and Abraham expelled Hagar and Ishmael, Sarah died, and Abraham arranged for her burial, secured a wife for Isaac, remarried, had additional children, and died peacefully and happily of old age.

But either that writer, or group of writers, or more likely his or their editors, or maybe even editors working later (the distinction between writer and editor was much fuzzier in those days than it is today), were not satisfied. There was one action-packed scene after another, and plenty of worry and wonder about whether and when and how God's promises would be realized. But there was nothing to tie it all together. The editors wanted something, somewhere, a scene or series of scenes, a story within a story, to connect the story's past and the story's future. Without that scene, without some sort of climax, they feared that readers might feel as if the story didn't end, but just faded away.

They knew where they wanted to go. but not how to get there, and that's when they came to G. He jumped at the opportunity. What writer wouldn't have? It's a great story, a gripping family saga that took on, in the most unabashed way, some of the great issues of its day, of any day—migration and dislocation; family, sex, and marriage; sibling rivalry and inheritance; might, inequality, and right; crime and punishment; war and diplomacy; honesty and duplicity; jealousy, love, fear, death, doubt, and belief—all complicated by the comings and goings, the commands and the promises, the blessings and curses of an unfamiliar and mysterious God.

G liked what he read but agreed with them that something was missing. After several readings, he even had a hunch about where it should go. You can see it for yourself simply by plotting the events in Abraham's life on a time line. He was seventy-five, Sarah sixty-five, when God called them out of Haran. They traveled to Canaan, then Egypt, then back. A decade passed. Twice God emphatically renewed his promise, yet Abraham remained childless. That's when Sarah suggested he sleep with her maidservant. A year later, Ishmael was born. Another decade passed, thirteen years to be precise. Abraham was ninety-nine when God promised him Isaac, commanded circumcision, and destroyed Sodom and Gomorrah. About a year later, Isaac was born and Ishmael and Hagar were cast out.

Next thing we know, Sarah dies—at the age of 127. And we are led to believe, or expected to believe, that after all those things nothing worthy of note happened between the expulsion of Hagar and the death of Sarah except an easily managed conflict with Abimelech over a few wells. A gap of thirty-seven years. I suppose from a purely practical point of view the structure is just fine. Isaac, the child of God's promise, is alive and well. Ishmael is out of the way (though not so far out, in body or mind, that he does not later join his brother at their father's funeral). Abraham is getting along with his Canaanite neighbors The author could move on to Rebekah, Esau, and Jacob. But if the stories of Abraham and all the stories after them were all work and no play, all function and no form, they would not have taken as many pages to tell or turned out as magnificently as they did.

That is not to suggest G had an easy time of it. At first, he too was unsure how to proceed. He knew it had to be short. The story was already long and in places repetitious, with some of the repetition essential and some not. It had to be dramatic, but not so dramatic that it changed the course of the entire saga, parts of which had (apparently) already been written. It had to reveal something essential about Abraham and his relationship to God, and he had some ideas about that, good ideas he thought, but all the good ideas in the world do not necessarily make one good story, and anyone who has been through it will know what it was like, and probably prefer not to think about it: how many false starts he had, how many times, after getting a second and third line down, he thought, Yes, that's it, I've got it, only to look back later and realize that *it* wasn't it at all.

Even after he decided to make it a test and got the form of the first line right, he couldn't get Abraham's response right. He was certain that he would say something, but he could not figure out what or how, and until he could figure that out, he couldn't move on. It was only after God called and Abraham said simply, "Here I am," and God commanded and Abraham said absolutely nothing, and then rose early the next morning and still said nothing, that the words started to flow, and not as they usually did, in fits and starts, but smoothly, as if some much more fluid writer than he was moving his hand.

And they flowed in a wholly unexpected direction.

And yet he liked the way it came out. He liked the way the opening—your son, your only one, whom you love, Isaac—echoed in language and theme so much of what had come before, starting with God's call—Go forth from your land, from your birthplace, your father's house. He liked the way the plot—the sudden threat and ultimate resolution—at once paralleled and recast and advanced so much of what had come before. He liked God's utter (and very human) capriciousness and Abraham's inhuman intensity (and guile). He liked the pace, the economy, the suspense, the combination of crystal-clear surface and unfathomable depth. He liked (and you tell me what writer wouldn't give something precious in exchange for?) the perfect pathos of Isaac's question about the lamb. He liked the sound of the words and, even more, the space between them, the gaps, the silences. He had imagined the story would be short, but he never imagined that it would be *so* short, or that so much of its impact would come from what wasn't there. He read the lines over and over, aloud, and he would not have been too embarrassed to admit that he was hypnotized by the sound of his own voice.

He made one copy and passed it on to his editors, telling them, "Here's my latest draft. I am still working on it." Then he took a break. He wanted to come at it a few days hence, with a fresh set of eyes. He did, and as so often happens, the spell had worn off. Here I have to be honest, or at least careful. I don't want to let all that has gone down since distort my report. He still liked it, as a story, as words on the page, elegantly arranged. It was a good start, but he wasn't finished. There were things, big things, wrong with it. In the context of the life of Abraham alone, it was deeply flawed. He couldn't leave him or it as they were. He went back to work and came up with a new version, a version he was much happier with.

But it was too late.

The writers he was working for, to a man, liked the draft he shared as much as he had liked it, at first maybe more, but without any of his subsequent reservations.

"Look," G said, "I like it too. But it's no good. Abraham's silence is all wrong."

"Wrong?" they said.

"Wrong that he just set out," he said.

"Wrong that he obeyed God?"

"Not that kind of wrong," G said. "Or not just that kind." He knew that people could disagree about that. They did then. They still do today.

"What other kind is there?"

"I mean I got Abraham wrong. I got Abraham wrong as a character, inside the story. Even if God had wanted him to saddle his donkey, and call for his servants and Isaac, and split the wood, all without saying a word, it was not like Abraham not to say a word. Even if you have no other qualms about his silence, you must admit that it was not consistent with his character."

"Character?" they said. "You are saying that it was out of character for Abraham to do what God commanded?"

"Yes," he said. "His first words to God were a question. His last were a question. And God's last words to him before he asked him to offer Isaac were in answer to his question about Ishmael, meant to reassure him that he would take good care of his firstborn too. It's just not right. Leave it like it is and it will be obvious to everyone that this story doesn't belong."

"He left home without saying a word," they said.

"Yes. He did. I admit it. But think about it: he was a semi-nomad already on his way to Canaan. The command to keep moving was not of the same magnitude or significance as the command to sacrifice his son."

"You are overanalyzing," they said.

They would not think of revising it in any significant way.

3

~~~

He protested. He implored. He pleaded. "The story could be, would be, terribly misunderstood," he said. His pleas—we can deduce—fell on deaf ears. There was nothing he could do. But he was not good at doing nothing, so he tried to go back to work. But he couldn't. Every time he sat down to write, he thought of the story and he couldn't think of the story without thinking about the other ways it might have come out. He tried reading, to take his mind off it, but no matter whom he read, no matter what he read about, the sound of the words, the look of the words, the order of the words, made him think of writing, and writing made him think of his writing, and his writing made him think of Abraham and Isaac. And he couldn't think about Abraham and Isaac without a huge wave of restlessness and regret.

Days passed, months, then years. His wife encouraged him to move on, to look forward, not back. It seemed to her that he was letting one disappointment, however large it loomed, spoil the many satisfactions of a pretty good literary life. But he was distraught and didn't even want to talk about it.

The men he had written for, on the other hand, talked about nothing else. They were jubilant, so proud of the final product. They sent him a copy and urged him to read it. They urged everyone to read it.

He couldn't even look at it.

His friends did too.

"Have you read it?"

"I can't," he said.

"Oh, you should. You won't be able to put it down."

"I can't bear to," he said.

"Why not?"

"My story."

"Your story?"

"The story of Abraham and Isaac."

"Which one?"

"The sacrifice story. It came out all wrong."

G's friend shrugged. "It is a great big book," he said, "a huge anthology of the literature of Israel." And it was: not all of it by any means, but the work the editors considered the best of it. There was—in addition to legend—genealogy, biography, and history. There were legal codes, cultic rituals and regulations, poetry, even the lyrics to some songs.

"You should read it," G's friend said. "There is some remarkable writing in there."

He couldn't and didn't.

He ate. He slept. He went to his table but never stayed for long. He walked more. He talked less. His wife was worried. Nothing she could say or do was the right thing to say or do, until what she did, whether out of frustration, or exasperation, or simple curiosity, was to start reading the book herself. She was a fast reader, and in no time she had read it from beginning to end. At which time she joined his friends and editors in urging him to read it himself.

"I can't," he said.

"Why not?" she asked.

"My story."

"Your story?"

"Abraham and Isaac. It will be terribly misunderstood. I can't even think about it."

"It's not two dozen lines," she said. A small part of Abraham's story, which is itself just a small part of whole. It is completely overshadowed by Creation and the Great Flood that comes before it, and after by the saga of Esau and Jacob and Laban and Jacob's wives and his sons, Joseph and all his brothers. Then the drama of slavery and liberation and revelation and forty years of wandering in the wilderness.

"Yes," he said, "but it's the climax, the pivotal moment of Abraham's life."

"Maybe so," she said, "but if it makes you feel any better, you should know that it doesn't seem to have left a lasting impression." In all the history that follows, despite more references than anyone could count to the God of Abraham and Isaac and Jacob and God's covenant with Abraham, Isaac, and Jacob and the land God promised to Abraham, Isaac, and Jacob, there is not one explicit reference to—she paused for emphasis—"your story."

"No mention?" he asked.

"No."

"Not one?"

"Not that I noticed."

That surprised him, and it was only then that he took a look for himself. At first he just scrolled through the book, a passage here, a passage there. Skimming or scanning the way, today, you might see a scholar searching to see if he'd been cited in another book's footnotes or bibliography or thanked in the acknowledgments. Then he scrolled some more. He was a slow reader, but very thorough, and in a few days of searching he found a handful of passages that might conceivably be interpreted as allusions to Abraham's story. One of the authors of the chapters on Isaac's son Jacob refers, cryptically, to the "terror of Isaac." And though he could imagine someone arguing that the phrase was nothing more than a synonym for the "God of Isaac," he had a hard time believing that it was just a coincidence that, with hundreds of references to the God of this and the God of that, it was only when referring to Isaac that the words "God of Isaac" became "terror of Isaac." Elsewhere, God tells Isaac that he would bless him because his father had listened to his voice and obeyed his commandments. And much later Moses reminds God of his promises to Abraham, Isaac, and Jacob, going so far as to mention multiplying Abraham's "seed like the stars of the heavens" and giving his seed all the land forever. He even notes that God himself swore those promises—"You swore by Yourself"—as God had sworn atop Moriah. But Abraham had done many things God asked, and God had made many promises. However clear those allusions seemed to G, or seem to me, in neither instance is there an explicit reference to Abraham's seeming willingness to sacrifice his son. Even in the books that recount the history after Moses and the crossing of the Jordan—the annals of the judges and the kings, the chronicles of the fall of Israel and later Judah, exile and return, then chapter after chapter of prophetic literature, wisdom literature, lots more poetry and song—there is still only fleeting mentions of Abraham and only oblique references to the story of Abraham and Isaac.

She was right. He had to admit it. He also had to make sure she understood that when it came time to decide what to include and where it should go, the anthology's editors had obviously been more concerned with portraying Israel's history as a nation, and ultimately a nation under one God, than with its literary history. Unlike the editors of most modern anthologies of literature, they did not necessarily organize the contributions chronologically. We don't know for certain which parts of the anthology, or even which parts of which parts of the anthology, were written when. G suspected that at least some of what came after his story had been written before it. If large parts of it had been written before, it might mean nothing that it wasn't referred to again.

"It may be that it was not referred to," G said, "because it was not there to refer to. I hadn't written it yet."

"Now you sound sorry," she said. "One minute you moan about how the story came out, about being read and misunderstood. The next you regret not being noticed."

And she was right again. The truth is that he was not wholly without an ego. For all his reservations, when push came to shove, he didn't want to be completely ignored. "What writer wouldn't be a little sorry?" he said.

"Maybe a writer who wrote a story about a father who nearly sacrificed his son—when it is entirely possible that God expected him to object, or at least stop the sacrifice himself," she said.

"Thanks," he said. "I got it wrong. I wanted to revise it. You know I did."

"Relax," she said. "If and when readers do notice, they will do it themselves."

"Do what?"

"They'll revise it."

"Revise it?"

"Yes. They'll revise it. They seem unable not to. Read it. The whole thing, and you will see for yourself."

So he did. He read, several hours a day for several weeks, and he saw. He saw exactly what she meant. With all due respect, it took careful reading, but no prophetic powers. If all you had in your hands was the anthology—no later translations into Aramaic, Greek, Latin, Syriac, Coptic, Arabic, or Persian—no commentary, no theories about how the book was put together, or when or by whom, no inside knowledge of the degree to which editors revised as they combined, juxtaposed, and synthesized writings produced by different schools or different traditions in different places at different times—nothing but the writings themselves, you would know it. You would know that this was one revisionary people.

They revised to elaborate, revised to elucidate, revised to answer questions, revised to interpret, revised to criticize, to accentuate, to update, to differentiate, and to explain. They revised myth, legend, and history. They revised rituals and regulations. They revised legal codes and even commandments (there are two versions of the Ten Commandments). They revised critical elements of their theology. They revised the names of people and places, including the name of the mountain where God gave Moses the Ten Commandments.

They revised the physical relationship between God and the people at Sinai (or Horeb). They revised the name of God.

Now, one might suspect that a people so bent on revising had no reverence for tradition. But just the opposite is true. These people revered tradition so deeply that they did whatever they had to do to keep it alive. So when times and ideas and circumstances and sensibilities changed, they revised it. But even when they revised it dramatically, hoping to substitute one tradition for another, even one image of God for another, the writers and editors—whether priestly editors or scribal editors or prophets or judges or kings or maybe even queens—did not believe that they had the right, or the authority, or the power, to excise that which they were revising or presenting an alternative to.

We don't know, especially for the early years, what got left on the cutting-room floor, or exactly which writers and editors did what to which texts. But one thing is clear: if the editors had been intent on imposing their view, a single view, a party line, intent upon covering up conflicting perspectives, we would not have had the book—then in many scrolls—that G had in front of him. Nor would I have the book I have in front of me today, in anything remotely resembling its current form.

We would not have both Chronicles and the parts of Samuel and Kings it revises. We would not have Deuteronomy and the parts of Exodus (and Numbers and perhaps even Leviticus) it revises. Or all of Deuteronomy, for in several significant ways that book revises, or records multiple traditions, itself. We would not have two versions of Creation, two versions of the Flood, two versions of the rebellion in the wilderness, two versions of Jacob obtaining Shechem, or, closer to home, two versions of God's covenant with Abraham, two versions of the expulsion of Hagar and Ishmael, three versions of Abraham or Isaac giving their wives to a pharaoh or king. In sum, we would not have multiple versions of more stories, and pieces of stories, and laws, and rituals, and reasons for laws and rituals, than anyone could possibly keep track of. Nor would we have so much evidence of the different perspectives, in time and over time, that marked the development of theology and law: Was Israel holy or did it simply aspire to holiness? Was the god of Abraham, Isaac, and Jacob one god of many or the one and only? Was God merciful or just or both? Did God hear Israel's prayers, accept their sacrifices, wherever they were offered, or only in one sacred place? Did we observe the Sabbath to mark Creation or the liberation from Egypt?

If revisionists had been nonchalant about tradition, let alone hostile to it, we would know only the end of the story, not how the nation got there, and the book would have been a small fraction of the length that it is.

What did all that mean for G? These people, his people, revised, but they didn't erase. "Face to face the Lord spoke to you on the mountain out of the fire," Moses says in one famous line of Deuteronomy. "I stood between the Lord and you at that time to convey the Lord's words to you, for you were afraid of the fire and did not go up the mountain," he says in the next. G liked the story but deeply regretted its meaning. He regretted its meaning but didn't want to discourage people from reading it. It was in the anthology—a great book if there ever was one—to stay, but if at any time people took note of it and were bothered by it, they would revise it. Maybe his children, maybe his children's children, maybe their children after them. Sooner or later, someone would revise it.

4

~~~~

And G's wife was right.

Someone did revise it.

Just not as G had hoped, for it soon became clear that his editors were not the only readers or writers at peace with Abraham's response to God's call.

Consider one of the first surviving revisions of the story, the one that came in the book of Jubilees, a revision of the entire early history, from Creation to Moses. It appeared in the second century BCE and took its name from the calendar reform the author advocated. He wanted to date all of Jewish history (every momentous event, every festival, every birth, and every death) precisely, dividing all time into Jubilees, periods of forty-nine years made up of seven segments of seven solar years.

It may be somewhat misleading to call Jubilees a revision. Every indication is that its author (whom I am going to call Jubilees for the sake of simplicity) or his editor or publisher thought of it as the original. I don't know who believed that. But those who did, however devout, were not seasoned readers. Except in the places, and there are many of them, where the author borrowed verbatim, his voice was different, his style was different, his point of view was different (the biblical narrator is omniscient; Jubilees's is Gabriel, God's angel of presence, channeling God and dictating to Moses on Sinai), his obsessions (among them the calendar and the end

of time) were different. Most pertinent, his Abraham was different, different from the Abraham in the pages of the book we call
Genesis.

If I have persuaded you of anything—just one thing—I hope
I have persuaded you that Abraham was one complicated character. Seventy-five years old and he hitched his wagon to a God
who appeared out of nowhere and said next to nothing about who
he was, where he'd come from, or how he expected Abraham to
behave. It was a bumpy ride and three decades later Abraham was
still trying to figure out what he had gotten himself into.

G's hope and expectation was that readers coming along later
would see that Abraham's response to God's command was out of
character. That they'd ask, "Would he have set out without saying a word?" But what Jubilees saw as out of character were large
chunks of the chapters that came before. His Abraham was born
halfway between Ur and heaven, with an instinctive sense of how to
get the rest of the way. Even as a small boy, he understood (in addition to advanced astronomy and agronomy) the errors of the earth,
especially idol worship and uncleanliness. He urged his father to
embrace the one true God, and when all else failed, he set fire to
the house where Terah's man-made gods were stored. Most strik-
ingly, in Jubilees's telling, Abraham approached God to talk about
a covenant—not the other way around. Like the biblical Abraham,
Jubilees's Abraham occasionally had doubts, but he never gave his
wife to a pharaoh or king (she was taken from him), laughed at
anything God said, or questioned God's judgment, not even about
the sinners in Sodom.

Some will say the makeover was predictable. Abraham was a
founder, and though writers occasionally gain a few minutes of
fame and a small fortune by debunking founders, the surer path,
at least over time, is to turn them into saints. Jubilees was hardly
the first or only writer of his age to apply posthumous polish to a
portrait, not even the first to apply it to Abraham. The author of
Nehemiah, a fourth-century BCE text and one of last books to be

added to the anthology, jumped right from Creation to Abraham, and what he found worthy of note was that Abraham had done exactly what God had asked him to do. Ben Sira, whose extremely influential book of wisdom, composed early in the second century BCE, was ultimately not included in the Jewish canon, gave Abraham pride of place in his passages praising famous men. Sira called him "the great father of a multitude of nations," who, when tested, was found faithful, by which Sira meant obedient and devoted, inclined to walk in God's way.

Then there was the book of Judith, another second-century composition, a gripping work of historical fiction about a beautiful and devout widow—she feared God with great devotion—who used her good looks and charm to single-handedly turn back a brutal siege by Holofernes, a commander in the army of the neo-Babylonian king Nebuchadnezzar. Holofernes's troops had surrounded the Israelites and seized their springs and wells. The streets were littered with the bodies of the dead and dying. The people urged their leaders to surrender, and some of them promised to do so if God didn't show his mercy in five days. Judith would have none of it. She exhorted her fellow citizens not to give God a deadline, not to put him to the test, not to bind his purposes, not to think they could know him or move him as they might an ordinary man. Instead, they should simply be strong to the bitter end: "In spite of everything let us give thanks to the Lord our God, who is putting us to the test as he did our forefathers. Remember what he did with Abraham, and how he tested Isaac . . . For he has not tried us with fire, as he did them, to search their hearts."

Jubilees worked in an adoring tradition. (One poet, a contemporary, boasted that he had heard the story of the "far-famed Abraham" "a thousand times.") Still, Jubilees did as much to elaborate upon and advance that tradition as anyone in his day whose work has survived. His Abraham simply could not have looked better in what Jubilees imagined were God's eyes. Yet his purity and goodness were problematic when it came to the biblical version of the story. If Abraham recognized the one true God from infancy and never wavered, if absolute obedience was his defining trait, the story's first line makes no sense. Why would God need to test him? And, by Jubilees's time, that question rubbed up against another: Even if Abraham wasn't such an angel, why would God need to test him or anyone else? What about Abraham wouldn't Jubilees's all-knowing God know?

Well, Jubilees was nothing if not inventive, and daring, an exegetical escape artist, able to wiggle out of every imaginable jam. He answered those questions by employing a character he'd introduced much earlier in his story, Prince Mastema, a dark fallen angel, a character he may have first encountered in Job. Mastema was jealous of all the swooning over Abraham in heaven, all the talk about his faithfulness despite affliction. So he taunted God, suggesting that Abraham loved Isaac above all else. He told God to test him, to see just how devoted to God he really was.

Now, Jubilees's God was no fool. He knew that Abraham had proved himself through many trials and tribulations: he had left his home, suffered famine, nearly lost his wife to a pharaoh and his nephew to cantankerous kings. He had submitted to circumcision and sacrificed his older son, Ishmael, and Ishmael's mother to the strong will of his wife. "And," Jubilees wrote, "in everything through which he tested him he was found faithful. He himself did not grow impatient, nor was he slow to act; for he was faithful and one who loved the Lord." (Note that the Abraham of old loved Isaac and obeyed God. Love of God, Abraham's and everyone else's, comes a little later in the story.)

So why did God ask him to sacrifice Isaac? Jubilees shows us, but not until after his Abraham rose early, saddled his ass, split the wood, called for Isaac and his lads, and set out on his three-day journey. With Gabriel and Mastema at his side, God watched as Abraham built the altar, placed the wood on it, bound Isaac, placed him on the wood, and stretched forth his hand to take the knife to slay his son. Only then did God tell Gabriel to tell Abraham to stop.

Why?

In Genesis, God's messenger says: "Now I know that you fear me." But in Jubilees's revision we hear God's instructions, and in those instructions God deleted the "now": "Tell him not to let his hand go down on the child and not to do anything to him, because I know that he is one who fears the Lord."

So Gabriel called from heaven and said, "Abraham! Abraham!" Abraham was startled and said, "Yes?"

Gabriel said: "Do not lay your hands on the child and do not do anything to him, because now I know that you are one who fears the Lord. You have not refused me your first-born son."

Note the return of the "now": coming out of Gabriel's mouth it causes no trouble. If someone now knows something about Abraham that he didn't know before, it is Gabriel and Mastema and the other angels. And sure enough, "the prince of the Mastema was put to shame." And Abraham lifted up his eyes and looked and, behold, he saw a single ram caught by his horns, and Abraham went and took the ram and offered it as a burnt offering instead of his son.

Then, just to make sure that there was no misunderstanding about what God knew and when he knew it, Jubilees altered God's blessing: "All the nations of the earth will be blessed through your descendants because of the fact that you have obeyed my command. I have made known to everyone that you are faithful to me in everything that I have told you. Go in peace." Here Jubilees's trick is the "to everyone," which ensured that the verb "YDTY" would be read as *yidda'tî* ("I have made known") and not *yāda'tî* ("I know"). Biblical Hebrew has no vowels. Without them, Jubilees's "YDTY" could have been pronounced and understood either way. But not when it was followed by "to everyone." We don't "know something" to everyone. We make something known to everyone. We show them.

Jubilees's God knew everything. He was not testing Abraham. He was demonstrating his devotion.

Now let me make it clear just in case it is not. Jubilees was not some woolly-headed religious reformer, softening up God, looking for an end run around religious observance. Or an irreverent writer having fun with sacred characters. Just the opposite: he was a serious fellow, a revivalist at a time when the attitudes, values, ideas, language, even customs and manners that Philip of Macedon and his son Alexander had brought from the West were taking root in Near Eastern sand and soil. I imagine Jubilees speaking to Jews so smitten by Greek ways that they had begun to wonder if they really had to observe all those tiresome commandments in order to be good Jews. Trying to bring the wayward back into the fold, Jubilees stressed the primacy of law and ritual observance. He wrote and revised to show that the law, particularly the calendar, the schedule of festivals, was manifest in the early chapters of biblical narrative as well as in the later chapters that are explicitly concerned with cultic rules and regulations.

Jubilees's Abraham offered Isaac on the fifteenth day of the first month, the same day of the year that Jews in Egypt would later sacrifice a lamb to keep the Destroyer away from their firstborn. He thereby located the origins of the paschal offering in the religious life of the first Jew. His Abraham marked the near sacrifice with a seven-day festival (three days from Beersheba to Moriah, three days back, one day for Sabbath), a festival that just happened to coincide with the seven-day festival Jubilees knew (and we know) as Passover. In his telling, the connection between the events and their commemorations was not the least bit forced: Sarah's firstborn son, and with him Israel's future, was delivered from the machinations of Mastema and redeemed with a lamb. Later, the Jewish people, God's firstborn, were delivered from the Destroyer by the blood of the lamb. The lesson was clear: Obey his laws, do what he tells you to do, and God will take care of you. Abraham observed Passover. You should too.

5

<center>~~~~</center>

Jubilees took Abraham's obedience for granted. What needed to be explained was God's command. For Philo, a stoic Jewish philosopher living in Alexandria two centuries later (in the first half of the first century of the Common Era), it was the other way around. If Philo wondered why God asked, or was troubled that he did, he never let on. His attention, like mine, was focused on Abraham's response.

But there we part ways. He was as comfortable as Jubilees was with Abraham's obedience. His project was to explain it, show what it was made of, part of his larger project of demonstrating, in one fell swoop, the greatness of the Jewish tradition and its universal relevance, the harmony between the written law of Moses and the philosopher's unwritten natural law. You see, Philo shared Jubilees's devotion to Judaism but not his aversion to Hellenism. What he did was take Abraham's obedience and translate it into Greek.

God commanded, and Abraham obeyed.

No whining, as Abraham had whined when God said he was going to make his name great and he asked how: How will I be great when I am going to die childless?

No anxious questions, like those Abraham had asked when God promised land and he asked how he was going to know that it was really his.

No qualms, like those Abraham had expressed when God

announced his intention to destroy Sodom, or divided devotion: remember when God promised a son through Sarah and Abraham responded by saying that he hoped that Ishmael would live in God's favor.

No hesitation: I am thinking of the moment Sarah told him to send Ishmael away.

God commanded and Abraham obeyed. Abraham's fondness for the boy—his only legitimate son, the child of his old age, a wonderful boy—was indescribable. Yet Abraham "showed no change of color nor weakening of soul, but remained steadfast as ever with a judgment that neither bent nor wavered." He simply set out to do what God had asked him to do. Isaac's question about the lamb would have reduced most men to tears, or struck them dumb. Either way, Isaac would have known where the lamb was. Not Abraham. He didn't alter his voice, his countenance, or his intention. He looked at his son with a steady eye, assured him that God would provide, and went about his business.

Philo loved the story. He considered it the greatest moment in a long life of great moments. He couldn't imagine a nobler example of the wise man suppressing emotion for the sake of reason, the reason that the stoic philosopher considered the unwritten law of nature and essence of God and the human soul.

Just one thing bothered him: not what Abraham did, but why God says he did it: "Now I know that you fear me." The word "fear" provided the opening for cynics and skeptics whom Philo criticized but didn't name, lowlifes who loved nothing more than dragging everyone down to their level. They either misunderstood the story or intentionally twisted its meaning. "So what?" they said. Many a man had sacrificed a child. Some had sacrificed several. What's so special about Abraham almost sacrificing one?

And Philo, as well versed in Greek history, poetry, and drama as he was in the books he attributed to Moses, would have known the stories.

Leos, one of the founders of Athens, son of Orpheus, sacrificed three daughters in a successful effort to end a famine. By one account, the daughters volunteered and went exuberantly to the altar.

Aristodemus of Messenia sacrificed one daughter when his city was struck by a plague. He didn't have to. The lot had fallen to another man's child. But when the father of that young woman whisked her off to Sparta, Aristodemus (ignoring the protests and pleas of the girl's fiancé) rushed his daughter to the top of the city gates.

Then there was Iphigenia, about whom accounts vary widely. Her father, Agamemnon, had learned from an oracle that Artemis was angry, and in her anger she was holding back the wind that the Greeks needed to get their ships to Troy. Nothing short of sacrifice would appease her. After much back-and-forth between Agamemnon and his brother (Menelaus), then Agamemnon and his wife (Clytemnestra), then Agamemnon, Clytemnestra, and Iphigenia herself, Iphigenia insisted against all argument upon giving her life for her country. Some versions of the story end with her on her way to the altar: "With my own blood in sacrifice I will wash out the fated curse of God." In others, the ax actually falls and blood flows, but it is the blood of a deer, a deer Artemis left behind when she whisked Iphigenia away.

King Athamas of Orchomenus had two wives and four children. His second wife wanted the children from his first marriage, Phrixus and Helle, out of her way. So she ruined (by roasting) the seed for the season's crop, causing a famine, and then, when she learned that her husband had sent a messenger to the oracle to determine what the gods wanted, she bribed the oracle to say that the gods wanted Phrixus and Helle. The children were saved at the last moment by a flying golden ram. Helle fell off en route to safety, giving the Hellespont its name. Phrixus made it safely to the city Aia, where he sacrificed the ram to Zeus in gratitude, was warmly received by the king, and was given the king's daughter in marriage. The fleece of that very ram was later the object of Jason's quest, but that's another story.

Closer to home, in the book we call Judges, there was Jephthah, who in battle with the Ammonites made what most commentators since have characterized as a reckless vow. If God delivered his enemies into his hands and saw to his safe return home from battle, he'd make a burnt offering of whatever or whomever came out to greet him. Much to his dismay, his daughter was the first one out the door. He was bereft, but he kept his vow. Further along in Israel's history, the king of Moab, under siege by Israel, sacrificed a son atop the city gates.

Philo knew men had sometimes sacrificed children. But, he insisted, Abraham's sacrifice was different, not just one more sacrifice but a novel form of conduct. Abraham didn't do it mindlessly, out of tradition. It was not tradition where he came from. Or out of a desire to impress fellow citizens or subjects. He did it without fanfare or witnesses, without telling a soul. Or—as the vast majority of men did it—in a moment of crisis and fear, in the hope of getting something from God.

Abraham did it simply because God asked him to do it. (That God asked may have been the biggest difference, but not one that Philo noted.) Abraham did it solely to demonstrate his perfect piety, his devotion, and his love.

Well, to get from fear to love, Philo had to put aside the book of Genesis the minute Abraham raised the knife, before God stopped him and explained why it wasn't necessary for him to go through with it. And that's precisely what Philo did. He then moved, as he believed any true philosopher ultimately would, beyond or beneath the story's literal meanings, its local meanings, to its allegorical meanings, its universal meanings, the meanings only wise men can see.

Isaac's name, Philo wrote, means "laughter"—not the carnal laughter of the body but the ethereal laughter of the mind. All laughter and joy ultimately belong to God. Only he is completely happy, free of the sorrow that humans so often live with, or the fear of sorrow to come. When God asks for Isaac, Abraham doesn't hesitate. He understands that Isaac, like laughter and joy, belong to God. But for that understanding, for his piety and his love, God rewards him. He stops the sacrifice, thereby sharing some of his laughter and sparing Abraham some fear and grief.

That's ingenious, and lovely in its way, but it is not the story I know or the larger cycle of stories of which it was, and remains, a part. Abraham certainly knew his share of fear and grief. But a purely happy God, without frustration, sadness, or regret? That's not the God of Genesis. Between sunset on the sixth day and Moses's farewell address, you'll have as hard a time finding a happy God as you will have finding a man, woman, or child who loves him.

Don't get me wrong. I have grown fond of Philo. I admire his learning, and though some say his knowledge of Hebrew was minimal or nonexistent, thereby rendering meaningless all his allegory based on the deep meaning of particular words, I, knowing so few languages myself, would be a horrible hypocrite to hold his ignorance of Hebrew against him. Long after his death, many now-famous men adopted his distinction between literal meanings and allegorical meanings, the carnal and the spiritual, to say some really nasty things about the Jews. But I'd be the last writer on earth to argue that a writer is responsible for every last thing posterity does with his or her words. Writer to writer, I regret that he didn't pay more attention to his prose. The language is stuffy and there is a tedious sameness to the structure of his sentences. It can be a small act of stoicism to read him. Still, I can't help but admire the precision, rigor, and dogged persistence of his analysis. He was a reader, a real reader, for whom every writer has a special place in his or her heart.

I only wish he didn't like G's story quite so much. For all his interpreting and allegorizing, for all his effort, perfectly understandable, to turn a story of fear and obedience into a story of reason and love, he actually left it pretty much as he found it on the page. That's partly because he too fell for the story's silences. And even more because he, like Jubilees, took Abraham's response for granted. Philo himself was a brave man. At the age of sixty, in the fortieth year of the Common Era, the final year of the reign of Caligula, he risked his life to protest vicious violence against Alexandria's Jews. Yet it never seems to have occurred to him that Abraham's standing up to God, asking him what he was thinking, might also, in the face of his fear, have been a stirring example of stoicism, reason, piety, and love.

6

To get a sense of Philo's comfort with the story, all you need to do is turn to Flavius Josephus, the Jewish priest (born Yosef ben Matityahu), general, rebel leader (for a while), later advocate of accommodation with the Romans, and self-proclaimed prophet, who, late in the first century of the Common Era, toward the end of a long and eventful life, settled down in Rome under the patronage of the emperor Vespasian, then Titus, and finally Domitian, to write history: first a history of (and our primary source for) the war with Rome; then a general history of the Jews, starting with Creation; and finally a short memoir—three works to which anyone interested in late Second Temple Judaism or Jewish history will at one time or another turn.

Philo took aim at writers who insisted that there was nothing extraordinary about Abraham. He left the story as he found it but put the great man's deeds in context, revealing what he took to be the story's hidden meanings, showing skeptical or cynical readers what they couldn't see. Josephus, though no less admiring, worried that his readers might conclude that Abraham (and his God) were extraordinary, but in a horrible way, the former bloodthirsty and the latter murderous. To lessen the likelihood, he added scores of lines to the story, many of them lines of dialogue, saying what G had left unsaid.

God appears, enumerates the many good things he has done for

Abraham, and asks for Isaac back in sacrifice, at which point Josephus jumps in to make God's motives clear. " 'He' simply wanted
to 'make trial of' and 'manifest his piety'—to show that Abraham
had his priorities straight. What better way to do that than to show
that he 'put the doing of God's good pleasure even above the life of
his child.' " Later in the story, right after God "forbade" Abraham
to slay his son, Josephus allows God to explain his motives himself:
He didn't ask out of some "craving for human blood." He didn't
make him "a father only to rob him in such impious fashion of his
offspring; no, He simply wished but to test his soul and see whether
even such orders would find him obedient."

As for Abraham, Josephus didn't deny, couldn't deny, wouldn't
want to deny, that when God asked for Isaac, Abraham set out without protest or pause, making all the preparations without saying a
word to anyone about God's commandment or his own resolve to
obey it (thereby demonstrating a readiness that, according to one
standard translation, even God found "surprising"). But Abraham's
ardor had nothing to do with eagerness. It was simply a sign that
he understood that everything he had, he had thanks to God, and
as a result "in everything we must submit to his will." And that's
why, after he built the altar, Abraham turned to Isaac and launched
into a long address, emphasizing that none of this was his plan. He
had prayed for Isaac for years and rejoiced when he arrived. He had
hoped Isaac would live a long life, take care of him in his old age,
be his heir. Unfortunately, God had plans of his own. He, who had
given him Isaac, now wanted him back. The silver lining was that
now Isaac would not die in an ordinary way, whether in war, from
disease, or by accident. Instead, he would be "sped" by his own
father to God, the Father of all, through the rites of sacrifice.

Spelling all that out, including some things that seem obvious,
Josephus provided an early demonstration that when it comes to
storytelling, more is not always better. But he was a historian, with
the historian's desire to tell the whole story and the historian's
reluctance to let good research, or any research, go to waste. If he

had evidence, whether from the teachings of Moses or the traditions that had grown up around them, he would be inclined to use it. If that evidence allowed him to interpret or explain something, he would be inclined to interpret and explain. It is partly a matter of pride. What is the good of knowing something if no one knows you know it? And partly, control. Why take the chance that readers will explain it for themselves—and get it wrong. That's why so many history books are so long.

But there was more to Josephus's verbosity than a professional preference for sound over silence. He wrote a mere half century after Philo. He read him, learned and borrowed from him, admired him, and in writing his history of the Jews he thought of himself as contributing to Philo's project, explaining and extolling the Jewish tradition. But he was writing in a different, and much more dangerous, world. The Romans had laid siege to Jerusalem, destroyed the Second Temple, suppressed the revolt, and set out to extinguish every last bit of Jewish resistance, if not every last Jew. Palestine was awash with Jewish blood.

Josephus was a survivor. He had survived a shipwreck that took the lives of hundreds of fellow passengers. He had survived the siege of Jotapata, a small hilltop town north of Nazareth, on the Roman general Vespasian's route to Jerusalem. After the breach of the walls, Josephus and four dozen Jotapatans took refuge in a cave. His compatriots concluded that if death and surrender were their only choices, they'd prefer to die. Yet Josephus had mixed feelings about that kind of martyrdom (his elaborate arguments against it anticipate almost every Jewish objection to it in the centuries ahead), and after a suicide pact that involved the drawing of straws and the death of all but the man Josephus was supposed to kill before he killed himself, he and that other man came out of the cave alive. He was captured, imprisoned, and sentenced to death, but Vespasian spared his life when Josephus persuaded him that he, Josephus, would have been dead already, in mass suicide, if God hadn't wanted him alive to deliver an important message: that he,

Vespasian, would ultimately ascend to the throne. Vespasian took Josephus on as his hostage and interpreter, freeing him when his prophecy came to pass. By the time Josephus started writing history, he was a Roman citizen, living on a pension and in luxury at the emperor's expense. But his people were still in trouble. The task of demonstrating, to his Roman audience, the antiquity, the preciousness, and the relevance of Jewish history was more pressing than ever. It might be a matter of life or death. Josephus had every reason to try to explain exactly what Abraham and his God were thinking.

And what Isaac was thinking. In Josephus's hands, even Isaac (whom I have always imagined as a small boy, just old enough to carry the wood and ask, as a small boy might, about the lamb) is loquacious, a young man, fully aware of his duty. Writers before Josephus had implied that sometime before Abraham bound him Isaac had realized that he himself was the lamb. The author of Judith had his (or her) hero urge his or her fellow citizens, suffering miserably and on the verge of surrender, to "remember what God did with Abraham, and how he tested Isaac." A tested Isaac had to have had some time to think about his future, or lack thereof. And Philo interpreted the story's haunting refrain, "And the two of them went together," to mean that they had walked together at the same pace, in the same place, in mind as well as body.

Josephus's Isaac left less to the imagination. He responded to Abraham's address with an address of his own, assuring his father that he understood, and then some. The way he saw it, if he wasn't willing to go along with God and his father—if he "should not resign himself up readily to both their pleasures"—he wouldn't be "worthy" of having been "born" in the first place. The fact is that he would have been willing "even if" the idea to offer him up had been his father's alone. And what father, not wanting to sacrifice his son but concluding that he had no choice in the matter, would not take some solace in the thought that his son understood? With those words, Isaac immediately made his way to the altar.

Just to be sure that readers understood that Isaac was speaking of his own free will and accord (which was also to understand that the middle patriarch, the son of Abraham, the father of Israel, was not simply a prop in this momentous play, a lamb being led to slaughter), Josephus gave us his exact age. Isaac was twenty-five, old enough to argue, fight back, or simply run away if he had had any objections to his aged father's plans.

Josephus's Isaac was a knowing and willing victim, but his knowledge was narrow. He knew one ancient virtue, obedience: son to father; father and son to God. What God commands, you do, even if he commands you to do something that he himself will characterize as "impious" shortly after he stops you from doing it. Other first- and second-century Isaacs knew more, perhaps none as much as the Isaac of the writer we know only as Pseudo-Philo, a Jewish writer whose one extant work, in a Latin translation, was shelved and passed along with Latin translations of Philo of Alexandria and for many years attributed to him, though I don't know how. Their approaches to scripture are nearly as distinct as their styles.

Pseudo-Philo was as drunk on words and scripture as Philo was stone sober. He was an ecstatic rewriter of the Bible, whose retelling of the big story, from Creation to Saul, often reads as if he had found fragments of several sacred scrolls and then, without a copy of the original to guide him, or any interest whatsoever in restoring it to its original form, set out to produce an updated edition. His treatment of the near sacrifice falls into three different chapters. Today a generous reviewer might say that he chose to organize his book thematically, as opposed to chronologically, and there would be much truth to that. From Pseudo-Philo's point of view, there was meaning to the madness.

Pseudo-Philo's God, like the God of Jubilees's, was prodded by jealous angels to ask for Isaac, and his Abraham set out immediately. When, along the way, Abraham told Isaac the plan, the boy was momentarily confused, even dismayed. He reminded his father that it was the sweet smell of burning lamb that God seemed to love. And the best of the flock was set aside for slaughter in order to atone for wicked deeds of men. Man, on the contrary, was supposed to inherit this world. "Why then," he asked his father, "should you be saying to me now, 'Come and inherit eternal life and time without measure?'"

We will never know how Abraham would have explained it, for Isaac answered his own question before his father had a chance to say a word: "Why if not that I was indeed born in this world in order to be offered as a sacrifice to him who made me? Indeed, this will be my blessedness over other men—and in me the generations will be proclaimed and through me nations will understand how God made a human soul worthy for sacrifice."

Just in case anyone misunderstood what Isaac was saying (and at least in the English translation of the awkward Latin translation of a text that scholars assume was first composed in Hebrew, it would be easy to misunderstand or not understand at all), eight chapters later Pseudo-Philo retells the story of Jephthah, the mighty warrior of Gilead, who, desperate for an edge in a difficult battle, vowed to sacrifice to God "whomever comes forth from the doors of my house to meet me." Alas, it was his daughter, his only child, and he rent his clothes and moaned and groaned about his fate.

His daughter (who here, unlike in Judges, has a name, Seila) urged him to get hold of himself. "Who is there who would be sad in death," she asked, "seeing the people freed?" Remember, she said, the days of the fathers, "when the father placed the son as a holocaust"—a whole burnt sacrifice—"and he did not refuse him but gladly gave consent to him, and the one being offered was ready and the one who was offering was rejoicing."

Here Isaac is not merely appended to a story about Abraham's obedience. Or to Jubilees's story of a demonstration of the same, or to Philo's story of God's sharing his happiness and joy with those who display perfect piety, devotion, and love. Rather, he himself stands at the center of a story about the dignity of human sacrifice, of an innocent boy dying, as a sin offering, for God. And though Pseudo-Philo gave Isaac a voice and theological imagination that would have been impressive even at twenty-five, he was not alone in imagining Isaac that way. If you find that hard to believe and you have a strong stomach, grab a Bible that includes the Apocrypha and take a look at the second and fourth books of Maccabees. The former is an abridgment of a long-lost Jewish history. The latter is an essay in stoic philosophy—a celebration, not unlike Philo's, of the elevation of reason above passion—grounded in a portion of that same history, a graphic account of the earliest Jewish resistance to Antiochus IV, who ruled the Seleucid Empire for ten years, starting in 175 BCE, and whose persecution of the Jews contributed to the Maccabean revolt.

Antiochus defiled the Temple, forbade circumcision and the observance of the Sabbath, and made it a capital crime just to say "I am a Jew." It isn't clear what he was thinking. Some say he stumbled into a Jewish civil war, mistaking the revolt of exurban traditionalists against Hellenized Jerusalem Jews for a revolt against his rule. Some say that after Rome curtailed his invasion of Egypt, he coveted the Temple's gold. Some, including one historian who knew him, say he was not thinking at all. He was insane. Whatever his motivation, his decrees and his deeds made a bad situation in and around Jerusalem worse, and in histories of the revolt against him, and against Greek culture and Greek rule, Jewish writers celebrated the Jewish martyrs who suffered publicly and, when called upon, died for their God.

The second book of Maccabees recounts the murder of two women who ignored the prohibition of circumcision. They were paraded around the city with their newborns at their breasts and then hurled from the walls. Another group of Jews sneaked off to a cave to observe the Sabbath. They were burned alive. Both 2 Maccabees and 4 Maccabees tell the tale of Eleazar, an aged scribe, respected in Jerusalem by pagans and Jews alike. Antiochus's goons force-fed him a piece of pork. He spat it out and led his captors to the rack. Still eager to spare his life, they urged him to substitute kosher meat for the king's. He refused and urged other children of Abraham to die, like Isaac, nobly for their religion. Beaten, scourged, cut, stabbed, burned to the bone, and about to expire, he lifted his eyes to God and said, "You know, O God, that though I could have saved myself, I am dying in these fiery torments for the sake of the Law. Be merciful to your people and let our punishment be a satisfaction on their behalf. Make my blood their purification, and take my life as a ransom for theirs."

Seven other victims of Antiochus were brothers, sadistically and grotesquely tortured—with wheels, joint dislocaters, rack and hooks, catapults and cauldrons, braziers, wedges and bellows, thumbscrews and iron claws—one after another in front of their mother, who was proud to her own dying breath of her sons' piety and resolve. She took strength from the example of Abraham, the first Jewish parent to sacrifice a son to God. Like him, she put religious reason—her love and fear of God—above her sympathy for her sons. Her "sympathy for her children" was great, the chronicler wrote, but it did not sway her, "for she was of the same mind as Abraham." "For God's sake also," she said, "our father Abraham was zealous to sacrifice his son Isaac, the ancestor of our nation; and when Isaac saw his father's hand wielding a knife and descending upon him, he did not cower." Meanwhile, one of that woman's sons implored his brothers: "Remember whence you came and at the hand of what father Isaac gave himself to be sacrificed for piety's sake."

Clearly, we are not in Genesis anymore. Not that all the stories there are suitable for children. Horrible things happened and worse were threatened. But the details were generally left to the imagination. Two writers, at the very least, had a hand in recounting the Flood. Neither thought it necessary to describe a single person drowning. As for blood, there's not much of it. Cain killed Abel. His blood cried out, but just metaphorically. Jacob's sons slew the citizens of Shechem (as they were recuperating from circumcision) in revenge for the rape of Dinah. Without a drop of blood. In Exodus, the blood certainly starts flowing (water turned to blood, the blood of the lambs smeared on the doorposts, the blood of the firstborn), and in Leviticus there is so much animal blood splashed around altars that today the squeamish tend to pass right over those pages. In Deuteronomy, the specter of spilled blood and a whole lot of other really nasty stuff hovers above the would-be disobedient. Nevertheless: nowhere in the first five books is there precedent for the virtually pornographic depiction of that poor mother cheering as the king's henchmen gouge, scalp, skin, fry, boil, and dismember her seven sons.

But here's the essential point: Even if the contributors to those books had been into that kind of thing, it never would have occurred to them to portray suffering or dying young as something that happens to good people who live their lives by God's laws. The chapters of scripture on Abraham, Isaac, and Jacob, like the chapters and books that follow them, are full of mixed signals and outright contradictions. Different writers took different positions on some pretty weighty questions of history, theology, and law. I could show you passages that suggest that God wants false prophets put to death immediately and others that suggest he wants those accused of false prophecy to have fair trials. I could show you passages where God says that the sins of the fathers will be visited upon the children and others where he says they absolutely will not. I could show you passages where it is clear that the author thought that the god of Abraham was one of many and others where it is just as clear that the author thought he was the one and only God. But if there was widespread agreement about anything, it was that God takes care of those who obey him and at the very least abandons those who do not. The blessings in Deuteronomy are reserved for those who walk in God's way. The curses are the punishment for those who go astray. The godly prosper on earth. The ungodly fail. To be sure, those self-effacing children of God in Maccabees, and their mother, insist that they are suffering for their sins. But there is not a hint that they have done anything wrong. If they suffer for sins, they are the sins of others.

Times change. Persecution changes too, and the authors of Maccabees may have been trying to make sense of and give theological meaning to a form of persecution that the Hebrew scriptures didn't fully explain: the persecution of Jews not as Israelites or Judeans, people who occupied a coveted city or plain, or controlled a coveted well, but as Jews, people who worshipped a particular god in a particular way. Antiochus's victims believed in God and observed all his laws. Yet they suffered, suffered for doing exactly what God told them to do. And yet despite their suffering, and perhaps earthly failure, they wanted to believe that God still loved them, that their suffering, individual and communal, was a clear sign that he loved them: He punished them immediately instead of waiting until their crimes reached great heights. He tested them, disciplined them, but did not forsake them. And he would reward them for their suffering with eternal life.

I can see where they were coming from, but as a reader and writer trying to understand Abraham and Isaac, I can't hide my discomfort with the development. I expected Abraham to protest or at least ask God why he had made such an inexplicable demand, a demand that seemed to contradict his promise and confound his own grand plan. I am sorry he didn't. You might think I am dreaming, that in the context of his place and time my expectation of a questioning Abraham is an impossible stretch. But is it any less of a stretch to say, as some writers had begun to say, that Abraham was zealous to kill Isaac and that Isaac was the first Jewish martyr, not just ready but glad to die to sanctify God's name?

Even some writers who celebrated martyrdom understood the point I am trying to make. After the emperor Hadrian suppressed the Bar Kokhba revolt in 135 CE and renewed the Roman crusade against the Jews (those not sold into slavery were prohibited from entering Jerusalem, circumcising their sons, observing the Sabbath, even studying Torah), several writers recast the story of that Maccabean mother and her sons. They gave her a name, Miriam, and portrayed her as resisting not Greek but Roman persecution. But like the unnamed mother, Miriam was perfectly devout, her sons brave and true to God. When the time came for her youngest to die, she urged the emperor to kill her too, right then and there, but he (contemptuously citing Leviticus) refused. Miriam squeezed the baby to her breast and gave him a message for his greatest grandfather: "Do not preen yourself [on your righteousness], saying 'I built an altar and offered up my son, Isaac.' Behold, our mother built seven altars and offered up seven sons in one day. Yours was only a test, but mine was in earnest."

~~~~

Now, someone looking back at all this revising at the turn of the millennium might be struck by an apparent paradox. Writers took every imaginable liberty with the story of the near sacrifice. Some took unimaginable liberties. Yet as they did, they went out of their way to say that the entire anthology, the literature that they revised, was not just complete but perfect—every letter, every number, every word, every phrase, every juxtaposition, every omission, every repetition, every flight of fancy, every seeming contradiction, every error of transmission or translation, every slip of the pen, every compromise with an editor, every surrender to exhaustion or frustration or a deadline or darkness at the end of the day—intentional, purposeful, and meaningful, the completely conscious and perfectly realized design of its author.

And get this: some of them suggested or said (or simply assumed that everyone knew) that the entire thing, not just the cycle of stories about Abraham, not just the stories before and after that cycle, not just the laws, rituals, and regulations, all those building plans and codes, but all the myth, history, poetry, philosophy, and even prophecy—they said all that had been dictated (the first five books to Moses), revealed (to the prophets), inspired, and (according to some) actually written by a single writer, black fire on white fire, a ghostwriter; not my ghostwriter, however, but rather another, in many people's minds the first, last, and greatest of all ghostwriters. God. Not everyone said all that, by any means. But most everyone did.

Wouldn't you know it? Nineteen lines that the author struggled with, then lost control of and wanted to change but was not able to, nineteen lines that he regretted like he had never regretted anything he had written before, in time came to be considered not just perfect, to the letter, but divine.

I take the compliment on his behalf, and appreciate the irony. The history of literature is full of it. But I am less interested in the irony than the paradox—the paradox of divinely inspired writings that (centuries after the Scriptures were redacted and the canon closed) every Tom, Dick, and Harry (or Jubilees, Philo, and Josephus) felt free to revise. Or, to be more precise, the reason why, in the minds of generation after generation of writers, copyists, editors, and translators at the turn of the Common Era, there was no paradox at all: they did not think of themselves as revising a thing. The glory of Jewish literature, Josephus explained, the history no less than the law, was not simply that it comprised exactly twenty-two books "containing the record of all time," each of them written by a prophet who had obtained his knowledge from God. It was also that throughout "long ages" no one had "ventured either to add, or to remove, or to alter a syllable." (The Greeks, by contrast, possessed "myriads of inconsistent books," "mere stories, improvised according to the fancy of their authors.") What we might see as adding (say, in the scores of words of direct speech that Josephus added to his rendition of Genesis 22), Josephus and other writers saw as explicating, interpreting, illuminating, finding the real and true meaning of a text that was difficult, deeply mysterious, even intentionally cryptic, its true significance often shrouded, whether in indirection, hidden meanings, or even baffling contradictions. It was a text that they believed often said something different from what it appeared to say, meant something different from what it appeared to mean, taught something different from what it appeared to teach. Without judges, sages, wise men, priests, and eventually rabbis to interpret, decipher, and explain it, we would be lost.

Ancient interpreters assumed the text was perfect and they assumed it was mysterious, but I don't think there was anything inevitable about the marriage of those two assumptions producing dramatic revision or transformative interpretation. Would it be a crime to leave a perfect story mysterious? I don't think so. In literature, as in painting or music, even history, not every mystery has to be solved, not every enigma has to be interpreted, explained once and for all. There are many stories, to say nothing of poems and even more paintings, that I don't fully understand, or understand at all. It wouldn't occur to me to change a word or a brushstroke. In fact, I would be no more likely to insist on knowing what they mean than I would be to ask or insist upon knowing the cause or meaning of the layers of light—orange, purple, pink, red, azure, and gray—that form in and around the clouds over the river out my window at sunset so many nights. I am not saying no one should ever inquire, nor even that I myself never do, but simply that it isn't a crime just to look and lose yourself in the view, letting go of the need to know, as I often do standing in front of a work of abstract art, or reading some of my favorite poetry—

> The palm stands on the edge of space.
> The wind moves slowly in the branches.
> The bird's fire-fangled feathers dangle down.

—or listening to certain classical music. I enjoy the sound and sense and allow the rest to remain mysterious.

But here's what I have to remind myself. Back then, readers of the Bible were not reading for pleasure, or first for pleasure, or just for pleasure. G did not intend to write an instruction manual—*What to Expect When You Are Expected to Sacrifice Your Son*—but those who translated, interpreted, and rewrote his story assumed not just that it and all the other old stories were perfect and mysterious but also that they were relevant and instructive, their lessons and morals as timely and applicable on the day they were being read as they had been on the day they were written. G didn't write a how-to guide, but they were reading or listening to figure out how to live their lives.

Here one might fairly ask (as friends of mine often do) if I understand that ancient interpreters assumed that their sacred texts were perfect, mysterious, significant in every detail, endlessly instructive, and in one way or another divine. And I understand that those assumptions not only provided an opening for improvisation but actually made it likely, perhaps even necessary, as writers sought to straighten time's crooked lines, bring theological unity and moral clarity to messy biblical characters, plots, and meanings, and tweak texts they took to be perfect until they were perfect for their purposes, in their minds. And I understand that all the straightening and tweaking was not a by-product but often the very purpose of biblical interpretation. If I understand all that, why go on and on about it?

My answer is this: I am still thinking about Genesis 22 from the perspective of poor G, centuries earlier, imagining and eagerly anticipating the day when his story would be revised. That day had come. But put yourselves in my shoes, as I put myself in his: When, at the turn of the millennium, all those Jewish writers decided that suffering like that mother's seven sons suffered could be a sign of God's grace, that sacrificing one's son could be a way of showing one's love, that dying for God could be a way of glorifying him, that the suffering and dying of people in one generation could serve as expiation for people in another, that God's chosen people, however defeated in this world, would all be together in the next, I can't help wishing that instead of revising or reinterpreting the story of the near sacrifice, instead of making Abraham zealous and Isaac willing, they had left the story of Abraham and Isaac alone and come up with one of their own.

"Be careful what you wish for," some sage said. In this instance they did.

~~~~~

Now, there are people, really smart people, who in our day have spent a significant amount of time arguing, in a scholarly sort of way, about whose atoning sacrifice came first: Did the Jews borrow the idea from the early Christians or did the early Christians borrow it from the Jews? All agree that by the time of Jesus, Isaac's role in the story had grown enormously. But had it developed to the point where some readers and writers imagined Isaac not just as a willing victim but a willing victim whose messianic suffering and death would result in forbearance and remission of sins for time immemorial? And, if so, was that Isaac on the minds of the earliest Christians when they tried to make sense of the death of Jesus? Or did that Isaac emerge only after the followers of Jesus imagined that their beloved rabbi was God's beloved son, the messiah who had died for mankind's sins and was raised up again so that through him we could all be saved and reborn?

Believe me when I say that I don't have a stake in the outcome of that debate. I think of it as I might think of some intricate evolutionary puzzle, complicated not just by the absence of key pieces of evidence but also by tremendous uncertainty about the dates of the pieces that we have. Several Aramaic translations of the Bible (called Targums) portray a willing Isaac. They go so far as to explain, perhaps for the first time, why, if Isaac was so willing, Abraham needed to bind him. The reason is that he had asked

Abraham to bind him—so that he would not tremble or flinch, confusing Abraham or causing the knife to slip, or accidentally kick
Abraham, or (unintentionally) spoil the sacrifice (which had to be
perfect, unblemished) in some other way. What's more, at least
one Targum suggests that as a reward for his obedience, Abraham
had asked for, and God had agreed to provide, not just deliverance
but redemption, a remission of the sins of future generations. But
there is no agreement on the dates of those translations, and even
if there were agreement—agreement, say, that came after Jesus—
scholars would still argue about whether or not translations drew
on older sources that didn't survive or older understandings of the
story that were never recorded.

Meanwhile, among the Dead Sea Scrolls, the trove of sacred
literature discovered in the Qumran caves, there is a brief retelling
of Genesis 22. Its technical name is 4Q225–227, but because of
several critical correspondences, including a character named Mastema accusing Abraham before God, some scholars call it Pseudo-
Jubilees. Pseudo-Jubilees is dated to the turn of the era, and one of
its many intriguing aspects is an extra line of speech by Isaac. After
he asks about the lamb and Abraham answers, Isaac has more to
say. But what? Some scholars believe he says, "Tie me up" or "Bind
me well," which would indicate that at least one early Isaac was
aware of Abraham's mission and at peace with it. Unfortunately,
certainty is hard to come by. It seems clear that after Abraham
answered his question, Isaac said something. But we don't know
how Abraham answered. The line is missing. (He might have said,
"God will provide the lamb." Or he might have said, as he says
in some of the Targums, "God will provide the lamb, but if he
doesn't, you, Isaac, will be the lamb.") And the supposition that in
Pseudo-Jubilees Isaac asked to be bound is based entirely on one
Hebrew letter, a letter that might have been the first letter of quite a
few words other than "tie" or "bind," words that might well have
been followed by words other than "me up" or "me well." What's
more, as James Kugel, an extraordinarily wise and trenchant bibli-

cal scholar, has recently observed, that one letter, and thus Isaac's imagined request, doesn't come precisely where literary analysis and logic would lead us to expect it to come in the story.

Those are just a few questions about a few pieces of the puzzle. There are scores of them. Even when the words are all decipherable and the dates widely agreed upon, scholars debate the relative influence of what is known: not just ideas about Abraham and Isaac but the whole complex of turn-of-the-millennium Jewish ideas (and contemporaneous pagan, especially mystery cult, ideas) about the son of man, the end of days, the suffering servant, the coming of the messiah; about martyrdom, death, atonement, salvation, and resurrection.

It is a complicated debate and, once you delve into it, fascinating, but my attention is fixed on the rewriting and revision of one short story, and all I really need to say, at least for now, is that in light of the rewriting and revision between Jubilees and the advent of Christianity, you don't need to be a biblical scholar to understand what the first Christian Jews did with it.

The earliest Jewish interpreters, whatever their other differences, all stressed Abraham's piety, his devotion, his love, and especially his obedience, not just to specific commands but to all of God's laws. He was repeatedly tested and he repeatedly passed. At least in hindsight, it should not be surprising that the first Christians, while hardly gainsaying obedience to God, let alone devotion, sacrifice, and love, folded all that into faith. Abraham's greatness lay not so much in what he did—his obedience to God's commandment—but in the faith that made it possible for him to do it, that made the unbearable bearable: the faith that one way or another God would keep his promise.

Not that the very earliest Christian writers made much of the story. As far as I know, no one wrote a treatise on Abraham and Isaac or devoted a chapter to it in a treatise on some larger incident or theme. No one even bothered to retell the story from beginning to end. Abraham appears in crucial places in the Gospel of John and the Epistles to the Romans, Hebrews, and Galatians, most notably in arguments about the supremacy of faith and in confident early Christian claims to be the true heirs of Abraham, the beneficiaries of God's blessing. But the near sacrifice is mentioned explicitly only in the very Jewish-leaning Epistle of James and the very Christian-leaning Epistle to the Hebrews, where the author, whose name we don't know, appears to address a group or community of fellow Jewish Christians, whom he feared, or whom he had been told, were backsliding, rethinking the meaning of Jesus's life and death and (more crucially) their commitment to the new community in the face of the demands and dangers of Jewish-Christian life and faith. At the heart of his Epistle was a carefully constructed and perfectly polished, if not especially balanced, comparison of the old Temple sacrifices to the sacrifice of Jesus, the eternal priesthood of the church to the Levitical priesthood, the new covenant to the old, of faith to law.

To make the case for faith, "the assurance of things hoped for, the conviction of things not seen," the author turned to history, the faith with which men (and women) of old won God's favor. Abel by faith offered a more acceptable sacrifice. He died, but because he had that faith he still speaks. Noah, warned by God about events he could not possibly have foreseen, built an ark and became heir to the world to come. Abraham left his home for a place unknown, for a land of pure promise. By faith, Sarah received the power to conceive Isaac, despite her age. And then, "by faith Abraham, when he was tested, offered up Isaac, and he who had received the promise was ready to offer up his only son of whom it was said, 'Through Isaac shall your descendants be named.' He considered that God was able to raise men even from the dead; hence, figuratively speaking, he did receive him back."

Thanks to Abraham, the story continued: By faith Moses cast his lot not with Pharaoh but with the people of Israel. By faith the people of Israel crossed the Red Sea as if on dry land. After them, men and women of faith "conquered kingdoms, enforced justice, received promises, stopped the mouths of lions, quenched raging fire, escaped the edge of the sword, won strength out of weakness, became mighty in war, put foreign armies to flight. Women received their dead by resurrection. Some were tortured, refusing to accept release that they might rise again to a better life. Others suffered mocking and scourging, and even chains and imprisonment. They were stoned, they were sawed in two, they were killed with the sword; they went about in skins of sheep and goats, destitute, afflicted, ill-treated—of whom the world was not worthy—wandering over deserts and mountains, and in dens and caves of the earth." They did not receive what God had promised, but they retained their faith in things unseen.

The author of the Epistle to the Hebrews introduced no new characters. Imagined no new scenes. Put no new words in the mouths of Isaac, Abraham, or God. He neither added nor took away. He contributed just two lines to a growing body of exegesis. But to change the meaning of words is to change the words, and two lines of New Testament Epistle, long attributed to Paul, were not just any two lines of exegesis. By the time Augustine got to them in *City of God,* most of the church fathers had had their say, and many people read the story in a whole new way.

My feelings about all of the early Christian talk of faith are mixed.

Naturally, I understand that many readers had a difficult time with the story.

I have had a difficult time with it myself.

And though my particular reservations may not have been widely shared, I can't help thinking that many people, including some of those who loved to crow about Abraham's greatness, actually had a hard time imagining, from the inside out, how he could have done what he did. Think about it: A sick child is enough to cause, in parents, intense anxiety if not the deepest despair. But we don't always get to choose our trials, and in his shoes (asked to do the last thing on earth I wanted to do, yet afraid not to) I'd consider the kind of faith imputed to Abraham to be the greatest of blessings. I can't help thinking that the idea that Abraham's response to God was rooted in faith (faith that God would keep his promise, faith that he'd ultimately get Isaac back) made it more comprehensible, a difficult story easier to bear.

And it wasn't as if those who talked and wrote about Abraham's faith didn't have evidence. Commentators had long noted that Abraham was faithful, by which I think they meant devoted and obedient. It was, for many, his defining trait, and though being completely obedient to God is one thing and having complete faith in God is quite another, the distance between them was not great, especially to people writing and reading Greek, where the same word—*pistos*—could easily convey either of those two different ideas about Abraham. What's more, earlier in Abraham's life, some time after the battle with the kings, in a passage the early Christians frequently cited, Abraham appears to have had faith and been rewarded for it. The word of God had come to him in a vision: " 'Fear not, Abram, I am your shield. Your reward shall be very great.' And Abram said, 'O my Master, LORD, what can You give me when I am going to my end childless.' " God told him to look toward the heavens, and then promised him descendants as numerous as the stars. "And he trusted in the LORD, and He reckoned it to his merit."

I could argue until I was red in the face, reminding people that chapter 15 is one thing and chapter 22 another. The former mentions trust explicitly. The latter mentions fear. If trust were the key, God would have said so when he stopped him—would have said, "Now I know that you have faith in me." And he would have rewarded him for keeping that faith, rather than for obeying his command.

I would argue in vain. Abraham's faith lay at the root of everything else, the early Christians would say. On the way to Moriah, it was simply assumed. And if you can't grasp that, recall the words with which Abraham took leave of his servants: "You stay here with the ass. The boy and I will go up there; we will worship and we will return to you." Not "I" but "we."

I might point out that there are other ways to interpret those words, obvious ways, as even some Christian commentators acknowledged. But it would be more than a little presumptuous of me to insist that one couldn't legitimately read them as trust or faith. In the third century, Origen, the Alexandrian scholar and theologian, imagined a perplexed observer asking Abraham what he was actually saying to his servants: "Are you saying to the servants in truth that you will worship and return with the child, or are you deceiving them? If you are telling the truth, then you will not make him a holocaust. If you are deceiving, it is not fitting for so great a patriarch to deceive."

"I am speaking the truth," Origen's Abraham replied, "and I offer the child as a holocaust. For this reason I both carry wood with me, and I return to you with him. For I believe, and this is my faith, that 'God is able to raise up even from the dead.'" In fact, Christian interpreters said, it was Abraham's faith that allowed him to see ahead: "His character was considering the slaughter," Bishop Succensus wrote, two centuries later, "but his faith declared and spoke the truth about the outcome." When Isaac, observing that his father had the fire and he had the wood, asked about the lamb, Abraham's faith spoke the truth again: "God will see to the sheep for the burnt offering, my son." If that was not an expression of faith, Christian commentators asked, or prophecy grounded in faith, what would be?

I could say, again, that faith is not the only way to read Abraham's response. That I don't think that was the author's intent as he was writing, nor his or his editors' or first readers' impression as they read. But it should be pretty clear by now that neither the author nor his editors nor his first readers got to say what the words meant once and for all. And that's a good thing. Among the wonderful things about the story is the work it leaves for readers to do.

Faith that God would not make Abraham sacrifice Isaac is one thing, faith in resurrection another, and there's no evidence that Abraham knew anything about it. In his world, as I understand it, individuals died. Families, communities, and nations lived on. His hope for posterity was grounded in God's promise of descendants as numerous as the grains of sand on the shore. That's why he was so upset when it seemed as if he wasn't going to have any. But if Jubilees's Abraham could know some of God's laws even before God approached him (and all the rest of them five hundred years before Sinai), I suppose there is no reason why the Christian Abraham couldn't understand God's power to raise the dead.

I can see where they were coming from and where they ended up. I can understand how they got there. Yet I still read the story, above all else, as a story, and I can't help thinking that when the author of Hebrews recast it as a story about faith, he robbed it of its drama, or what was left of it after Jubilees decided that God, knowing everything, knew that Abraham would do exactly what he had asked him to do.

Now Abraham knows the outcome too.

Sure, it was difficult for him to go through the motions, to rise early, saddle the donkey, gather and split the wood, hike for the three days with the boy bounding, obliviously, at his side, ditch the servants, answer Isaac's question, and finally build the altar and bind him. But if the outcome was not actually in doubt, if Abraham believed that in the end God would keep his promise, what distinguishes the story from a dog-eared children's story where the harrowing beginning and middle are made palatable by the knowledge, foreknowledge after the first read, that everything works out in the inevitable end?

And then, along the same lines, there is the problem of God's blessing. If God knows that Abraham is perfectly faithful and Abraham has unshakable faith, what is God testing or demonstrating? However arbitrary or unknowable the grounds for Abraham's initial election (and Noah's before him), God made these people work for their blessings. Jubilees's God might have been able to read Abraham's mind, but there is no evidence that Abraham could read God's. And even if he could, why would God reward him so richly for doing something that Abraham knew he was not going to have to do? Years later a wise man would speculate that God doesn't throw dice. The jury is still out on that one, but I think it even less likely that he plays charades.

To Christians in the first few centuries of Christianity, it wasn't a game. It was history, sacred history, and if you knew how to read it, there was no mystery about its meaning. The Hebrew past was a shadow, a prefiguration of things to come: In Sarah's miraculous pregnancy, they saw Mary. In her beloved son, Jesus. In Abraham's willingness, God's own. In the three-day journey, the three days between crucifixion and resurrection. In the wood that Isaac carried, the cross. In Abraham's promise that God would provide a lamb, the lamb of God. In the ram, Jesus again. In the thicket the ram was caught in, his crown of thorns. In Moriah, Golgotha. In the sacrifice, the Eucharist. In Isaac's offspring—singular, Jesus. In the descendants of Isaac, the child of promise, Christ's church.

That's a dicey way to do history. When we look to the past, our expectations and desires shape when they don't determine what we see. If I go looking for evidence that Abraham had questions and doubts about God, I'll find it. But if I am not careful, I'll miss or minimize the importance of the moments he appears to have had none, all those times he did just what God asked when God asked it. If I go looking for evidence that the present was prefigured by the past, I'll find it. But if I am not careful, I'll miss or minimize the importance of all the floats that don't seem to have a place in history's inevitable parade. If I reduce people and events to their conscious contribution to a future that they themselves didn't necessarily anticipate, plan for, or even dream of, odds are that I will not understand them. Christians, elevating the ideal of faith in their own time, looked back and found it everywhere, including in Abraham's words to his servants ("We will return to you") and to Isaac ("God will see to the sheep"). But isn't it possible that the poor man was simply dissembling, with every good reason not to say "You stay here, I'll be back after I sacrifice Isaac" or "Actually you are the sacrifice, my son"—so that the former didn't stop him and the latter didn't flee.

That said, historians make that kind of mistake all the time. The early Christians may have taken a tendency or temptation and transformed it into a theory and method, but they were hardly the first or only or last people to read the present back into the past, to look back and see nothing but earlier versions of themselves. (Many Jewish interpreters would also come to see the Jewish present prefigured in the Jewish past, types in the patriarchs and anti-types in their descendants.) If I seem cranky, or crankier, about the Christian interpretation of the near sacrifice, I am. But it is not because of their presentism, or my sense of what makes for a good story, or their idea of faith. I can live with all three. What I can't live with, or what I would prefer not to live with, what bugs me and often infuriates me, is not the idea of prefiguration but rather supersessionism. The idea that the present superseded the past, the Christians the Jews. The idea that with the sacrificial death and resurrection of Jesus, God's blessing had passed from the descendants of the flesh to the descendants of the spirit, from people of the law to the people of faith, from the people enslaved in the earthly Jerusalem to the people living free in the Jerusalem above, from the people of God's promise to the people of God's curse, from the physical offspring of Isaac to the spiritual offspring, Jesus, and through him the church.

Recall that in Genesis all the nations of the earth were to be blessed through Abraham and his descendants. But the authors of several of the texts we know of as the Gospels insisted that not all of Israel was of Israel—or as Paul, author of the Epistle to the Romans, put it, not all the descendants of Abraham and Isaac were the children of Abraham. The Jews made the mistake of pursuing righteousness through the law rather than through faith. They stumbled over the law and never made it to faith. As centuries passed and the church fathers studied ancient history, they found that that stumbling, the Jewish spiritual blindness no less than the Christian scrambling toward Christ, had been foretold. And they found that stumbling even on the way to Mount Moriah. The Jews, wrote Cyril, the powerful patriarch of Alexandria from 412 until his death in 444, followed God by law but were unwilling by faith to follow Christ, who went to his death for all. "For 'from part of Israel there was rigidness,' which is signified by means of the ass present with the servants. For the ass is the representation of their final unreasonableness. And their rigidness is the child of unreasonableness." The Jews were the ass: the earthly, the dumb, the blind, the servants Abraham left behind.

Yikes. Philo, whose ideas had an enormous influence on early Christianity, had written doggedly of the distinction between the physical and the ethereal, the carnal and the spiritual, the body and the soul, the literal and the allegorical, the earthly and the heavenly, and there's no doubt what the philosopher took to be the higher realm. But there is also no doubt that Philo, a devout and fully observant Jew, believed that the body, the letter, the literal, was here to stay. To say that you prefer your church and its stories to another church and its stories is one thing. But to say that your church annuls another church (completes it, voids it, supersedes it) is quite another. And when that other church and its people are still with you—in other words, when the superseded past is still with you—well, that reading of history is a recipe for disaster.

Now, remember that when I speak of the early Christians, I am speaking not of men and women on the street but their chief spokesmen, the men we call the church fathers, several dozen different writers living over several centuries in dozens of places all over the Mediterranean world. Gather together even a small sample of their writings about Abraham and Isaac and you will find a magnificent variety. Some were interested in God's command. Some, Abraham's response. Some, the journey. Some, the servants. Some, Isaac. Some, the near sacrifice itself. Some, the ram, and some, God's blessing. Some imagined what an ordinary man might have felt, or even said to God. Some imagined what Abraham might have said to Sarah to comfort her or calm her down. Some explained why Abraham hadn't said anything to Sarah. Some imagined how his spirit would have warred with his flesh on the three-day journey, which, like the teasing form of God's command, was intended to make the test harder to bear. Some imagined that Isaac had known everything. Others, that he had known nothing at all. Some dug deep into the details of story. Others scoured the old for clues to the new.

When I step back from the story, I am reminded that the early Christians argued about everything: They argued about the divinity of Jesus. They argued about the relationship between Father, Son, and Holy Ghost. They argued about Jesus's incarnation and his body (was it earthly flesh or some more heavenly substance?). They argued about whether flesh and the Jewish deity who created it was good or bad. They argued about whether the God of the Israelites and the father of Jesus were one and the same. They argued about where the spirit and light and word of God resided and how, if they didn't reside in each of us, one gained access to them. They argued about the relative importance of faith and works in the attainment of God's grace. They argued about whom God spoke to and who could speak for God. They argued about the status and role of bishops. They argued about whether Christians should share a specific set of beliefs and, if so, what those beliefs should be. They argued about which books should be included in the canon, and they argued about how those books should be interpreted, according to the plain sense or by means of symbol, type, figure, or allegory. They argued about who gets to say.

They argued a lot about the Jews. In the second century, Marcion was among those who considered the story of the near sacrifice and every other story in the Old Testament vile, the god of the Jews a lower god, perhaps a false one. Huge portions of the New Testament also drew Marcion's scorn. He liked Luke and ten letters, all of which he attributed to Paul.

How often Marcion and other early Christians actually argued *with* the Jews is not entirely clear. Some scholars say that Christians and Jews had nothing to do with one another after the first century, not even disputation. They say that the Christian polemic that looks the most like argument—explicitly anti-Jewish polemic—was actually aimed at other Christians, those who clung to Jewish practices, or at pagan converts who adopted Jewish practices, or at pagans who used Jewish history or theology to refute Christian claims. Others say that on the ground, even in churches and synagogues, there was every kind of encounter, argument, rivalry, coexistence, identity, and exchange. The latter believe that the Gospels were not just originally Jewish but fundamentally Jewish, grounded in Jewish tradition and teaching and belief. The very distinction between Christian and Jew, some say, remained blurred for centuries.

Marcion was excommunicated, but over the next two centuries

other forms of heresy and every sort of schism convinced many clergymen that the church needed canon, law, and binding creed. Yet in the fifth century, the bishop of Hippo, Augustine, was still doing battle with dualism, and in his arguments against Manichaeism, a heresy he himself had flirted with before his conversion to Christianity, he defended the literal truth of the Old Testament and insisted that the God of ancient Israel and the God of the new Israel were one and the same. He also argued against the likes of John Chrysostom of Constantinople and Severus of Minorca, who insisted that Christ's teachings led inexorably to the elimination of the Jews. "Slay them not," Augustine famously said. Jews should be allowed to live and practice Judaism, but his reasons are telling: The Jews were living, physical evidence of the truth of the teachings of Moses, the authenticity of antiquity. They actually existed. At the same time, their subsequent exile, dispersion, misery, and degradation were daily living proof of the fate awaiting those who rejected Christ and remained slaves to the law.

The sacrifice of Isaac, as the church fathers were inclined to call it, did not figure in that or any other major debate among Christians. Notwithstanding many differences in emphasis and some differences in interpretation, they all agreed that the story was about a father, Father Abraham, a lover of God and a man of perfect faith, who set out, at God's command, to sacrifice his beloved son. Whether his and his son's willingness merely prefigured God's sacrifice or actually precipitated it, the outcome was the same: God stopped him, but for his faith God rewarded him and his offspring. The Father of all fathers so loved the world that he gave his only Son, his own beloved son, so that whoever believes in him should not perish but have eternal life.

I understand why, looking back over the four centuries between the death of Jesus and the appearance of Augustine's *City of God*, centuries in which the church won converts, worked out creed and canon, and became the religion of the Roman Empire, so many people have been inclined to see Christianity exactly as the Christian faithful themselves saw it, as the latest and the greatest. Israel's covenant of Moses's law was the past; the Christian covenant of faith, the present and future. Jews were the aging parents, Christians the vigorous child. There was an obvious chronological logic to that view of the relationship—the Jews had been around longer—and, to Christians, an equally obvious appeal.

What that view missed was that the religion of Israel was not in decline or frozen in time. With the destruction of the Temple in 70 CE, the suspension of daily ritual sacrifice, and the dispersion of the priesthood, Jews certainly did hold on to one part of their past—the revelation at Sinai—as if it were their last remaining connection to God. But it was less a desperate clinging than a passionate embrace, and like so many of those it was fruitful. By the time Augustine characterized the Jews as artifacts, flesh-and-blood fossils, irrefutable evidence of biblical truth, Jewish interpreters were deep into a long and remarkable renaissance, a renaissance in which they paid homage to the past, to revelation and to tradition, by using it to create something new. So much so that instead of thinking of Judaism and Christianity as parent and child, it might be more useful to imagine siblings, siblings in a large, fractious family, struggling for the attention and affection of their parents—or Parent—and their share of the inheritance, which included not just a priceless set of sacred texts but the power and authority to say what they meant.

Now, a person living today or much closer to our time than to late antiquity should be excused for thinking that those Jewish interpreters, however often at odds with Christian interpreters, all thought about Abraham and Isaac (and every other Bible story) the same way. That's because when people speak of the Jewish interpreters of late antiquity today, they often refer to them not by their names but simply as "The Rabbis." When people speak of the fruits of their labor, they often refer to "Rabbinic Tradition" or "Jewish Tradition" or just "Tradition."

Sometimes that is nothing but an innocent form of shorthand. It is easier, especially when referring to the rabbis of the first millennium, to say "the rabbis" ("according to the rabbis," "in the words of the rabbis," as "the rabbis liked to say," or simply, "the rabbis said") than to drop a name (Gamaliel "the Elder," Yishma'el b. Elisha, Meir, Judah ha-Nasi, Haninah bar Hama, Shmuel bar Nachman, Mar Shemuel, or scores of others) in the instances when we have a name, a name few laypeople are likely to recognize. Other times it is a rhetorical sleight of hand, an attempt to end a debate, clinch an argument, settle a dispute, link one's position on a matter of ethics or ritual or law to an unassailable authority. In either case, the phrase suggests that Tradition is singular, monolithic, and perfectly clear; that the rabbis (one generation after another, one century after another, producing more than a thousand years of interpretation, not just in Palestine and Babylonia but in Syria, Greece, Italy, Spain, France, Germany, Macedonia, Asia Minor, Byzantium, Persia, Alexandria, and everywhere else on earth there were Jews) thought or spoke as one, walked in lockstep.

Yet as anyone who has taken even a cursory look at the literature the rabbis produced knows, nothing could be further from the truth. What we call rabbinical or Jewish tradition was, from the first, just like biblical tradition: multiple, dialogical, polysemous, sometimes even riotous. The Mishnah and Tosefta are voluminous compilations of (and ongoing debates about) the oral law, the law God spoke at Sinai but Moses didn't record, transmitted from generation to generation and ultimately organized into six orders (seeds, festivals, women, damages, sacrifices, and purity) and sixty-three tractates (topics like blessings, Sabbath, marriage, divorce, torts, oaths, courts, offerings, and ritual slaughter). The Gemara is the commentary on the Mishnah and Tosefta, and the two Talmuds, one redacted in Palestine and one in Babylonia, combine the Mishnah and the Gemara. The *midrashim* are the body of literature that has recorded or re-created century after century of commentary (midrash) on the written Torah itself, whether the narrative portions of the written Torah (*midrash aggadah*) or the law (*midrash halakhah*).

Because the Talmud is the commentary on the Mishnah and the Mishnah is often the commentary or elaboration upon the written Torah, the Talmud inevitably contains commentary on the written Torah. In other words, it contains midrash, and in the Talmud's midrash, Abraham and Isaac come up from time to time. In one instance, a question about the appropriate penalty for a person who ignores the words of a prophet sparked (or was later linked to) a discussion of the surest ways to distinguish true prophecy from false, which sparked (or was later linked to) a discussion about the attentiveness with which Isaac listened to Abraham, which sparked a discussion about the possible reasons for God's test. But from the middle of the first millennium, most of the Jewish commentary on Abraham and Isaac came in midrash proper, interpretation of the written scriptures themselves, interpretation drawn from lessons and homilies delivered and discussions that took place in the schools and Torah academies and synagogues that were fast becoming the center of Jewish life.

First-millennium midrash has come down to us in many different forms. Some of it reads like raw transcripts of conversations, some like collections of sermons, some like loosely connected collections of short stories, some like pumped-up parallel narratives of entire books of the Torah. But invariably it, just like the commentary on the oral law, was a literature of dialogue and debate launched by questions: questions about word choices, questions about juxtapositions, questions about repetition, questions about inconsistencies, questions about contradictions (including contradictions between different versions of the same biblical story and contradictions between how biblical characters behaved in the past and how readers were supposed to behave in the present), questions about the meaning of obscure, archaic, confusing, puzzling, or just plain troubling passages, questions about gaps, questions about practical ramifications of passages in ethics or ritual or law, questions about the tension between oral and written Torah, questions about exactly what happened in a story and why.

One of the first questions rabbis asked was an old one: Why did God test Abraham? He already knew he was righteous. When rabbis wanted to, they answered it without adding or taking away a word.

Some answered, as Jubilees had answered, that God had simply wanted to demonstrate Abraham's obedience, to elevate him, like a banner, for all the world to see. Perhaps God also wanted to justify, a hundred years after the fact (one form of biblical backdating), his initial call and blessing. Abraham's performance made it more difficult for readers (turning from the end of Genesis 11 to the opening of Genesis 12) to conclude that God's choice had been arbitrary.

Others said that God always tests the righteous, the way a potter tests the strong vessels (the weak would shatter) and a farmer yokes the strong cow (the weak would let him down). When it comes to people, the philosophically minded added, such tests allow the righteous to transform potential into actual, good hearts into good deeds. God was pretty sure and maybe even certain that Abraham was good. But Abraham was not without a will of his own. He didn't have to be good. God gave him the opportunity to see what he was made of.

Others said it was simpler than that: God tested Abraham to increase his fear of him.

Why did Abraham, who had plenty of servants, saddle his own ass?

Because love upsets the natural order of things, just as hate does. One rabbi hoped that one would counteract the other: "Let the sword taken in the hand of our father Abraham" when he stretched forth his hand to slay his son "come and counteract the sword grasped by Pharaoh" when he threatened to destroy the Jews.

Why did Abraham take two servants with him?

Several reasons, two of which were quite practical. If he had taken only one and that servant became ill, Abraham, in caring for him, would have become the servant of his own servant.

Another reason: If he had taken only one and that servant needed to leave his side to relieve himself, Abraham would have been left on his own.

Why did God lead him on for three days?

So no one could diminish Abraham's deed by saying that he had obeyed in shock or confusion at God's command, rather than carefully considered obedience.

Another reason: Because God always comes through on the third day. See Jacob in Genesis. The three spies in Joshua. The books of Jonah and Esther. Or the prophecy of Hosea: "After two days he will revive us, after three days he will raise us up, so we can live in his presence."

. . .

Other questions, or variations on those very same questions, prompted rabbis to modify or elaborate on the words on the page, starting with questions about the meaning of the story's very first words: "After these things." Most early Christian commentators encouraged readers to skip right over that phrase. They said it was merely a way of moving the narrative forward, a little like "Next thing you know." If those words referred to anything, it was all the things that had happened since God first called. Most rabbis, by contrast, believed that only momentous "things" could have triggered so momentous a test.

"What things?" they asked, which was another way of asking "Why? Why did God ask?"

The first move many rabbis made was to employ a second meaning of *ha-devarim* ("these things"), which, from the Hebrew root *d-b-r* ("speak"), also means utterances or words. "After these words," God tested Abraham. God's command came in response to something someone said and, at least since Jubilees, Satan was a prime suspect. Some imagined him accusing Abraham of taking God for granted, throwing a great feast to celebrate Isaac's weaning but neglecting to set aside even a single bullock or ram for God.

God scoffed. Come on, Satan, if I were to tell him to sacrifice his son, he would not refuse.

Others said it was the "words" of Abraham himself, full of remorse for celebrating without making an offering to God. God told him to relax. I know that you are worthy. Watch, I'll show you and everyone else, once and for all.

Others imagined Isaac and Ishmael arguing about who was the more beloved son.

"I am more beloved than thou, because I was circumcised at the age of thirteen," Ishmael said.

Isaac said no, it was he, circumcised at eight days.

"I could have protested, yet did not," Ishmael said. "You had no choice."

"All you did was lend God three drops of blood," Isaac said.

"Were the Holy One, blessed be He, to say unto me, 'Sacrifice thy-self before Me,' I would obey."

God said, "This is the moment!"

And Abraham rose early in the morning.

Why early?

Some said: Because he delighted in God's commandment and was eager to do what God had asked. Others: Because all God's chosen rise early. Jacob rose early in the morning. Moses rose early in the morning. Samuel rose early in the morning.

Others still: Because Abraham wanted to leave before anyone tried to stop him.

What prompted Isaac to ask about the lamb?

Satan. The last thing he wanted to see was a demonstration of Abraham's greatness. He approached them along the way. Abraham first. "Are you crazy?" Satan asked. "God gives you a son at one hundred, and you are going to sacrifice him?"

Abraham ignored him.

"And what if he asks you something harder?" Satan asked.

"I'll do what he asks," Abraham said.

"And tomorrow he is going to say, Ha, you are a murderer."

"I will live with it."

Getting nowhere, Satan turned to Isaac.

"I doubt that's where we are going," Isaac said, "but if so, so be it."

"You mean you don't care if all that was due you will go to Ishmael?" Satan asked.

Isaac did a double take, and it was only then that he asked about the lamb.

In some versions, Abraham tells him that God would provide the lamb. In others, that he himself would be the lamb. After which, in every version, both of them walk on together.

The moral of that story in the minds of many rabbis: Evil doesn't have to do all that it is intended to do to cause trouble.

Once atop Moriah, "Abraham built an altar," suggesting to the rabbis that he built it alone, without any help from his vigorous and ever-obedient son. Many wondered why. Some said it was because Satan had not surrendered after appealing to the two of them directly. Rather, he turned himself into a river, blocking their path. When they tried to ford it, the water rose, which tipped off Abraham. He chased the angel away, but he was still wary, and that's why, when they arrived at the site, Abraham told Isaac to hide, fearing that Satan would try to maim him in some way, perhaps by pelting him with stones, leaving him unfit for sacrifice.

It was one question after another, and some of the answers to the simplest questions surprised me.

At long last, some rabbis had come to see the unlikelihood— what I took to be the unlikelihood—that, in response to God's command, Abraham would have said nothing more than "Here I am." Many imagined a dialogue to explain why God had taken so many words ("Pray, take your son, your only one, the one you love, Isaac") to introduce his command when just two—"Take Isaac"— would have done the trick.

"Take your son," God said.

"Which son?" Abraham asked. "I have two sons."

"Your only son," God answered.

"Isaac is the only son of his mother and Ishmael is the only son of his mother."

"The one you love."

"Is there a limit to the affections? I love them both."

"Isaac!" God said.

There were (always) other explanations. Some said, as some church fathers said, that God was simply trying to increase the suspense, make the test harder, bring Isaac ever closer to Abraham's heart. Many noted that God had employed the same tactic in his very first words to Abraham: "Go forth from your land, your birthplace, and your father's house." He could simply have said, "Go. I'll show you where."

Others said just the opposite: that he had used the extra words to soften the blow.

How those lines of imagined dialogue were first delivered or received, I can't say. It is not impossible—in fact it seems likely—that at least some rabbis were going for a laugh, gently mocking Abraham (who had somehow divined God's will) for stalling. No matter. We mock people for their human foibles. If it was mockery, I'd be happy to think that in every generation there have been some who have acknowledged the mystery, strangeness, even inhumanness, of Abraham's silence.

Other rabbis imagined Abraham's attempt to buy some time coming after God told him what he wanted him to do.

"Sacrifice Isaac?" he asked. "I can't. I am not a priest."

Get on with it, God said, citing one of David's psalms: "You are a priest forever."

At last someone besides Satan was giving voice to what some, yesterday no less than today, might consider reason, trying to slow the mad march to Moriah. Abraham ultimately departed, but God's good angels picked up where he left off. They protested the unfairness of it all. They wept. It was unnatural for a man to kill his son, they cried. Especially a man like Abraham, who showed hospitality to strangers, observed the Sabbath, remained true to Jerusalem. If he was not a man of merit, no man ever was, or would be. In some versions, Abraham wept too and his tears fell into Isaac's eyes, blinding him momentarily and thereby saving his life. The heavens had opened up above him. Had he gotten a good look at the Shekhinah—the divine presence—that look would have been his last.

Several rabbis, whose words have been preserved in the one of the oldest tractates of the Mishnah, suggested that on the way to Moriah, Abraham had prayed for Isaac's life. Atop the mountain, God answered his prayers. Nonetheless, subsequent generations of rabbis imagined that after God stopped him, Abraham called him out on his prevarication: "Yesterday you said that through Isaac my seed would be acclaimed. Then you retracted and said, 'Take now thy son.' Now you say, 'Do not raise your hand against the boy.'"

And God (anticipating Psalm 89) said: "Oh Abraham, I will not violate My covenant, or change what I have uttered. I said, 'Take now thy son, etc.' But did I tell you to slaughter him? No, I said to 'take him up.'" (The literal meaning of the word for sacrifice, *olah,* is "what is brought or taken up.")

"You have taken him up," God said. "Now take him down."

Other rabbis found other ways to demonstrate that Abraham had completely misunderstood God's command. Rabbi Samuel ben Nahmani, in the name of Rabbi Jonathan, did so by unpacking a powerful passage in Jeremiah, in which God chastises the people of Judah for sacrificing children to Baal. Those were sacrifices, God insists, that "I never commanded, never decreed, and which never came to My mind." The word "commanded," the rabbi said, referred to the king of Moab (who had sacrificed a son in the heat of battle). The word "decreed" referred to Jephthah (who had sacrificed his only daughter after returning home safely from battle). "Never came to My mind" referred to Abraham. The idea that God had commanded Abraham to sacrifice Isaac was preposterous. The thought had never even entered God's mind.

Abraham, however, was not mollified. When God's angel stopped him, he asked, "Who are you?"

"I am an angel."

"God told me to do this," Abraham said. "God Himself will tell me to stop."

Which is why God said and the Bible reads, "By My own Self I swear."

Another interpretation for the word "swear": After Abraham stopped and sacrificed the ram, he insisted that God himself swear that he would never test him like that again.

God swore, repeating his promises, at which time Abraham said to him: You've had your say. Now I would like to have mine. You told me to sacrifice Isaac. I could have protested. I didn't. When you said take your son, I might have said: Yesterday you promised to make my children as ubiquitous as dust. Through Isaac. Yet now you say sacrifice him. Yet "I did not do this, but suppressed my feelings of compassion to do your will." I bound him and laid him on the altar, and I hope that when Isaac's people are in trouble, you will "remember that binding in their favor and be filled with compassion for them."

God promised to remember—or to respond to a reminder. He knew, he said, that in the future, Isaac's descendants would fall into the clutches of sin and, as a result of their sins, become the victims of persecution. He would judge them on Rosh Hashanah. If they wanted him to remember the binding of Isaac, they should blow upon the shofar: "On the New Year they take the shofar and blow on it, and eventually they will be redeemed by the ram's horn."

Abraham and Isaac's descendants have paid heed, and then some. They sound the shofar not only on Rosh Hashanah but also every day (but the Sabbaths and the last day) of the entire month of Ellul, which leads up to it. They have incorporated Abraham's plea—"Remember"—not only into the penitential prayers and liturgical poems they recite from the first day of that month through the last moments of Yom Kippur, but also into their daily and weekly prayers throughout the year, including the prayers that immediately precede and follow the reading of Genesis 22 in weekday morning services: "Just as Abraham our forefather suppressed his mercy for his only son and was willing to slaughter him in order to do Your will, so may Your mercy suppress Your anger from upon us. . . . May You overstep with us the line of Your law and deal with us with the attribute of kindness and the attribute of mercy. In Your great goodness may You turn aside Your burning wrath from Your people, Your city, Your land, Your heritage."

All that cheers me. Even the demand for redemption in the future based on Abraham and Isaac's merit cheers me. It isn't so much the idea of it. I came of age, perhaps naively, thinking that we all earn our own blessings and curses. I understand now that way back when, the issue was hotly contested. Read the book of Exodus, where God, in blazing anger over the Golden Calf, threatens to destroy the Israelites and Moses implores him not to: "Remember Your servants, Abraham, Isaac, and Israel, how You swore them by Your Self and said to them: I will make your offspring as numerous as the stars of heaven, and I will give to your offspring this whole land of which I spoke, to possess forever." For a different view, turn to the book of Ezekiel. The prophet argues that "the righteousness of the righteous shall be accounted to him alone, and the wickedness of the wicked shall be accounted to him alone."

What I welcome in Abraham's insistence that God remember is not so much the idea of the merit of the fathers—how could I be happy that we all benefit from Abraham's willingness to do something I wish he hadn't done?—but rather the unmistakable implication in Abraham's words that God had made an excessive and mind-boggling demand. After all, God had already reaffirmed his promise—his blessing and the descendants—even sweetening the deal with the reassurance that Israel would seize its "enemies' gates." But here and elsewhere Abraham, and the rabbis through him, suggest that as payback for the test that Abraham has just endured, all God's previous promises weren't enough. Abraham wants pardon for future crimes, absolution for the ages, a guarantee that the covenant and the promise at the heart of it would be irrevocable.

There is more, and I could go on, along similar lines, for pages. But if I did, I might mislead you, contributing to just the kind of distortion I have warned you against. For every late-antique take on the story that suggests that (as far back as the first centuries of the first millennium) there were rabbis who believed that God should not have asked and Abraham should not have obeyed, there are several other takes that remind me that theirs was a minority view. In fact, some of the very riffs I find reassuring resist glib readings. Recall that some rabbis imagined Abraham weeping, his tears flooding Isaac's eyes. But just to make sure that no one mistook his compassion for reluctance, those same rabbis or their editors quickly added: "Yet even so, his heart rejoiced to obey the will of his creator."

So much so that sometimes God had a hard time getting him to switch gears. That's why, in the minds of many rabbis, God said, "Do not raise your hand against the boy" when the mortal danger to Isaac came not from Abraham's hand but from the cleaver he held in it. It turns out that the tears of God's angels had ruined the knife.

"Then I will strangle him," Abraham said.

"Lay not a hand upon the lad."

"Let us bring forth a drop of blood from him," Abraham pleaded.

"Don't do anything to him," God said. "Nothing. Not a blemish"—punning on the words *me'ummah* ("anything") and *mum* ("blemish").

Abraham stopped. But he was disappointed, and in his disappointment he prayed:

As he sacrificed the ram, he said: "Do Thou regard the blood of the ram as if the blood of my son were being poured before Thee."

As he skinned the ram, he said: "Do Thou regard this as though it were the skin of my son Isaac, which is being flayed before Thee."

As he coated the ram with salt, he said: "Do Thou regard this as though the salt were being poured on my son Isaac."

As he offered the limbs of the ram, he said: "Do Thou regard this as though these were the limbs of my son Isaac being offered to Thee."

As he burned the ram, he said: "Do Thou regard this as though the ashes of my son Isaac were heaped up on top of the altar before Thee."

In those prayers and others like it, the rabbis, through Abraham, wanted God to see the ram not in place of Isaac, not instead of Isaac, not as a substitute for Isaac—a valid exchange, a ram instead of a boy—but the ram as if he were Isaac. To help God see it that way, some rabbis imagined that the ram's name was Isaac. Others imagined that Abraham had asked God to pretend that he had sacrificed Isaac first and then, after Isaac, the ram, the ram in addition to, not instead of, Isaac.

And that's not all. In addition to rabbinical riffs in which Abraham asks God to let him take some blood, and riffs in which Isaac expresses his hope that a portion of his blood would suffice for the atonement of Israel, there are riffs in which Abraham actually takes Isaac's blood: "And Abraham bound him on the altar and then took the knife in order to slaughter him, until a quarter of his blood left him."

And another: "And there were Abraham's eyes on Isaac's eyes, and Isaac's eyes on the very heavens, and tears falling, pouring, from Abraham's eyes until he stood virtually to his height in a pool of tears. He said to Isaac: My son, since you have already begun to give up a quarter of your blood, may your Creator appoint some other victim in your place."

Exegesis of crucial passages of Scripture moved in the same

direction, including the interpretation of Exodus 12:13 ("When I see the blood I will pass over you, so that no plague will destroy you when I strike") and Exodus 23 ("For when the Lord goes through to smite the Egyptians, He will see the blood . . . and the Lord will pass over the door and not let the Destroyer enter and smite your home"). What blood? Anyone who knows the story of the exodus from Egypt would swear it was the blood of all those lambs smeared on the lintel and doorposts of Jewish homes. But it was not only that blood: it was also, according to many rabbis, "the blood of Isaac's binding (*akedah*)." "That is the blood meant, for it says, 'Abraham called the name of that place, the Lord will see.'" What did he see? "He saw the blood of Isaac's sacrifice."

Then there's the line in Chronicles that explains another crucial moment of deliverance, when God was about to destroy Jerusalem on account of the census that David had ordered. He "sent a pestilence upon Israel, and 70,000 men fell." Then he sent "an angel to Jerusalem to destroy it, but as he was about to wreak destruction, the LORD *saw* and renounced further punishment and said to the destroying angel, 'Enough! Stay your hand!'"

"What did he see? The blood of Isaac's sacrifice."

Other writers, including those who translated the book of Chronicles into Aramaic, had a slightly different view: What did the Lord behold? "He beheld the ashes of the Akedah of Isaac."

And where, rabbis asked, did God see Isaac's blood and ashes? On Ornan the Jebusite's threshing-room floor, some answered, where, after God's angel retreated, David built an altar and offered a sacrifice and vowed to build the Temple: "Here will be the house of the Lord and here the altar of burnt offerings for Israel." And that's where his son, Solomon, built the Temple, on the threshing-room floor. And where was the threshing-room floor? Where else? On Mount Moriah.

And centuries later, after the return from exile in Babylonia, when the Israelites rebuilt the Temple, how did they know where to put the altar and what to do with it? "Said R. Eleazar: They beheld the altar all built and Michael, the Great Prince, stood by it sacrificing on it." But R. Isaac Napaha disagreed: They rebuilt it themselves, and they knew they had found the right spot when "they beheld Isaac's ashes, that these lay on that spot. Isaac's ashes were the foundation of that altar."

And why were ashes placed on the head of each and every one of the participants in a public fast? There was "a difference of opinion" between "Rabbi Levi bar Hama and Rabbi Hanina," two authorities cited in the Babylonian Talmud. One said it was to show God that we know that before him, "we are all like dust and ashes." The other, to call to mind "for our sake Isaac's ashes."

If only I were not so squeamish about sacrifice, especially human sacrifice, I could just relax and take quiet satisfaction in the thought of all that those nineteen lines had wrought, the legacy of one very short story in history and literature, from Exodus to the establishment of Solomon's Temple to the establishment of Temple service to the rebuilding of the Temple and beyond. Who, now, would have the audacity to say that the story—which many rabbis now referred to as the "Binding of Isaac" (*Akedat Yitzhak*) or just the *Akedah*— had been neglected or ignored?

But I am who I am. I am appalled by many of those takes on the story, and I can't help wondering how many first-millennium rabbis felt the same way. Unfortunately, I have no way of knowing. I am not, in most instances, reading transcripts of conversations, or complete sermons, or even narratives written by a single author. Far from it. I am reading edited compilations of conversations and passages from sermons and scenes from stories, perhaps edited compilations of compilations, exegesis passed from rabbi to rabbi, rabbi to students, rabbi to congregations, for generations and sometimes centuries before it was collected by editors who cut and pasted and added and updated with abandon and only occasionally cited their sources and only inadvertently dated them. One interpretation follows another with the simplest transition ("another inter-pretation"; "Rabbi So-and-so said") or no transition at all, and it is the same whether the latter interpretation supplemented the former or complemented it, implicitly dissented from it or flatly contradicted it.

Every once in a while I get a hint (in a word—"No!"—or phrase—"Enough of that!") of one rabbi's view of the interpreta-tion of another. But most of the time I come away only with each rabbi's own view, set before or after the view of another (and that other might well have lived long before or long after). I know (any reader would know) that the rabbis loved language, loved puns and other fun with words and numbers, loved multiple meanings, loved associations and interpretations based on the juxtaposition of words, and on the sound of words, and on the repetition of let-ters and roots and words and phrases in passages near and far. But whether particular rabbis loved or were at peace with explanations and associations and revisions that were mutually exclusive, or sim-ply different from their own, I can't say.

I have no idea what the rabbis who imagined Abraham stall-ing thought of the stories in which he rose early and rushed to do the deed. What those who imagined him weeping as he took leave of Sarah thought of the stories in which he was giddy with excite-ment, eager to obey God's command. What those who imagined him praying to God to spare Isaac (let alone taking God to task for asking) thought of the stories in which he pleaded with God to let him go through with it. What the rabbis who imagined God with a good reason to ask and a determination to see Abraham obey thought of the stories in which God contended he hadn't asked and never would.

I don't know. I don't even know what the rabbis who associ-ated Isaac's deliverance with the sacrifice of the paschal lamb and redemption of the Jewish firstborn in Egypt thought of the rab-bis who associated it with the shofar and atonement of Rosh Hashanah. Or what any of those rabbis thought of the rabbis who believed that the twice-daily lamb sacrifice in the Temple, built on Mount Moriah, was a reenactment of Abraham's substitution of a lamb for Isaac.

What I do know is that the rabbis who compiled and edited the collections of rabbinical commentary we call *midrashim* brought the widest range of interpretations and narrative together on the page, offering us many different, often contradictory ways of thinking about the story without trying to resolve the contradictions or get us to think about it one way or another. It bears repeating that neither they nor the rabbis whose words they purported to preserve thought of themselves as revising Scripture. But in their endless asking and answering, they created a vast archive of anecdote, of lexicography, of scene, of dialogue, of cognates and analogy, countless precious nuggets of narrative, commentary, and exegesis. Or, more accurately, they contributed volume upon volume to the existing archive, an archive that in one form or another (the histories of Josephus and 2 Maccabees; the rewritten Bibles of Pseudo-Philo and Jubilees; the philosophical essays of Philo and 4 Maccabees; the historical fiction of Judith; the interpretative translations beginning with the Aramaic Targums; the self-conscious revision of early parts of the Bible by later biblical writers, copyists, translators, and editors; and the explanations of the text offered by teachers at public readings of the Torah going back a thousand years) was nearly as old as the texts themselves. Recall the scene, the gathering before the water gate after the return from exile in Babylonia, recorded in the book of Nehemiah. Ezra was asked to read from the teaching of Moses, and while he did, the Levites explained the teaching to the people: "They read from the scroll of the teaching of God, translating it and giving the sense; so they understood the reading."

That archive was a great repository of tradition. It was tradition. And yet, as each succeeding generation of exegetes drew, commented, and elaborated upon the material in it, consciously or unconsciously transformed minor keys into major, selected elements of interpretation and narrative that made the most sense to them and combined those elements into single-author commentaries or wove them in creation-to-nation narratives, elevated some motifs, neglected others, brought new ways of thinking and new tools to bear on old problems, or simply saw old stories and old problems in a fresh light, that repository of tradition was also the raw material out of which new tradition was made.

Consider the small and simple contribution of Johanan ha-Kohen, a liturgical poet who lived in the land of Israel in the seventh century. Drawing on both Bible stories and midrash, he imagined a dialogue between God and his daughter, the Torah, about possible suitors. She surveyed the field and found a lot to love, but she also found reasons (Noah drank too much and cursed his grandson, Canaan; blind old Isaac was like a judge who took bribes; Jacob deceived his father) to reject one after the other. In the end she chose Moses, but I can't resist noting her reason for passing over Abraham, for whom her father had made a strong case. She, too, thought the world of him, and she, too, knew that he was "good and perfect in his ways":

> But he did not beg for mercy for his only son.
> He wished to spill his blood like a cruel man
> In order to fulfill your will wholeheartedly
> As he was certain that God is good and merciful.
> He should have, however, begged to spare his only son
> And save him from the burning coals.
> No mercy would have been shown his son if the Lord of
>   mercy had not taken pity.

In just a few lines of verse (*piyyut*), Johanan transformed a story about Abraham's responsibility to God into a story about his irresponsibility to his son.

That was not a common way of looking at the story or Abraham in the middle of the first millennium. Yet the poem was out there. Later it was incorporated into Shavuot services in Ashkenazic synagogues, where it remained for centuries. It was out there, along with the rest, and I love that it was there, and I love the reason it was there, which I have to admit is the very same reason that the commentary that disturbs me was there. I love that the rabbis had so much to say and weren't afraid to say it. I love that they weren't cowed by the age or authority of the story or any other ancient story, by its status or stature in anyone else's eyes, or by their own tremendous reverence for it or by their reverence for their teachers and for the teachers who had come before them. I love the attitude even when I don't love the expression; love the form—the way they talked about the story and the way they did things with it—even when I don't love the content.

Scripture was Scripture, holy, sacred, divine. But teachers and students, preachers and congregations, writers and readers, shaped the way people understood it, sometimes altering the meaning by altering the plot (a story in which God says he never intended for Abraham to sacrifice Isaac means something different from a story in which God explicitly rewards Abraham for his willingness to do so), sometimes altering the plot by altering the meaning (a three-day journey in which Abraham is silently scheming to come up with a way out means something different from three days in which he is eager to obey God's command, and both are different from days in which he is certain—"We will worship and come back to you"—that God was not actually going to make him sacrifice his son).

Scripture was Scripture. The law revealed in it, oral and written, though also subject to seemingly endless debate and (over time) subject to all sorts of revision, was, at least by the Middle Ages, thought in each moment of time to be fixed and binding.

But the stories in Scripture were neither fixed nor binding. Their meaning was plainly not (and has never been) the meaning for all.

13

~~~

The archive I am imagining was not exclusive to Jews. Christian interpreters made contributions to it throughout late antiquity, and every indication is that as they prepared sermons and lectures and wrote pastoral letters and apologies—arguing among themselves and explaining to others who they were and what they believed— they drew on it too. Their first contribution was the late first-century idea that the story was all about Abraham's faith. Several centuries later, some turned their attention to Sarah.

They didn't have much to work with. G had left her out of the story, and the earliest Jewish interpreters, from Jubilees to Josephus, had followed his lead. And by their lights who can blame them? The story wouldn't have been much of a story if the sacrifice had been aborted in the first few lines. How do you say "Over my dead body" in classical biblical Hebrew? And though Abraham might have been torn, God would have understood. He might well have said exactly what he had said a chapter earlier, when Sarah ordered Abraham to cast out Hagar and Ishmael, and Abraham was distressed: "Whatever Sarah tells you, do as she says, for it is through Isaac that offspring shall be continued for you."

The first rabbis were no more inclined than Second Temple sages to tangle with her. But questions remained. How, for one, did Abraham get away from a mother so protective of Isaac and his prerogatives that she banished his older brother for misbehaving at the boy's weaning? They imagined Abraham scheming. He thought: She never allows the boy out of her sight. "After all, she was a woman, with a woman's mind, and she flew off the handle at every little thing; imagine if she got wind of this." But if he was just to leave with Isaac, without saying a word, she'd kill herself. So late in the afternoon on the day Abraham received God's command, he asked her if it would be okay for him to take Isaac for religious instruction. There was a school a few days away. He himself had known God since the age of three. The boy was ready. Sarah was pious, and she agreed. "Go in peace," she said. But he didn't want to take any chances that she'd change her mind. So "Abraham rose early the next morning."

The more pressing question was how Sarah died. Her death is reported in the very first lines of the very next chapter of Genesis, and the proximity of two such momentous events simply could not have been a coincidence. To explain it, many rabbis turned, once again, to Satan, who, having failed to persuade either Abraham or Isaac that what they were doing was crazy, figured Sarah was his last hope. Some said he had approached her disguised as an old family friend and told her where her husband and son had gone. She cried out, the same cry that she imagined would soon come from her son—three short sobs (explaining one way of sounding the shofar, the three short blasts called *shevarim*). Her heart stopped on the spot, and her soul flew out of her. Others said Sarah had taken off after them, making it only as far as Hebron, where she learned that Isaac had been spared, and she died, on the spot, of joy. Others still said she had awaited their return at the door of her tent. But Isaac lagged well behind Abraham, and when Sarah saw Abraham approaching without him, she assumed her son was dead. She fainted, and never came to. In a fourth version, she lived long enough to hear Isaac tell the tale:

"You mean if it were not for the angel you'd already be dead?" she asked.

"Yes," Isaac said, and she shrieked six times (explaining the six additional blasts of the shofar required as a minimum in addition to the three mentioned in the Torah). Then she died.

Thus Genesis 23:1: "And Sarah's life was a hundred and twenty-seven years, the years of Sarah's life. And Sarah died in Kiriath-Arba, which is Hebron, in the land of Canaan, and Abraham came to mourn Sarah and to keen for her."

"And where did Abraham come from?" many rabbis asked. "Why wasn't he with her?"

"He came from Mount Moriah."

And how old was Isaac at the time of the binding? Each of the versions linking God's test and Sarah's death had the additional virtue of allowing rabbis to answer that question definitively, and with a mature Isaac. Born when his mother was ninety, he would have been thirty-seven.

(And, for curious close readers wondering what Sarah was doing in Hebron when she died, when Abraham left for Moriah from Beersheba and returned there: see the second Satan version above.)

If there was a first-millennium rabbi who considered the possibility that Abraham might have taken Sarah into his confidence, his words have not been preserved. A few bishops, by contrast, did consider it, only to conclude that Abraham had had no choice but to keep her in the dark. Writing in the fifth century, Basil of Seleucia detailed Abraham's deliberation: "'She is pious,' he thought, 'but I fear her nature. Although seeing the piety, I fear the love. The woman is pious, but she is a mother. It is a terrible thing when mothers are overpowered by the weakness of nature. I fear lest she defile the sacrifice through weeping. . . . Lest beating her face, she ruins the sacrifice and does violence to God.'"

The church fathers could be nasty about Sarah's nature. Gregory, bishop of Nyssa in the last quarter of the fourth century, believed that Abraham had considered her "entirely untrustworthy," a judgment in which he concurred, noting that Adam had not been "aided in the least by accepting Eve's advice." But for many commentators, especially in the Christian East, nastiness about Sarah's nature was tempered by typology. If Abraham was a type of God and Isaac a type of humanity saved by the lamb of God (or linked with the lamb as a type of Christ), there had to be a role for Sarah, and there was: she prefigured Mary, and however faint the shadow in the eyes of those with the dimmest vision, she was worthy of representation if not always respect. Even Gregory paid her the respect of imagining what she would have said to Abraham had he confided in her: "Do not become a wicked story for the world. This is my only born son . . . my first and last child. Whom will we see after this one at our table? Who will call his sweet voice to me? Who will call for mother? Who will attend my old age? Who will wrap up my body after my death? Who will heap up a mound over the body?" He's the "bloom of youth," fruit of great prayer, branch of our succession, remnant of our people, staff of our old age. She asks Abraham to kill her first: "Let the eyes of Sarah see neither Abraham as a child killer nor Isaac killed by his father's hands."

I like Sarah's warning about the wicked story, and her last line too. (And I am struck by the echoes of Homer and Sophocles in the writing of a bishop who suggested that his education was unadulterated, all Christian.) Still, I can't help thinking that the main reason Gregory gave Sarah a voice was to use what he took to be her weakness as a foil, magnifying Abraham's strength.

I much prefer the Sarah of the fifth- and sixth-century verse homilists and hymnists, Christians whose literary and liturgical language was Syriac, a dialect of Aramaic. These writers, perhaps inspired by the great Syriac theologian and hymnist Ephrem (who maintained that the only reason Abraham hadn't told Sarah about the sacrifice was that God hadn't commanded him to), not only imagined what Sarah might have said to Abraham but also let her say it for herself. And say it she did, in verse homilies so dramatic and so full of direct address, dialogue, and physical movement that some scholars believe they might have been acted out on a stage. It seems certain that they were sung in church, and on feast days in Syriac churches they may well have been sung by women.

In one homily, Sarah, seeing Abraham and Isaac packing up, asks where he is taking her only son. She reminds him that she has never discouraged him from doing what is good. You brought in the poor, she says, and I looked after them. Some of the poor "turned out to be angels." You fetched a calf; I kneaded the unleavened bread. "We were as one person, with a single love." But now, "when you have in mind a journey, why is the child going with you, and why are you not revealing your secret to Sarah your faithful wife who in all the hardships of exile has borne trials along with you?"

"I wish to slaughter a lamb and offer a sacrifice to God," Abraham replies.

Sarah asks him to leave Isaac behind. If anything is to happen to him, she says, I'd be "unjustly deprived of the single son to whom I have given birth. . . . You are drunk with the love of God—who is your God and my God—and if He so bids you concerning the child, you would kill him without hesitation."

Don't worry, Abraham says. Like me, you are "pure and full of faith." God is in charge. He does what he wants, on earth as well as in heaven. If he wants Isaac back, he'll take him. I have vowed to do what God asks. And I will. But it is a lamb I plan to sacrifice. Don't delay us any further with all your talking. "I shall take with me two young men so that you will not worry over Isaac, (thinking) that I am handing him over to slaughter."

They set out, but Isaac has overheard all that, and after Abraham orders the servants to remain at the foot of the mountain, he begins to pepper his father with questions. Where are we going? Why are we going alone? What are you going to do to me? You said we were going to slaughter a lamb, but where on this mountain are we going to find one?

The Lord will provide the lamb, Abraham says. So Isaac begins to gather wood and Abraham begins to build the altar and tend to the fire. They work together, rejoicing in their respective tasks, but in the hymnist's telling, they are emphatically not of one mind. They have entirely different ideas about the work they are doing and entirely different expectations, and when Abraham grabs Isaac, binds him, and raises the knife, Isaac cries out, first to his father— "Instead of the lamb you have made me the lamb"—and then to God.

Another hymnist, the Syrian-born Romanos, who is believed to have lived in the sixth century, wrote in Greek and began his hymn in the traditional Greek fashion, with hypothetical speech. His narrator asks Abraham, "How did you not say?" and then goes on to suggest what Abraham might have said to God. Then Abraham introduces Sarah, warning God to be careful, lest Sarah overhear them. Abraham tells God that she wouldn't believe that he had understood him correctly.

"If he who gave were to take away," she would ask, "what has he given? Old man, just leave to my care what belongs to me; when he who called you wants him, he will let me know." She would remind her husband that God had sent an angel to inform her that she would soon bear a child. He would send another to inform her that her son would soon die. "I will not trust the child to you; I will not give him to you." If God wants a sacrifice, let him take a sheep. She would promise Isaac that it would not happen: Abraham would have to kill her first. Then he could murder his son. But he won't, she would say. Your father won't.

Among the remarkable things about Romanos's hymn, and among the things that has led scholars to suspect that his influences included the Syriac hymnists or a common source, was that from that point on in the hymn, the apparatus of hypothetical speech falls away and Abraham and Sarah talk directly to each other. Abraham warns her not to anger God by speaking that way. "He asks of us what belongs to him already." Don't blemish the sacrifice with tears. "God wants him, and who can keep him from God?" He is strong enough to slay him while he's locked in your embrace. Show him your good will by giving him up. I could cry too, he says, "wet all earth with my tears. . . . Or does it seem to you that it is only your offspring that is doomed? Isn't he my son as well to whom I gave life?"

"You have been his begetter and you will be his slayer also?" she asks.

God rules over all, Abraham replies. "He has demanded of me a gift of that which was given to us only for a short time."

Like the Syriac hymnists, Romanos gives Sarah her say, but neither he nor they were done with her. In Romanos, she turns to Isaac and tells him to go. If God wants you alive, she says, he will not kill you. "Now I will be glorified: I will be called blessed for offering a gift of my womb to him who gave you to me." Go, she tells Isaac, "and become the victim of God, together with your begetter—or rather, your murderer." She has faith that as he left her, he'd find his true father. And she had faith that he'd be back, one way or another. If not in this world, then in the world to come.

One Syriac homilist imagined that Sarah had begged Abraham to allow her to go along with them: to carry stones for the altar, to bind Isaac with locks of her white hair, to dig the hole for his grave. If he would not permit her to go all the way, she would "remain at the foot of the mountain until" he had "sacrificed him and come back." She grabs Isaac and tells him to listen to his father, to do what he says. "If he should actually bind you, stretch out your hands to the bonds, and if he should actually sacrifice you, stretch out your neck before his knife, stretch out your neck like a lamb, like a kid before the shearer. See my son that you do not put your father under oath when he draws out his knife against you, lest his mind be upset and there be a blemish in his offering. And listen my son to the words of your mother, and let your reputation go forth unto generations to come." In tears, she embraces him and kisses him and says, "Go in peace."

Part of me wishes that Romanos and that Syriac writer had stopped with lines like "I will not give him to you" or "You are drunk with God." But if they had, their innovation would actually have been less notable than it was, limited to the way they gave Sarah a say, in direct speech, and the words they gave her to say. That's because what I welcome today, what looks to me like Sarah's good sense, was actually firmly established tradition, deeply devout writers diminishing her by giving voice to her motherly instincts and womanly nature, her lesser understanding and love of God. In the middle of the first millennium, at least a few writers moved beyond that tradition, making Sarah Abraham's equal in faith— and, no less remarkably, making Abraham her equal in doubt.

In Romanos, Abraham is at first as reluctant as Sarah to obey God's command. He worries that anyone who were to see him slaughtering his child would think him mad. He wonders how he could possibly bind and murder the boy whose "swaddling clothes" he had "untied," the boy he had nurtured and hoped would be his heir. He goes so far as to say that he will not do it, leaving it ambiguous whether he intended to refuse or he knew that he ultimately wouldn't have to.

Sarah's argument with Abraham is the extension of his argument with himself, and Romanos devotes the same amount of space to the two of them, and the same amount of space to her change of heart as to his insistence that she should have that change of heart. Then he does something equally striking: he gives Sarah the last word. She had predicted that Isaac would return safely, and when he does, she dances "with joy" and says: "May he who made you appear before me, my child, receive my spirit."

Here, again, Romanos may have taken his cue from the Syriac homilists, who also end with Sarah. One Syriac writer imagined that, upon his return, Isaac had reported right to his mother, telling her what had happened, and insisting, rather unconvincingly, that she need not have been worried. God sent the lamb, Isaac says, and Abraham offered it in my place. "He stretched out his hand to the knife, and it reached the very neck of your darling, and had there not been the voice, I would yesterday have been killed, and they would have been looking for my bones in the fire."

Sarah faints, and when she comes to she is sobbing, speaking to Isaac as if he had died. "Welcome in peace slain one come alive, upon whom the Lord's right hand had compassion. The fingers which fashioned you in my womb have now delivered you from the knife." You were slain by Abraham, but "God in His mercy gave you back."

A second Syriac homilist imagined an even more dramatic ending. Early on, when Sarah had asked where he and Isaac were going, Abraham told her not to mind: "This secret to-day women cannot be aware of." Sarah groaned. She not only wanted to know, but to go, to participate. Abraham ignored her, but on his way home, he decides to call her bluff. He tells Isaac to stay behind, so he can "spy out her mind and her thoughts."

Sarah receives him ("Welcome, O happy one, who has sacrificed my only child on the pyre"), fetches water to wash his feet, and asks him to tell her what happened. "Did he weep when he was bound, or groan as he died?" She imagines that he was looking for her, his eyes wandering over the mountains, expecting her to save him. Now she wants to know everything.

Isaac did not cry or groan, Abraham reports, but he did ask for you.

"I was wishing I was an eagle or had the speed of a turtle-dove," she says, "so that I might go and behold that place." She would have liked to see the fire and to "bring back a little of his blood to be comforted by its smell," and a lock of his hair and an article of his clothing and some of his ashes. As she speaks those words, Isaac appears. She embraces him and welcomes him back to life. Isaac explains what has happened and she thanks God for giving him to her "a second time."

Once again, Sarah had the last word, and that is not the only sign of her elevation. Abraham has been tested once, but she has been tested twice, once by God and then again by her husband. She passes with an unimaginably high score: "I do obeisance to that voice which delivered you, my son, from the knife," she says in the hymn's final lines. "I praise Him who saved you from burning on the pyre. Henceforth, my son, it will not be Sarah's son that people will call you, but child of the pyre and offering who died and was resurrected."

. . .

I marvel at those strange hymns, and sometimes I ask myself why. After all, their authors took the Sarah of the Hebrew Bible, a woman who, though hardly without faults, would at least have had the good (and to me wholly imaginable) sense to say no to God, and transformed her into a woman of almost unimaginable Christian faith. One minute she calls Abraham drunk with God. The next she is at least as drunk as he is, "burning," as one Syriac writer put it, with a desire to sacrifice her son.

But history moves in unpredictable and often surprising ways. I am grateful for Sarah's voice and the depth and complexity of her feelings, and the complexity of the feelings she brought out in Abraham, and I am grateful for the esteem in which these writers, whether women or men, held her. All the more in light of the condescension of so many of their Jewish and Christian contemporaries. I myself am not moved by the hymnists' and homilists' ideas or feelings of faith, let alone by their burning desire, but if their ideas and desire were to be held up as the highest virtue—heralded and rewarded—I think that it is a virtue that Sarah should have the right to choose. Above all, I take solace in the thought that once her angry and incredulous words were out there, added to the archive, and once Abraham's doubts were out there with them, and even Isaac's anxiety and sense of betrayal, there was no telling what others might do with them.

That Sarah was new to me. So was that one hymnist's anxious
Isaac. But so much else was familiar that as I read, I felt as if I
had been transported to a great reunion, held in the middle of the
first millennium, to mark five hundred years or more of biblical
exegesis. Syriac Christians hosted, but they invited Greek-speaking
Christians from near and far (including Ephrem Graecus and Gregory of Nyssa and John Chrysostom of Constantinople and Basil of
Seleucia and Amphilochius of Iconium and Irenaeus of Lyon and
Clement and Origen of Alexandria). And, hard as it may be for
some to believe, they invited a host of Jews.

Looking around the room, I recognize men who told the story
as a test of obedience and men who told it as a test of faith. Men
who imagined that Isaac was a wise and willing victim and men
who imagined him wondering, anxiously, what in the world his
father was up to. Men who understood why Abraham didn't say a
word to Sarah and men who didn't—believing that she too would
have proven to be a model of Christian faith. At one table Jews
who translated Hebrew scripture into Greek and Aramaic shared
trade secrets with Christians who translated it into Greek, Latin,
and Syriac and, after that, Greek to Coptic. At another, bishops
who (perhaps influenced by Melito, bishop of Sardis) devoted their
days to identifying typology, all the bits of history that pointed
to and culminated in Christ, mingled with bishops (including Ire-

naeus) who borrowed the Jewish concept of *zekhut avot*—the merit of the fathers—to make sense of the sweep of sacred history: Abraham's sacrifice didn't merely prefigure God's, it brought it about. Because Abraham was willing to sacrifice his son, God actually sacrificed his.

In the ballroom's low light, a pair of priests, who (like many rabbis) imagined Isaac asking to be bound and angels crying out to God as Abraham reached for the cleaver, might have been mistaken for rabbis, who (like many priests) saw, in the wood that Isaac carried, the cross that condemned men carried to their own executions. And if that wasn't surprising or confusing enough, after a few drinks, Greek and Syriac Christian commentators, who could be vicious about Jews in their writings and sermons (as Romanos himself, probably Jewish-born and later baptized, was in his homilies about the Passion), took to the stage and sang songs of Abraham and Isaac with lyrics that might have been written by a rabbi.

Swept up in the revelry and feeling a little bit giddy, I was tempted to offer a toast. Here's to the very height of biblical hybridity and interdenominational exchange. How could anyone read those hymns and still say that the early Christians weren't paying close attention to the Jews?

Afterward I would have felt silly—not on account of what I'd said about the priests and rabbis but for imagining I could know the height of anything like that. Only when we are hiking or mountain climbing, and even then only on clear days far above the tree line, do we know the summit the moment we are there. Those Syriac hymnists (and probably Romanos too) had sung their last song before Muhammad was born. At most the future prophet was a little boy, and no one could have seen the man and Islam coming.

And even if I had received a hot tip, had known that he was on his way and about to take the Arabian Peninsula by storm, had somehow got my hands on an advance reading copy of the Qur'an, the bounty of Islamic exegesis would still have taken me by surprise. Unlike the priests and bishops, who claimed that their new covenant and testament had fulfilled the old, Muhammad insisted his revelation was nothing but a midcourse correction, a reminder of a kind of submission to God that had preceded slavery and Sinai and the whole history of ancient Israel. He expressed great respect for the Hebrew prophets, right through Jesus, and the great books. His simply thought that the revelation those books recorded had been distorted and corrupted, by word and by deed, and that as a result the People of the Book, all the people of all the books, had lost their way. "There are illiterates among them who do not know the book," he said, "but only fancies, and they do nothing but conjecture. Woe to them who write the book with their own hands and then say: This is from God."

When I first read those words, in the opening pages of the Qur'an, I assumed the people Muhammad called illiterates were the very same ones I call exegetes: the ancient interpreters, the rabbis, the priests, all the people I've been telling you about, from Jubilees to the Syriac hymnists and Romanos. Muhammad's project was to set the record straight, return to revelation uncorrupted by interpretation and revision, to get back to basics, fundamentals, original intentions. That isn't my project, but that is what I assumed he was up to.

What I discovered, as I kept reading in the Qur'an, and then volume after volume of Islamic exegesis, especially the Hadith, the authoritative record of the words and deeds of the Prophet, is that neither Muhammad, who died in 632, nor the Muslim exegetes (scholars, jurists, theologians, and historians, one generation after another) who came after him were opposed to all interpretation and revision and elaboration and embellishment. They were opposed only to the interpretation and revision they were opposed to, elaboration and embellishment they didn't like. Muslims produced every manner of interpretation, every manner of revision, every manner of story about Abraham. They told about his emigration (from Babylonia to Syria), about his close encounter with a tyrant (who tried to steal his wife), about his relationship with Hagar and their son Ishmael; about Hagar and Ishmael's relocation to Mecca; about Abraham's visits to Ishmael and Hagar; about Abraham and Ishmael's building of the Kaaba, Islam's holiest shrine; about Abraham's calling on Muslims to make the pilgrimage to Mecca; and about Abraham's own first pilgrimage. And they told scores of stories about the near sacrifice of his son.

They told and recorded stories. If you were to read them, you would find not just liberal revision of ancient stories but familiar revision, starting with an Abraham who never had a question or doubt, never made a mistake, never wavered; an Abraham about whom Jubilees himself would have found an enormous amount to admire. You'll find an articulate, talkative, willing Isaac, and an Ishmael who (as in many rabbinic sources) maintained a close relationship with his father long after he left home, married, and began to father a great nation of his own. You'll find a crafty Satan, who tried to stop Abraham but was thwarted at every turn, often by Sarah, a woman of few words but almost all of them right there with her man. You'll find a "noble substitute" for Isaac. And for Abraham and Isaac's steadfastness in the face of a terrible trial, you will read about a reward that will make you think, at once, of Christian notions of vicarious atonement and Jewish notions of the saving merit of the fathers.

I don't mean to suggest in some sort of chauvinistic way that Islamic stories were completely derivative, cut and pasted from Jewish and Christian sources. They weren't. Like so many of the stories of the rabbis and priests, like so many of the biblical stories themselves, they were composites, made of prebiblical traditions, pre-Islamic Arabian oral traditions (including pre-Islamic monotheistic traditions), Jewish and Christian biblical traditions, and emerging and evolving Islamic traditions. There were many parallels, many borrowings, many adaptations, and in no time there were notable new directions.

For example: Several influential Islamic authorities cut through the confusion of countless rabbinic explanations of what prompted

God to ask. Turns out, he got the idea from Abraham, who had been so moved by the news of the imminent arrival of a pious son, and so grateful, that he immediately made an oath to God: When the boy came of age, he would sacrifice him. Several years later, Abraham dreamed that the time had come. He asked his son what he should do, and his son said: If that's what God wants, let's do it.

Islamic writers also contributed the fullest and most graphic descriptions of the story's climatic moment. Jewish exegetes didn't shy away from it—recall Isaac asking to be bound, angels weeping, Abraham expressing his frustration when God said stop. But the form of the early midrash, the painstaking examination of the meaning of single words, phrases, and discrete verses (and the movement from those words and verses to distant words and verses in Scripture and distant places and times in history in order to explain them) tended to provide a merciful distraction. The emphasis on typology or allegory in Christian interpretation had precisely the same effect.

In dozens of different Islamic versions, we do not stray.

Isaac asks Abraham to tighten his bonds so that he cannot squirm, to pull his shirt out of the way so it won't get soaked with blood and later cause his mother grief, to sharpen the knife and be quick so his death will be less painful, to return his shirt to his mother to provide her with comfort, and to give her his best wishes. Only then does Abraham draw his knife across Isaac's neck. But unbeknownst to Abraham, God has slipped a sheet of copper between knife and neck. The knife doesn't break the skin. Frustrated, Abraham flips Isaac onto his forehead (thereby helping readers understand why the description of the near sacrifice in many sources, including the Qur'an, deviates from the standard Islamic sacrifice ritual, where the victim is always placed on its side).

God commands Abraham to stop. He does, and he and Isaac sacrifice a ram instead. Not long after, father and son return to Sarah, who greets them and asks about their day. Abraham tells her where they have been, and her response, in one paradigmatic version, sounds like an Arabic version of the punch line of a Jewish comedian's joke: "You would sacrifice my son and not inform me?"

In other versions Isaac asks Abraham to lay him on his forehead (providing a second explanation for the deviation). Abraham heaps praise on his son for his obedience and grabs the knife, but God (or sometimes Gabriel) turns it to its dull side and then informs Abraham that he has already fulfilled his vision. In unison, Gabriel, Abraham, and Isaac shout, "God is most great."

To say that Isaac is a willing victim in these accounts does not say enough about his role. He seems to be calling the shots from the moment Abraham wakes from his dream.

"Are you obedient?" Abraham asks, vaguely.

"Yes," Isaac says. "Even if you wanted to sacrifice me, I would not try to prevent it."

Abraham retrieves rope and knife and off they go. Satan, taking the form of an old man Abraham recognizes, tells Abraham that he is doing the devil's work. Abraham tells him to get lost, so Satan tells Isaac that his father is about to sacrifice him. "If that's what God wants, so be it," the boy says. Satan leaves, thinking his last best chance is to find Sarah, and Abraham and Isaac go on their way. When they arrive, Isaac delivers a complete set of instructions:

Take my shirt off so it will not be bloodied, causing my mother to cry over me. Tie me up so I don't squirm in your arms, causing you pain (note that the Islamic Isaac's concern is for his father's comfort, not the Levitical requirement that a sacrifice be completely unblemished). When you place the knife at my throat, don't look, or you might be overcome by compassion. Give Mother my greetings, but spare her the details of the sacrifice so that she will not be sorrowful over me. "And when you see a young boy like me, do not look at him, so that your heart will not grieve on my account."

Hearing all that, a voice from heaven calls out, "O friend of God, how can you not be compassionate for this small child who speaks to you with such words."

"Don't distract me," Abraham says, thinking it is Satan speaking. He gets back to work, removing Isaac's shirt and binding him. As he puts the knife to Isaac's throat, he prays, "In the name of God the powerful and excellent."

God flips it.

Abraham turns to sharpen it.

God flips it again, and says, "O Abraham, take this ram and redeem your son with it. Sacrifice it as an offering. God has made this day a holy festival for you and your children."

The ram joins in: "O Friend of God, sacrifice me instead of your son, for I am a more appropriate sacrifice than he. I am the ram of Abel, son of Adam, who gave me as an offering to his Lord and whose offering was accepted. I have grazed in the meadows of the Gardens for forty autumns."

All that was left was God's blessing, and many Islamic interpreters, like many rabbis, implied, without coming right out and saying it, that in the biblical version of the story God is a little stingy. Abraham has nearly sacrificed his son, and God rewards him simply by reiterating promises he has made several times before. But the Islamic Abraham doesn't demand more. God, unprompted, offers it, and not to Abraham but to his son. In some versions he offers him a wish, any wish. In other versions, he offers him a choice, one of two: Either I'll forgive half the Muslim people, or I'll respond to your petition on anyone's behalf. Isaac chooses the latter: "Whenever a sinner who believes in you appears at the gates of heaven," he says, "pardon him on my behalf, and let him into paradise."

Who could resist the charm of Isaac's generous calculation? Or not appreciate the echo of a passage in the Talmud in which a rabbi imagined a future day when God, unhappy with his chosen people, would appeal to the patriarchs, starting with Abraham, to see if any of them were willing to take upon themselves responsibility for the sins of the current generation?

"Your children have sinned," God says.

Wipe them out, to sanctify the name of God, Abraham advises.

God turns to Jacob, thinking that a man with so many difficult children of his own might be more compassionate.

Wipe them out, Jacob advises.

Frustrated with both grandfather and grandson, God turns to the man in the middle and Isaac doesn't let him down. On behalf of the sinners, Isaac takes several different tacks: First, he chides God for saying "Your children have sinned." Plainly, Isaac reminds him, the sinners are your children too. Then he uses some fancy math to point out that they really hadn't sinned for very long. Finally he plays his trump card: He tells God that if he, God, himself would "bear all" the sin, it would be great. If he won't, Isaac says he would be happy to split the burden with him, half and half. But if God should say that he, Isaac, must bear it all, he would say: "I offered myself up before Thee as a sacrifice!"

Before I am accused, by a reader familiar with Islamic interpretation, of missing the forest for the trees, let me make one thing perfectly clear. I understand that most readers, settling into an easy chair with a representative sample of Hadith, would find all these small details, and even all the remarkable echoes and correspondences, less significant than one huge innovation, or correction: in many Islamic versions, Ishmael is the son whom Abraham promises to sacrifice. Ishmael is the son Abraham dreams God wants him to sacrifice. Ishmael is the son he nearly does sacrifice. And Ishmael is the son who asks God's pardon for his descendants through the ages.

How could that be?

Easy, as anyone who has stuck with me for this long should see. Even if an Islamic exegete's only source was the Hebrew Bible, he could have substituted Ishmael for Isaac with less effort than it had taken earlier commentators to imagine Abraham (to say nothing of Sarah) eager to see the sacrifice through or Sarah welcoming Isaac back from the dead. The word "Isaac" appears five times in Genesis 22. All it would take is a quick search-and-replace.

In fact, it was even simpler than that, for Islamic exegetes weren't working from the Bible. Their starting point was the Qur'an, God's words to Muhammad by way of Gabriel, and Muhammad recounted the story in his own inimitable way, at once more concrete and cryptic, a jazzy mix of figurative and literal, poetry and prose (that many Muslims insist is neither). In it, Abraham asks the Lord for a righteous son and his wish is granted. When the boy comes of age, Abraham dreams that he is supposed to sacrifice him. He asks his son for his view:

> He said, "My father, do as thou art bidden; thou shalt find me, God willing, one of the steadfast." When they had surrendered, and he flung him upon his brow, We called unto him, "Abraham, thou hast confirmed the vision; even so We recompense the good-doers. This is indeed the manifest trial." And We ransomed him with a mighty sacrifice, and left for him among the later folk "Peace be upon Abraham!"
>
> Even so We recompense the good-doers; he was among Our believing servants. Then We gave him the good tidings of Isaac, a Prophet, one of the righteous. And We blessed him, and Isaac; and of their seed some are good-doers, and some manifest self-wrongers.

You see: The trial had taken place even before the good news of Isaac arrived. The nearly sacrificed son would have to have been Ishmael, the older son, Abraham's only son at that time.

Of course not everyone read it way. For starters, whether within chapters or among them, the Qur'an only occasionally proceeds chronologically. What comes first is not necessarily what happened first. The narrator circles around and jumps around, usually putting stripped-down versions of biblical stories or brief references to biblical characters and stories in the service of the pedagogy, the point, the lesson, the argument, thereby leaving ample room for creative reading and interpretation. Generation after generation of

Muslim scholars and sages rushed in to fill that space, and they created myriad versions and variants of versions, including versions of what happened (in some Abraham does exactly what Isaac asks and in others he refuses to, insisting that he'll do only what God commands) and where it happened (Mecca, where Ishmael and Hagar lived, or Syria, where Isaac and Sarah lived) and exactly when it happened in relation to the building of the Kaaba and the call to pilgrimage (Shiite scholars have tended to set the sacrifice in the context of the very first pilgrimage to Mecca, and both sacrifice and pilgrimage in the context of Arabian pilgrimages and sacrifices that preceded Islam) and even what animal Abraham sacrificed in Isaac or Ishmael's place.

The earliest exegetes considered Isaac the victim, and they weren't embarrassed, as some later exegetes may have been, to cite Israelite tales (Torah) and the Gospels as authorities. Yet the appeal of the Ishmael in Mecca versions of the story is not mysterious. In the Bible, God made his covenant with Abraham and confirmed it (because you have done this) at Moriah. Ishmael, though banished, would be taken care of. He would be the father of many great nations, but the covenant was with Isaac and his children through the ages.

The early Christians started there, but they altered the definition of Abraham and Isaac's descendants, casting the Jews off as Abraham and Sarah had earlier cast off Hagar. One of the ways that Paul did that was by allegory: Abraham, he wrote in Galatians, had two sons, one by a slave woman and one by a free woman. Hagar represented the covenant enacted at Sinai, in Arabia. The Jews were her children, and she and her children, children of the flesh, all those who rejected Christ, were slaves in the earthly Jerusalem. Sarah represented the new covenant. Her children, children of the spirit, were free in the Jerusalem above. "Cast out the bondwoman and her son: for the son of the bondwoman shall not be heir with the son of the freewoman. So then, brethren, we are not children of the bondwoman, but of the free."

Ishmael was the genealogical link between Abraham and the Prophet, the progenitor of the Arab people. Is it any wonder that as Islam took root in the Arabian Peninsula and spread from there, many Muslims, scholars and lay, preferred the version of the near sacrifice that made Abraham's older son the son whose submission to God defined their faith and secured God's blessing? In favoring Ishmael, Muslims simply did what, for so many, comes naturally. They redirected the course of sacred history so that God's blessing ran their way.

Many, but hardly all. The debate between those who favored Ishmael and those who favored Isaac continued for centuries, with exegetes on both sides citing respected authorities (sometimes the very same authorities), ideally a chain of authorities with links extending all the way back to the Prophet. Some arguments were polemical and pointed:

"The Jews claim that it was Isaac, but the Jews lie."

"The proof for those who say that it was Isaac is that the Christians and Jews agree about it. The answer to that is that their agreement is no proof and their view is not acceptable."

The Jews "forced this understanding because Isaac is their father while Ishmael is the father of the Arabs."

But late in the first millennium and early in the second when Islamic scholars began compiling collections of oral traditions, many of them were as comfortable as the rabbis who edited compilations of midrash with disparate and contradictory accounts and explanations, laid out one after the other. It was not uncommon for Islamic scholars to report the arguments for opposing views accurately and at length before making the case for their own. And they appear to be have been at peace with multiplicity, or at least a certain kind of uncertainty: "Some people say that it was Ishmael," wrote al-Yaʿqūbī (a Shiite historian and geographer in the third century of Islam), "because he was the one who settled in Mecca, while Isaac remained in Syria. Other people say that it was Isaac because Abraham sent him (Ishmael) and his mother out when Isaac was a young boy, and Ishmael was a grown man with children. There are many traditions about each view and people disagree about them."

By that time the literature of Islam was as vast as the empire, and Muslims had a body of sacred exegesis they thought of as all their own, exegesis that, notwithstanding all the Qur'anic criticism of the fancies, lies, and conjectures of the Jews and Christians, was full of innovation and of invention, full of insight borrowed from the archive of oral and written exegesis, full of creative reading and writing—said to be, by way of the Prophet, the word of God.

One man's revelation was another's impossible fancy. One man's fancy, another man's revelation. It is a truth that's been churned into a truism, yet not a trite one when it comes to sacred stories and religious differences more generally. No one could be more attuned to it than I. Yet when I step back from all the narrative twists and interpretive turns I so enjoy tracking, from all the versions and variations and authorities and traditions, from the arguments about whether it was Isaac or Ishmael whom Abraham nearly sacrificed, or a ram, goat, or lamb that he ultimately did, it seems to me that there is at least one way in which most Islamic versions of the story really did deliver what Muhammad had promised: a return to fundamentals, foundations, a simple story of command, response, and reward.

No questions. No hesitation. No doubt. No gut-wrenching appeals from Sarah. When Satan told her where Abraham had taken their son, she was skeptical. She said that the boy's father was even more compassionate to him than she was. But if God had truly commanded Isaac's sacrifice, Abraham would go through with it. In one version she blames herself—for mistreating Hagar. But she does not try to stop it. Nor, after God stops it, does the Islamic Abraham ever take God to task for asking.

What is the Islamic version of the story about? It is not so much about faith. Nor the ideal of human sacrifice. Nor a prefiguration of a great sacrifice to come. Nor martyrdom. Nor even the saving merit of our forefathers. Rather, most Islamic versions of the story are, at root, about listening to God's voice. What God asks, his chosen people do. It was a trial, a test, and Abraham passed it, and in passing it, he became first and forever after the paradigmatic Muslim, the very definition of a Muslim, one who submits to God.

You don't have to look hard to find them: the Jewish riffs in early Christian commentary and the Christian riffs in the rabbinical commentary of late antiquity and the Jewish and Christian riffs in the Islamic commentary. They are hard to miss, and they would not be so striking to me if, over the centuries, Jews, Christians, and Muslims had always spoken the same languages, shared the same libraries, read the same books, and then gathered for ecumenical Bible study, tolerated difference in theory and practice, treated one another as equals, at least under the law, or lived together in peace.

But notwithstanding periods of calm and even tolerance (some say early Muslim Spain was as good as it got), they did not. Even when there was not punishing proscription or gross inequality, there was tension and periodic violence at the core of even the most tolerant communities. It is the history of conflict among Muslims, Christians, and Jews, and the widespread perception of difference, of separation, of sharp distinctions, of high walls and fences topped with wire, that makes instances of convergence and exchange worthy of note. If all were sweetness and light, we'd expect it and take it for granted. But we don't, because there were so many ways of seeing and thinking about sacred history each group wouldn't acknowledge, so many lines each group wouldn't cross (or imagine itself crossing), so many places each group insisted it would never go.

The rabbis responded to all the talk of Abraham's faith by making explicit what they hadn't thought needed to be said: the story of the Binding of Isaac was about listening to God's voice. They believed, just as the priests did, that God tested Abraham to search his heart. But what God was searching for was not some abstract sense that he himself would keep his promises but active obedience. In the words of the author (or editor) of the *Pirke de Rabbi Eliezer,* a rich rewriting of and commentary on Genesis and Exodus put together in the late eighth or early ninth century (though attributed to the late-first-century Eliezer, teacher of the great Akiva), God said he wanted to know if Abraham would be able "to keep all the commandments of the Torah."

Christian commentators insisted the sacrifice of Isaac had nothing to do with Moses's law, that shadow of better things to come. Someday, perhaps, the Jews would outgrow it, accept Christ, and leave the old Israel for the new.

Islamic scholars, meanwhile, shrugged off all Christian talk of shadows, of prefiguration, of types. What use could a Muslim possibly have for the idea that prophecy and sacred history culminated in Christ—five hundred years before Muhammad arrived on the scene? Unlike the Jews, they considered Jesus an important prophet, a messenger of God. But like the Jews, they believed that he had been a man. God was One. That may be why, when God granted the Islamic Isaac (or Ishmael) a wish as a reward for his and his father's submission, the boy wished that everyone who believed in God would be welcomed in heaven—except those who believed God had a son or some other partner.

Neither rabbis nor priests took the idea that Ishmael was the nearly sacrificed son seriously. To them, it was one more sign that when it came to history and sacred literature, the Muslims had a few screws loose. Whether they showed respect for Ishmael or mocked him, they all elevated Isaac. But not the same Isaac. Jews and Christians each had their own, and considering that by the end of the first millennium Jesus had come to be the biggest sticking point between them, what is remarkable about the Jewish Isaac is how much like Jesus he had become.

The rabbis had abandoned (if they had ever entertained) the Isaac I imagine, the small boy with no real role or obvious understanding. Their Isaac was a young man, thirty-seven years old, sharing the stage with his father, a knowing victim and a willing victim and sometimes not a victim at all, but rather an agent in the drama that nearly took his life. Sometimes he asked to be bound. Sometimes he stretched his neck toward the knife. Sometimes he bound (and thus nearly sacrificed) himself. Perhaps nowhere is his privileged place in the story clearer than in the version in which he, lying on his back on the altar, obtained a view of the divine presence that his father, standing above him with the knife, did not.

Christian exegetes were no less in awe. Isaac's miraculous birth was annunciated by angels. He bore his own cross. He was bound like a lamb. He was returned to his father (and mother) unscathed. He was the beneficiary of God's blessing, and in all those ways and more he was a type of Christ, of the church, of the body of Christ's faithful. In all those ways he remained dear.

But the story was about his father, who was tested through him. Not every exegete went as far as Melito, the bishop of Sardis, who in the second century insisted that Isaac had been completely "silent, bound like a ram, not opening his mouth nor uttering a sound." You may recall that a few hundred years later several Syriac hymnists imagined him asking a slew of anxious questions on the way up the mountain and then, upon his return, nearly killing his mother with a blow-by-blow account of his ordeal. But even at his most articulate, he remained a young boy who never usurped his father's role. "Abraham was fervent for the killing of Isaac," one hymnist wrote, while Isaac was "looking out for the lamb . . . both readily became workers for God . . . though their labors were not equal."

And no matter how much Isaac said or didn't say, knew or didn't know, he absolutely did not suffer. "Christ suffered," Melito wrote, "whereas Isaac did not suffer; for he was the model of the Christ who was going to suffer." Christ suffered, Cyril of Alexandria wrote two and a half centuries later, but Isaac, "having been placed on the wood," was "stolen away from death and suffering."

To understand the Christian insistence that Isaac did not suffer is in part to understand the power of typology, which limited the range of things commentators could say about him just as surely as it enlarged the range for Sarah. For Christ's death and resurrection, unharmed and unblemished, to be fulfilled, there had to be something unfulfilled; for his sacrifice to end all sacrifice and atone for the sins of humankind, there had to be a near sacrifice, a dress rehearsal, a ritual sacrifice that didn't quite do the trick. Isaac is "a type of the Lord," wrote Clement of Alexandria, "a child as a son; for he was the son of Abraham, as Christ the Son of God, and a sacrifice as the Lord, but he was not immolated as the Lord. Isaac only bore the wood of the sacrifice, as the Lord the wood of the cross." Isaac did "everything but suffer, as was right, yielding the precedence in the suffering to the Word."

But the more time I spend with the priests and bishops of late antiquity, the more I suspect that there was more at work than typology. After all, the Christian Isaac could have been stolen away from death without being spared pain and suffering. He could have suffered some without suffering as much as Christ. My hunch is that the Christian Isaac didn't suffer partly because of typology and partly because of exegetical competition between Christians and Jews. The Christian Isaac never suffered because the Jewish Isaac often did.

The rabbis said he had wondered, worried, and trembled. Sometimes he trembled exceedingly. They said he had asked to be tied so that his involuntary movements would not spoil the sacrifice. In at least one version he protested: "So this is the Torah you talked about to my mother Sarah when you said, 'I am going to take him to the schoolmasters!'" In more than one he cried. He sustained knife wounds, and he bled. Eventually, in some exegesis, he died.

Sometimes he died of fright.

Sometimes the moment the blade touched his throat his soul took flight.

Sometimes the sight of the heavens killed him.

Sometimes it was a loss of blood.

Sometimes he succumbed to the flames.

Sometimes it was, matter-of-factly and without elaboration, simple sacrifice: he was "slaughtered according to the rite."

In every instance God revived him, and when he came to, he realized that he had just been given a preview of the manner in which the dead would live again. He opened his mouth and recited the second benediction: "Blessed art thou, O Lord, who quickeneth the dead."

Today, friends and family and colleagues and neighbors and sometimes total strangers look at me in disbelief when I tell them that some rabbis imagined that Abraham had killed Isaac.

"No he didn't," they say.

"They imagined that he did," I say.

"What do you mean, they imagined that he did? The story is clear about that. God said stop."

"It's not what I mean," I say. "It is certainly not what I expected, or wanted; not how I hoped the story would be revised."

"It is not what happened," they say. "Everyone knows that Isaac didn't die. It is Jesus who dies, the Christians who celebrate a father actually sacrificing his son."

I understand their surprise and incredulity. The stories of death and resurrection are not the ones people are likely to learn in Hebrew school, or even in seminary. They realize that I am in a better position to know than they are, but they still insist I must be mistaken. How, they ask, could the rabbis or anyone else have come to that conclusion from the story as they remember it?

I send them back to the Bible, urging them to keep a few of the questions that some rabbis asked in mind:

Why the second angelic address? Why couldn't God have said everything he had to say the first time?

And why, in that second address, did God say, "Because you have done this and have not withheld your son, your only one"?

And most of all: How are we to understand the story's last line: "Abraham then returned to his servants, and they departed together for Beersheba." Where was Isaac?

The story left readers with questions. Some answered them with stories in which Isaac died:

God called again because Abraham didn't stop the first time.

Or Abraham did stop—he didn't lay a hand on him—and it was his literal obedience that sealed Isaac's fate. Remember that Abraham knew the rules the Torah prescribed for sacrifice as well as any Levitical priest. (Never mind that those rules would not be revealed, the priesthood established, for four hundred years.) He knew that the fire went first and the wood went on top of it. In Genesis 22, Abraham built an altar. He laid out the wood. He bound Isaac and placed him on the altar on top of the wood. If that's how it happened, if Abraham put the wood on the fire and Isaac on the wood, and then, as God commanded, he stopped and did not lay a hand on him or do anything to him, the incident would have ended with Isaac's ashes.

And that explains why God said, "Because you have done this thing and not withheld your son, your only one." Because one way or another, Abraham did do it, had done it. He had sacrificed his son.

And that explains why Isaac was not with Abraham when he returned to his lads and they rose and went together to Beersheba.

Some rabbis imagined that Isaac had been washed into heaven by the angels' tears, staying there until God brought him back to life and earth. Others imagined that God had lifted him into the Garden of Eden, where he remained—for three days, for three years (just in time to hook up with Rebekah), for however long it took him to recover from fear, from shock, from knife wounds, from the flames.

All reasonable people will acknowledge that there were, and are, other explanations, simple, straightforward answers to those questions. And they'll be relieved to know that one rabbi or another employed them all. Two examples should suffice. When God said, "Because you have done this thing and have not withheld your son," he meant only that Abraham had demonstrated his willingness—not that he had actually offered him. He had sacrificed the ram instead. As for Isaac at the end: Some said he had lagged behind. Some, conversely, that he had taken a shortcut home, eager to assure his mother that he was safe. Some said that Abraham had sent him to study Torah at the academy, the very academy he had told Sarah he was taking him to in the first place. And some (thank heavens, including no less an authority than Abraham Ibn Ezra) said what I would say if someone asked me: Isaac was right there, together with Abraham, in his charge. The author was simply thinking about Abraham and God.

The rabbis' questions provided a convenient opening for those who wanted to kill Isaac, but they did not make his death and resurrection inevitable. His death had to solve a larger problem than the problem posed by those lines, and I think it did. At least since 2 Maccabees, Abraham and Isaac had been associated with Jewish martyrdom, being prepared to die for God. They'd also been associated with the merit of the fathers, a merit that resulted not only in deliverance in times of trouble—from Pharaoh in Egypt, from the angel of death, from the Red Sea, from the destroying angel in Jerusalem after David's census—but also in the pardoning of sin, starting with the sin of the Golden Calf.

According to the author of Chronicles, Solomon built the First Temple atop Mount Moriah. According to many rabbis, the Jews returning from exile in Babylonia built the altar for the second atop Isaac's ashes. The Passover sacrifice, the two daily *tamid* sacrifices, perhaps all Temple sacrifices, were thought to be reenactments of Abraham's sacrifice, and after the Second Temple was destroyed, the daily and festival sacrifices were often evoked in and replaced by ritual and prayer: "Let our lips compensate for the bulls." The memory of Abraham's sacrifice was everywhere. Isaac, more than any other Jewish figure, was associated with the resurrection of the dead.

And yet, in Scripture and most early revisions and interpretations of Scripture, Isaac didn't die. Or didn't seem to die, and that left a gap, a growing gap, and perhaps a nagging gap between the meaning and significance in people's minds and the story as it appeared on the page. It was a gap that exegetes as early as Philo seemed to acknowledge (when he said that even though God had stopped the sacrifice, he accepted it as a complete sacrifice) and a gap that the creators of a significant body of midrash (when they imagined Abraham begging God to let him do it, or to let him extract a bit of blood, or at the very least to imagine that he had killed his son and then the ram) seemed intent to bridge.

And even if I am wrong in imagining intramural fretting, even if the gap were a gap that the rabbis could have lived with if they were living all by themselves (there were, after all, an infinite number of gaps between Scripture and interpretation), it was also a gap between a near sacrifice and the sacrifice to end all sacrifices that century after century of Christian commentators, in the pulpit, on the pages of their commentary, and in anti-Jewish polemic, would never let them forget: The Jewish Isaac didn't suffer. Without blood there is no atonement. Your sacrifice was just a shadow of the real thing, your merit not saving.

In a letter to his churches written a few weeks before Easter in 334, Bishop Athanasius of Alexandria went out of his way to warn Egyptian Christians not to observe Passover with Egyptian Jews. The bishop wanted to be sure they realized that the Jewish Passover (a Passover not of the Lord but of the Jews) was a ritual that God no longer approved of. Jews continued to celebrate the paschal offering only because they failed to understand that when Abraham offered his son, he was worshipping the Son of God, and that the ram he ultimately sacrificed represented Christ, and that while Abraham was tested through Isaac, it was not Isaac who was ultimately sacrificed but Christ: "For the sacrifice was not properly the setting to rights of Isaac but of Abraham who also offered, and by that was tried. Thus, God accepted the will of the offerer but prevented that which was offered from being sacrificed. For the death of Isaac did not procure the freedom of the world but that of our Savior alone."

~~~

So some rabbis imagined that Isaac, too, had died, had died on Mount Moriah.

I can't tell you who first imagined that, or even when. The blood and ashes go way back ("on account of his blood I chose them," God said of Isaac in Pseudo-Philo, probably in the first century). But the precise dating of particular motifs in first-millennium midrash is difficult when not impossible.

Nor can I tell you how many rabbis and laypeople imagined that he had died.

And notwithstanding my suspicion about competition between rabbis and priests, I can't access the relative importance of that competition compared to, say, developments within each tradition (rabbis and priests arguing among themselves) in particular places at particular times. To do that, I would need a proximity to writers and readers, teachers and students, preachers and congregations, theological debates and their specific settings, that I, leaping from one place and time to another, rarely have.

What I can tell you is that at the end of the eleventh century, the church's war of words against Jews and Judaism turned into the real thing. The pope, responding to a plea from the emperor of Byzantium, called for a Crusade, and an army of Christian soldiers, mustered throughout western Europe, set out to repel Muslim advances in Anatolia and then liberate Jerusalem. Jews were not the crusaders' initial targets, but it was not long into their journey that it occurred to them that while they traveled thousands of difficult miles to fight infidels, the greatest enemies of Christ were closer to home. They assaulted one Rhineland Jewish community after another.

Vastly outnumbered and virtually unarmed, the Jews had a limited number of choices. Some appealed to local clergy to protect them. Some tried to buy off the crusaders. Some fought. Some hid. Some fled. Some converted. And some, seeing no hope for survival as Jews, simply chose death. Of those, some killed family members and then themselves before the crusaders had a chance to. In the decades afterward, writers returned to those dark days in chronicles, memorials, penitential prayers, poems, and hymns, and when they did, they paid an extraordinary amount of attention and great homage to the men and women who took their own lives. They invariably likened them to Abraham and Isaac. And they sure seemed to be attempting to contest Christian calumnies against the Jews.

Several writers recount the killing in Mainz, where the Jews were set upon by a huge and (compared to some) highly organized band. The first martyrs "stretched their necks" to their tormentors, or simply let the crusaders kill them. Witnesses, seeing the first to die, concluded that because there was "none like" their "God," they would be better off taking their own lives. "The women girded their loins with strength and slew their own sons and daughters, and then themselves. Many men also mustered their strength and slaughtered their wives and children and infants. The most gentle and tender of women slaughtered the child of her delight. They all arose, man and woman alike, and slew one another. The young maidens, the brides, and the bridegrooms looked out through the windows and cried out in a great voice: 'Look and behold, O Lord, what we are doing to sanctify Thy Great Name, in order not to exchange You for a crucified scion who was despised, abominated, and held in contempt in his own generation, a bastard son conceived by a menstruating and wanton mother." Thus "the precious children of Zion, the people of Mainz, were tested with ten trials as was our Father Abraham. . . . They bound their children in sacrifice, as Abraham did his son Isaac, and willingly accepted upon themselves the yoke of fear of Heaven, the King of Kings, the Blessed Holy One. . . . Let the ears hearing this and its like be seared, for who has heard or seen the likes of it? Inquire and seek: was there ever such a mass sacrificial offering since the time of Adam? Did it ever occur that there were a thousand and one hundred offerings on one single day—all of them comparable to the sacrifice of Isaac, the son of Abraham."

In the ponds around the village of Wevelinghofen, "men, women, and children, grooms and brides, old men and women, slaughtered themselves and exposed their throats for their heads to be severed in sanctification of the One Name." One man, a saintly man well on in years, together with his son, "fled together into the water, and the youth stretched out his neck to his father for slaughter as they stood in the waters." The father recited the benediction for ritual slaughter, and the son answered, "Amen." And all those around them cried out, "Hear, O Israel, the Lord is our God, the Lord is One." "Behold, all ye mortals, the great valor of the son who, though not bound, submitted himself to slaughter, and how great was the fortitude of the father who was not softened by pity for so pleasant and handsome a youth," an only son. "Who will hear and not weep? The offering and he who offered him up were unanimous in their desire that their life-breath be stilled."

Writers not only likened the martyrs to Abraham and Isaac, they also went to great lengths to show that the martyrs had done so themselves. One chronicle describes a rabbi in Worms, where eight hundred lost their lives in two days, who cast his sacrifice of righteousness, his killing for the unification of God's name, not in the vernacular of his time and place but in the very language of the Bible. The man called out to his wife and all those nearby: "God gave me this son; my wife Zipporah bore him in her advanced age.

His name is Isaac. I shall now offer him up as a sacrifice as our father Abraham did his son Isaac." Zipporah asked him not to lay a hand on the lad—not yet. "Slaughter me first and let me not see the death of the child." The rabbi didn't want to delay. "He bound his Isaac, his son, and took the knife in his hand to slaughter him," reciting the appropriate blessing. The lad responded, "Amen." "And he slaughtered the boy. He took his shrieking wife and together they left the room. The errant ones slew them."

These were smart, learned, seasoned writers, and their analogies to Abraham and Isaac and other biblical heroes are not lacking in nuance. They call attention, in the most heartrending way, to differences between past and present, between Speyer, Worms, and Cologne, on the one hand, and Moriah on the other. They ask why the skies did not darken, as so many midrashists insisted they had darkened over Moriah. They ask why no angels cried: "Once over one Akedah, Ariels cried out before thee. But now how many are butchered and burned! Why over the blood of children did they not raise a cry?" They observe that, unlike Isaac, the victims of the Rhineland slaughter did not ask or need to be bound.

Over and over they note the difference in numbers:

On the merit of the Akedah at Moriah once we could lean,
Safeguarded for the salvation of age after age—
Now one Akedah follows another, they cannot be
    counted.

Repeatedly they suggest that while Abraham's sacrifice was great, theirs was even greater: "When were there ever a thousand and a hundred in one day, each and every one of them like the Akedah of Isaac son of Abraham?"

Considering how inclined chroniclers were to note differences, it could not have been an accident that none of them pointed out the biggest difference of all. No chronicler contests or qualifies or laments the analogy, argues that it is misleading, that Abraham didn't actually kill Isaac, that Isaac did not die. No one says what Miriam, the mother of seven sons in Hadrian's Rome, reenacting the martyrdom of the Maccabean mother, said to the last of her sons to die: "Go and tell father Abraham not to let it go to his head: 'Yours was a trial, mine was an accomplished fact.'"

We can't know, from the Crusade Chronicles or any other surviving source, precisely what the victims said in their final moments, let alone what they were thinking. Historians have been of many minds about the relationship between the experience and the stories told about that experience afterward. Nor can we know how many people took their own lives and the lives of loved ones, how many others were murdered, and how many converted to avoid certain death. And even if we knew the numbers, it is possible that our ability to comprehend their meaning has been impaired by the forced conversions, mass expulsions, blood libels, pogroms, inquisitions, mass murders, and attempted genocides in the centuries since. Even the highest estimates, in the low five figures, might seem small. Nonetheless several vital Jewish communities—Rashi had studied in both Worms and Mainz—were wiped out, and several others were devastated. It was a catastrophe, and whether chroniclers wrote in its immediate aftermath or decades later, they lived in its shadow. They couldn't see the future, but they feared that there was trouble ahead.

The crusaders had an explanation for Jewish degradation and defeat, and it was akin to their justification for their attacks on the Jews in the first place. Jews were being punished for their sins, especially the rejection and murder of Christ. Their suffering was a sign not of God's redemptive love but of his abandonment. The crusaders were simply the agents of God's wrath on earth, holy warriors, on their way to repel infidels and avenge crucifixion. All they had to lose was their lives, a victory in defeat that would earn them a remission of sins and eternal life.

Jewish survivors had a choice. They could concede their enemies' argument or use all the tools at their disposal to turn it on its head.

The story of Abraham and Isaac was one of their tools. The Jews had not been abandoned. They had been singled out, like Abraham, to do God's work. They were not being punished but rather tested, ten trials exactly like Abraham's. They had not sinned. They were the righteous, suffering for the sins of others. They were not defeated. Rather, they had sacrificed themselves exactly as Abraham had sacrificed Isaac. It was Abraham's sacrifice, not Jesus's, that was the greatest in the past, and theirs, not the crusaders', that was the greatest in the present. And theirs would be the greatest reward: "Happy is he who is slain or slaughtered and who dies attesting the Oneness of His Name," one chronicler wrote. "Such a one is destined for the World-to-Come, where he will sit in the realm of the saints." The martyrs had exchanged "a world of darkness" for "a world of light," a "world of sorrow for one of joy, a transitory world for an eternal world." Their chroniclers wondered how God could possibly restrain himself: "It was for You that innumerable souls were killed! May You avenge the spilt blood of your servants, in our days and before our very eyes—Amen—and speedily."

It was a multipurpose tool, a shield, a spear, a spur, and a standard against which they could measure their own achievement. Chroniclers used the story to contest Christian chauvinism. They used it to establish sacred precedent for the words and deeds of the Rhineland dead, for the line between acceptable and unacceptable forms of Jewish martyrdom remained contested, and not everyone believed that taking one's own life—as opposed to having one's life taken—fell on the acceptable side. They used it to glorify the Jewish tradition, and thereby persuade fellow Jews, including friends and neighbors who had converted, that their faith, its great past and its even greater present, was worth suffering and even dying for, a task that might have been complicated by their very own existence. After all, some of the early chroniclers were almost certainly among those who had decided not to sacrifice their lives. They used it to steel themselves for sacrifices to come. They used it to prod God into battle on their side ("May You avenge the spilt blood of your servants in our days and before our very eyes").

I deeply regret the stories in which Abraham killed Isaac. I regret the stories in which orgies of human sacrifice were staged to resemble Temple services, or baptisms in water and blood. I regret that in the wake of the First Crusade the weapon of choice was often a Jewish version of the passion, of righteous suffering and bloody atonement. Or a Jewish channeling of the spirit of the crusaders themselves, who were on their way to Jerusalem in the service and imitation of Christ, to take back the Holy Land or die the most glorious death trying.

It should go without saying that there is no moral equivalence between suicide and murder, the deeds of those who killed themselves and loved ones rather than convert and the deeds of those who murdered strangers because they refused to convert. Still, I regret the celebration of any kind of violence in God's name, and I despise the idea that the willingness to kill and die for God is the greatest form of devotion. There are places in the Hebrew chronicles and memorials where writers display understanding and sympathy for those who made other choices, including conversion, and places where they reveal, in the way they tell their stories, perfectly understandable mixed feelings about both martyrdom and survival. I wish that it had been possible for someone to figure out a way to use the story to celebrate or elevate the rabbinical imperative to live, which came, among other places, in the Talmudic interpretation of Leviticus 18:5 ("You shall keep My laws and My rules, by the pursuit of which man shall live: I am the Lord"). God doesn't want people to die by his rules and laws, many rabbis insisted. By his laws, he wants them to live.

But what writer, what chronicler, what memorialist, what poet, what composer of prayers, ever bore such a burden? What words had to do so much work in rallying a wounded and dispirited community in the wake of tragedy and in the face of ongoing threats from an unpredictable and merciless foe? How could I, with centuries of hindsight and so much safe distance, simply condemn them for borrowing some ideas about suffering and salvation, about water and blood, about punishments and rewards, from those among whom they lived and with whom they struggled, especially when some of those ideas or earlier versions of those ideas might well have belonged to them in the first place? Above all else, how could I blame them for wanting to believe that they, not those who persecuted them, were the agents of God in history, doing his work on earth? Who could blame them for wanting to demonstrate, in the complete absence of concrete evidence (the skies didn't darken, God's messenger didn't say stop, his angels did not weep), that their God was on the scene and on their side. I could regret the story but still try to understand it, and I did. I could hate the story but still feel for, even love, the storyteller, and I do.

Don't let the way I tell my story fool you. History does not unfold neatly, a chapter at a time. It is a great big carnival, a circus, a mall, a multiplex, a market, a bazaar. At the very same moment that some commentators said or suggested that Abraham had killed Isaac, others practiced and promoted ways of reading Scripture that made his death much less likely.

One was Egyptian-born Saadia Gaon, the first rabbi born outside of the land of Israel to head the great Hebrew academy in Sura. In tenth-century Iraq, he translated the Bible into Arabic and wrote commentaries in which he championed the plain sense (*peshat*) of Scripture. The Bible, he insisted, means what it says, and we should leave it as it was written—except in those instances when our senses, observation, experience, or intellect tell us that the plain sense can't be so. Or when the plain sense, "the popular explanation," of one passage contradicts the plain sense of another, the meaning of which is perfectly clear. Or when the plain sense contradicts Jewish tradition.

Here is one of his examples: A child could tell you that Eve was not the mother of all living things. Not the mother of the lion or the tiger or the bear. So Saadia maintained that it was fine to amend Genesis 3 to read: Eve was the mother of all living "and speaking." Similarly, anyone with an iota of intelligence could tell you why God couldn't, literally, be a "consuming fire." Fire is often man-made. It is sometimes feeble. It comes and goes. The author of Deuteronomy was using a metaphor, and therefore it was acceptable for interpreters to turn from the literal (*peshat*) to the figurative (*derash*) to understand and explain it.

And when, in the story of the near sacrifice of Isaac, God says, "Now I know that you fear me," every imaginable alarm goes off. Common sense, reason, our understanding of other biblical passages, and tradition all tell us that there is nothing that God doesn't know. The common emendation, "Now I have made known to the people that you are faithful to God," makes the story clearer, the Bible more internally consistent.

Coming after a millennium of every kind of interpretation and alteration, the liberties Saadia proposed might strike you, as they strike me, as tame. But he had to defend them, for in his day there were exegetes who insisted that even he strayed too far from the plain, literal, original sense of Scripture in which they thought all interpretation and Judaism itself should be grounded. Critics contended that the rabbis of the great academies and their oral Torah were merely handmaidens, valuable when they illuminated written Torah, superfluous when they did not.

The insurgents were called Karaites, and their movement, born in Iraq in the ninth century and later based in Jerusalem, had many adherents. But the rabbis, whose interpretations they often ridiculed and whose authority over the meaning of the words they rejected, didn't go away. They insisted that there was no reason to choose between interpretive freedom and tradition, oral and written. The challenge was to strike the proper balance between them.

In many minds, then and ever since, no one struck that balance better, or more gracefully, than Rabbi Shlomo Yitzchaki, or Rashi, the dean of the northern French school in the second half of the eleventh century. Rashi had a powerful yet playful intelligence, a command of classical midrash, and an ear for several languages and the meanings that emanate from the sound of words, all of which he conveyed in the loveliest prose. Today, rabbis often credit him for insight that he himself gleaned from the rabbis of late antiquity, from learned conversations that had taken place centuries before he was born. But his genius, when it came to Abraham and Isaac, was not revisionist daring or even interpretive originality, but rather the brilliant selecting, editing, and employment of earlier material, the winnowing of a universe of possibilities down to a beautifully arranged, interpretively sharp, and always morally instructive few.

Every Talmud features Rashi's commentary, and for centuries so did many Bibles. He was, and he remains, one very popular rabbi. But in his day his blending of figurative, homiletical, and literal— his use of figurative and homiletical to get to the literal—earned him many critics. One contemporary critic was Joseph Kara. "One should know," Kara wrote, "that when the prophecies were written they were written complete, with nothing missing and with adequate interpretation, so that subsequent generations would not be led astray by them. It is not necessary to bring a proof from anywhere else, including the midrash, because the Torah was given and recorded in perfect form, lacking nothing." Rashi's most famous critic was probably his own grandson, Samuel ben Meir (Rashbam), who lived in France in the first half of the twelfth century and insisted that readers could understand both the plain sense and the context without the sages.

Why is Abraham's knife called *ma'akhelet*? Rashi had given three reasons. First, because the root of the word (*akhal*) is the verb "to eat," and the knife eats the flesh it cuts. Second, because (as Rabbi Hanina had put it in the first century) the knife, through ritual slaughter, makes food (*okhlin*) fit for eating. Third, as many rabbis before him had noted, because Israel "eats" from the knife's reward. All the benefits that Israel enjoys it "enjoys only in the merit of that knife."

Rashbam insisted that Rashi's first explanation was sufficient in and of itself: "A knife is called a *ma'akhelet* based on the idea expressed in the phrase," in Deuteronomy, "My sword shall eat (*to'khal*) flesh." He didn't deny the legitimacy or occasional value of the figurative, but he believed that the figurative and literal should be kept separate. Rashi's mistake was mixing them on the page.

Abraham Ibn Ezra, the twelfth-century Spanish poet, astrologer, philosopher, grammarian, and philologist, pictured the plain sense of Scripture as a point at the center of a circle. That point was the meaning, in many cases a single meaning, consistent with reason, logic, and context (by which Ibn Ezra meant the meaning of surrounding passages). To get at that point, you had to start with a deep knowledge of Hebrew grammar and the precise meaning, in time, of particular Hebrew words. Unhinged from Hebrew, interpretation took flight, as it did when the rabbis of the great academies, sometimes with great philosophical insight, wandered round and round the circle but never zeroed in on it. Or when the Karaites ignored it, interpreting passages as they saw fit, according to their own needs. Or when the Catholic priests and not a few Jewish sages imagined that the point at the center of the circle was a riddle or a mystery, anything but what it appeared to be, at which time they invariably lost sight of it or buried it in a fog of explanation. Or when homilists, troubled by a difficult passage or a straightforward passage that was troubling, changed one word into another, one meaning into another, one story into another, a story simpler for them to explain and simpler for their students and congregants to understand.

Consider, as Ibn Ezra did, three words in the story's first line, "God tested Abraham." So simple, yet, he thought, so often misunderstood. Many rabbis said that what God had done was to elevate Abraham, raise him up, like a banner or a flag, for all to see. Some, from antiquity right through Saadia, said that God had demonstrated Abraham's obedience (even though the dimmest reader would realize that no one, not even Abraham's own servants, was there to see it). Others said that Abraham had misunderstood: God simply meant for Abraham to bring Isaac up to Moriah. As soon as he realized that Abraham had misunderstood him, he said, "Put him down." Those misreadings followed not only from an inattention to language and context, but also from an inability or unwillingness to admit that God would deliver and then rescind a command. But God did and God does. *Nissah* means "test." God tested Abraham, in order to reward him. Live with it, Ibn Ezra said.

Equally illustrative are Ibn Ezra's comments on Isaac's age. He acknowledged the tradition that Isaac was thirty-seven, and as tradition, he accepted it. But from a logical point of view he found it "unacceptable." If Isaac had been an adult, "his piety should have been revealed in Scripture and his reward should have been double that of his father for willingly having submitted himself to be sacrificed. Yet Scripture says nothing concerning Isaac's great self-sacrifice." Others put his age at five. That, too, Ibn Ezra found unacceptable. A five-year-old couldn't have carried the wood for the sacrificial pyre. Logic led to an approximation, something "close to thirteen," and to the conclusion that Abraham had "overpowered him and bound him against his will." The proof, Ibn Ezra wrote, lies in what Abraham said and didn't say: He "hid his intention from Isaac and told him, 'God will provide the lamb for a burnt-offering, my son.' Abraham knew that if he said, 'You are the burnt-offering,' Isaac would quite possibly have fled."

David Kimhi (Radak) was a distinguished rabbi and scholar from a distinguished family of rabbis and scholars, a family that, in response to the invasion of Spain by Moroccan Muslims (Almohads) in the middle of the twelfth century, and the subsequent persecution of Jews, literally carried the Spanish tradition to Provence. In Radak's view, there were times when Ibn Ezra went a little too far, reading more literally than Moses wrote. Radak was a rationalist who perceived multiple levels of meaning, and he believed that Moses fully intended to convey them all, a surface meaning for the masses and for the learned all kinds of depth. Radak brought history as well as philosophy, philology, and linguistics to his influential exegesis, and his sense of the place of Scripture over time provided him with a context for his understanding of the plain sense. In response to Ibn Ezra, he conceded the obvious: there were no witnesses on Mount Moriah. But to move from that observation to the conclusion that God had not intended to demonstrate Abraham's obedience was to miss one of the story's purposes for all those who heard or read it after it was recorded. It was a demonstration for the ages.

I could go on. I haven't mentioned Ramban (Nachmanides), back in Spain in the thirteenth century, who tried to tie it all together, South and North, Spanish, French, and German, classical and modern, philology, linguistics, theology, psychology, history, typology, and even what he took to be human nature. Or Rambam (Maimonides) in twelfth-century Spain, Morocco, and finally Egypt. In his *Guide of the Perplexed*, Maimonides used the story to correct what he took to be a widespread misunderstanding of the purpose of biblical tests. God tested not to learn something himself or to afflict in order to reward but rather to show men what they ought to believe and how they ought to behave. He tested Abraham and Isaac to show how far we must be prepared to go in the love and fear of God. Nor have I mentioned any of the other philosophically minded exegetes who followed in Maimonides's footsteps. One was grammarian and logician Joseph Ibn Kaspi, who was born in Argentière in 1280 but—driven by a unquenchable thirst for knowledge, an unhappy marriage, and children in far-off places—spent much of his life elsewhere in France as well as in Spain, Majorca, and (in search of instruction from Maimonides's family) even Egypt. Or the Kabbalists, who, beginning in the twelfth and thirteenth centuries, dug so deep into classical midrash in search of metaphysical meanings and especially the emendations of God that they sometimes left the rabbis of late antiquity looking literal. And even if I paused to identify and characterize each of them, my survey would still be superficial and skewed. There was also a vast body of Islamic exegesis in the first centuries of the new millennium and Christian exegesis in four modes (literal, allegorical, tropological, and anagogical) even before Martin Luther and all the other reformers entered the fray.

I fear trying your patience. What's more, for all the variety—
the various approaches of the academies in Iraq, Palestine, North
Africa, Spain, France, and Germany, the competing ideas about the
value and authority of the oral law and rabbinical interpretation,
the different approaches to the plain sense of the text (from the
narrowly grammatical to the boundlessly mystical), the contentious
debate among exegetes (including Saadia's criticism of the Karaites,
Ibn Ezra's criticism of Saadia, Rashbam's criticism of Rashi, and
Ramban's criticism of just about everyone)—I want to highlight
something a great many of the medieval exegetes had in common,
or a direction in which many of them seemed to be moving.

Where earlier generations of rabbis had reveled in multiple
meanings, many medieval exegetes engaged in a more sober search
for the one meaning. While earlier generations had focused on the
relevance of Scripture, its value as instruction the day it was being
read, many now focused on what they took to be its original meanings and contexts, its meaning to Moses and God. Where earlier
generations had been comfortable with the boundless association
of passages written at different times and describing different times
(where something that happened in Moses's Egypt or Josiah's Jerusalem could be used to explain something that happened a thousand years before), now many were engaged in a disciplined and
often quite literal analysis of vocabulary, grammar, and syntax in
time. Where earlier generations of editors had produced compilations of fly-on-the-wall rabbinical conversations and collections of
sermons, some now began to produce carefully edited commentary
of individual interpreters.

That shift in orientation neither began nor ended with medieval
Jewish interpreters. The rabbis were heavily influenced and encouraged by innovations in the study of science, medicine, philosophy,
and especially language, innovations that had their roots in the
Islamic world and spread (sometimes when Jews chose to leave or
were expelled) north and west from there. Then, too, if you will
allow me a rabbinical leap in space and time, what was Martin

Luther if not a Christian Karaite, calling for a return to the text and the spirit guiding each person's interpretation of it? Out with allegory, out with the hierarchy of priestly interpreters dictating meanings, and of course out with indulgences. Back to Scripture, Scripture alone.

I don't want to push the contrast between old and new, classical or medieval, too far. Rashi's commentary is rich with rabbinical riffs, direct quotations, or close paraphrases, which he often let stand without elaboration or comment of any kind. And for all their criticism of Rashi's use of classical midrash, neither Rashbam nor Ramban eschewed it entirely.

And, as always, literal and figurative were often only so in the eyes of each exegete. Writing in the early twelfth century, Rashbam criticized commentators who spun elaborate yarns to explain what had prompted God's test in the first place, including stories about Satan's goading and Isaac's bragging. They had all failed to recognize that the word *ahar* ("after," as in "after these things" in the story's first line) always referred to events immediately preceding the event at hand. Then he used that understanding of the word to spin an elaborate yarn of his own. God, he wrote, was punishing Abraham for swearing an oath of peaceful coexistence with King Abimelech, as Abraham had done in the scene immediately preceding God's test. That oath was a clear violation of the command (which God delivered some four hundred years later as Abraham's descendants wandered in the wilderness) *not* to make peace with any of the previous inhabitants of the Promised Land.

Three hundred years after Rashbam, Martin Luther insisted that the truth of the Bible and Christianity resided in the text alone. But if you open Luther's lectures to the chapter on Genesis 22, you will see that he didn't return to the text alone so much as the reinterpretation of it that came in the Epistle to the Hebrews, forever after the foundation of Christian talk of Abraham's faith. When the exegesis of the "saints" or even the Jews (whose writings came to him by way of the Frenchman Nicholas of Lyra) made good sense, he borrowed. When it didn't, he took off on his own. Often way off, as when he put himself in the story, telling us what he could or could not have done in Abraham's place, or when he imagined scenes that he was sure Moses must have left out of the historical record.

And what choice did he and all the other rebels have? As they elevated text above tradition, they created an interpretive vacuum, which they themselves then stepped in to fill. The Karaites' contribution to the archive of biblical exegesis was enormous, including some of the earliest line-by-line commentaries produced by individual authors. Luther's contribution to the archive was also enormous. His lectures on Genesis alone run to eight volumes, ninety-five pages of which are devoted to my nineteen lines.

Finally, and perhaps needless to say, the turn to individual commentary aimed at the plain sense of Scripture did not mean that every exegete arrived at the same plain sense, in matters large or small. When the angel of God called out ("Abraham, Abraham"), Rashi imagined that the repetition was a sign of love. Ibn Ezra and Radak imagined that it was a sign of urgency. And Ibn Kaspi imagined that it was a sign of relative significance: God and Moses signaling that the command to desist was more insistent than the command to sacrifice, that it was the command that really mattered. Nor did it mean that the rabbis who were in the business of editing collections of midrash believed that it was their job to separate the wheat from the chaff. The compilations of midrash published in the Middle Ages, including the *Midrash Ha-Gadol,* were as inclusive as ever, and when printing presses started churning out Bibles, each publisher tried to include more individual commentaries—alongside, above, and below the biblical text—than the next.

Nevertheless, exegetes who emphasized the literal and the contextual were here to stay, and they added immeasurably to the archive of biblical interpretation. They also contributed to a shift in the assumptions about the proper relationship between reader and Scripture. For the longest time, interpreters had tried to get close to the text by bringing it, quite consciously, to them, wherever they were. Now some of them were trying to move toward it. That didn't mean that they always succeeded. Nor did it mean that in moving toward it they were no longer interpreting it, remaking it in their own image, seeing things that weren't originally there. But it did mean that they had come to believe that it was their responsibility to move toward it and they imagined themselves doing just that.

What was in all that for me? Why would I, so long a champion of biblical revision, make so much of, let alone welcome, the arrival of exegetes so partial to what they took to be Scripture's plain sense? Those are fair questions, and my answer has several parts.

For starters, not even the most dyed-in-the-wool homilist is likely to resist the gift of a plain-sense interpretation when that interpretation corresponds to his or her own plain sense, or even more to his or her fancy. I love it when rabbis, reading literally, suggest that the meaning of the phrase "the two walked on together" is not that father and son walked as one, in mind as well as in body, but rather that Abraham kept Isaac close to ensure that he didn't try to run away. And I love it when Ibn Ezra tersely dismisses "those who say that Abraham slaughtered Isaac and left him on the altar and following this Isaac came to life": they are, he writes, "contradicting Scripture." And when the thirteenth-century Spanish mystic Ibn al-'Arabi argues that Abraham misinterpreted his dream, that God wouldn't and didn't command him to kill his son. And when Ibn Kaspi argues not just that the story's purpose was to uproot, undermine, and weaken the heathen practice of child sacrifice, but also that Abraham himself (even before he looked up and saw the ram in the thicket and decided, on his own, to offer it) understood that child sacrifice was an abomination to YHWH. I even applaud when Martin Luther, whose writings often make me want to scream, imagines that there had to have been a conversation between Abraham and Isaac at the altar, a difficult conversation, in which Isaac, "struck with amazement," reminded his father of God's promise. In any context I can imagine, Luther's scenario (like Ibn Ezra's before him) seems more likely—and more likely literal—than Isaac egging his father on.

But there's more. Attention to a story's plain sense can serve as a useful check on reckless revision, and a check also on destructive forms of typology, the explicit or implicit argument that the past is merely a shadow of things to come, always about something other than what it seems to be about, something in its future, something better. In the right hands it can encourage a proper respect for the past as the past, for distant and different ways of thinking and behaving (however much that thought and behavior contains the seeds of what's to come, however often even the simplest words and deeds have ethical, philosophical, theological, metaphysical, and mystical implications and dimensions).

Finally, remember where I started: remember that I was thinking about context before I was thinking about revision. It was my reading of Genesis 22 in the context of the ten chapters that came before it, in the context of that tumultuous quarter century of Abraham's life, all the questions he had asked God, all the worries and doubts that he had expressed, that made me think that Abraham wouldn't have done what he did in the way that he did it in the first place. That Abraham wouldn't have set out for Moriah without saying a word was the plain sense of the life and character of Abraham to me.

That is not to say that I have switched teams, gone over to the other side for good. I believe there are many different paths to interpretive enlightenment. I can bear long and learned explications of the origin and significance of single words with the best of them. Say, Ramban on the word "Moriah," which the author of Chronicles identified as the Temple Mount.

Why Moriah? Where did that place-name come from? Was it, as some Talmudic sages had said, that the word is a compound of the word for "instruction" and the divine name—and Jerusalem is the place from which instruction in the ways of the Torah spread around the world? Or that Moriah comes from *mora,* fear, and it was on Moriah that the ancients feared God and worshipped before him. Or, as Onkelos (the name associated with one of the most influential Aramaic translations of the Torah) and Rashi after him had said, that the incense offered in the Temple contains myrrh (*mor*) and other spices. Or, putting all the ancient *midrashim* aside, was it that the word "Moriah" meant "mountain of Myrrh," as in Song of Songs, "I will go to the mountain of myrrh and the hill of frankincense." That was probably the plain-sense explanation, Ramban concluded, for one simple reason: in Abraham's time there was myrrh on the mountain, but there was no Temple.

What I wouldn't give for that kind of command of the language and literature. But I would not be completely honest if I didn't confess that sometimes while reading passage after passage of that kind of analysis, my eyes glaze over and my attention strays. I might even daydream, almost irreverently, and imagine another commentator less concerned about where the word came from than how Abraham responded to the command to go there. "Excuse me, sir," he might have said. "I am but dust and ashes, a man of few words, and as such often misunderstood. Do you happen to remember, back before Isaac was born, when we stood on that hillside overlooking Sodom and I asked, 'Will not the Judge of all the earth do justice?'

"What part of my question didn't you understand?"

~~~

I have yet to find that Abraham in the literature of the late Middle Ages. But one of the remarkable things about the life of the story is that even though you can't always get the Abraham and Isaac you want when you want it, or even the Abraham and Isaac you need, you can always get something different from what you have. All the more if you are willing to turn to people working in different fields and forms. One obvious place to turn is the walls.

Visual artists were drawn to the story early on. The wall painting in the synagogue at Dura-Europos and the frescoes in the catacombs of Callisto and Priscilla go back to the third century. By the end of the fourth, bishops Gregory of Nyssa (in modern Turkey) and Augustine of Hippo (in modern Algeria, fifteen hundred miles to the west) had each noted that likenesses of the story—on wall paintings, mosaics, sarcophagi, and frescoes—were everywhere. Abraham's deed, Augustine wrote, was "so famous that it recurs to the mind of itself without any study or reflection, and is in fact repeated by so many tongues, and portrayed in so many places, that no-one can pretend to shut his eyes or his ears from it." Several hundred images from late antiquity survive.

Gregory believed that the artists of his day were out ahead of the exegetes who worked with words. Whether or not that was the case, the early artists frequently went their own way. They invariably pictured Isaac as a small boy. Either they had not heard, from the rabbis, that he was a young man, or they didn't believe it. And though it is hard to read the expression on the face of the small, simple figure of Isaac on the mosaic floor of the sixth-century synagogue at Beit Alfa, if pressed, I'd have to say he looks at least a little alarmed. The ram, by contrast, is relaxed and ready, and the early artists gave him a place, front and center, as a symbol of God's providence and deliverance, that he rarely attained in the stories or commentary of the rabbis or priests or (before too long) Islamic exegetes.

At least a few early artists gave Sarah a prominent place too, right up there with Abraham and Isaac atop Moriah. She is definitely in two of the late fourth- or early fifth-century images of the sacrifice on the walls of the chapel of the necropolis at El Bagawat (Egypt), standing right next to or just above Isaac, with a hand or hands raised in prayer. And she may well be on the scene in the sixth-century sarcophagus in a church in Lucq-de-Béarn. If so, she has her hand over her mouth, as if looking on, aghast. But the figures in that sarcophagus are indistinct, lacking essential detail, and is it hard to know for sure—hard to know if it is actually Sarah, hard to know if she is actually looking aghast. Someone wanting a close look at Sarah in the fifth or sixth century would do better with Romanos or the Syriac homilists.

What a difference a millennium could make. By the middle of the second, a veritable who's who of Byzantine, medieval, Gothic, Romanesque, Renaissance, baroque, and Dutch Golden Age artists had drawn or painted or etched or carved or shaped what they or their Christian patrons almost always called *The Sacrifice of Isaac*. They rarely added characters (in fact, most dropped Sarah from the scene) or dramatically altered the story's plot. They nonetheless managed to use ink, marble, wood, bronze, ceramic tile, stained glass, and oil to plumb the story's depths, its interiors, in distinctive ways.

Consider Abraham's demeanor. Many interpreters took great pride, in fact delight, in describing Abraham as unflappable, completely at ease. Neither his face nor his words gave any hint of reluctance, uneasiness, or dread, something that might have tipped Sarah off, made the servants suspicious, or alarmed Isaac. Painting that composure was no problem so long as artists imagined that he had been as calm and cool on the inside as he was on the outside, and some painters did. Expressionless, or nearly so. Moved only by the voice of God's angel. You can see that in the late oil paintings of the Florentine Andrea del Sarto, fascinating paintings in which there is certainly surprise in Abraham's face the moment the angel arrives, but a surprise that is as carefully controlled as the movement of the muscles in his big hands and arms and shoulders and neck and head. You can see the same self-control in the work of another Florentine, Alessandro Allori, a different and somewhat unusual take in that Allori painted a parade of scenes in one large canvas. In the penultimate scene, Abraham points up and ahead to the site of the sacrifice as if he were proposing a suitable spot for a picnic. Or Domenichino's *Sacrifice,* which looks like a still from a graceful dance. Even—or especially—in Caravaggio's rendering of what would have been Isaac's last moment of life, where Abraham's knife, shimmering with light coming straight from the heavens, is a blade's length from Isaac's neck and Abraham's hands are as steady as his gaze. Abraham looks at the angel intently, without revealing a bit of emotion, as if to say: If you've got something to say, say it, and quickly. I've got work to do.

But if you thought, as many writers did, that Abraham's composure, however impressive, simply had to be a cover, concealing inner turmoil or just plain fright, you had a problem. Or a choice, between inner turmoil and outer calm. Many artists sacrificed the latter for the former, painting an anguished Abraham, the inside on the outside, sad, sorry, frightened, torn, in despair, if not half mad. I am thinking of the sadness and perhaps resignation in the eyes and mouth of Donatello's marble Abraham, an early fifteenth-century sculpture all the more haunting for the subtlety of Abraham's expression. Or, less subtly, but not without great power of its own, the polychrome wood sculpture carved a century later by the Spaniard Alonso Berruguete, where a Christ-like Abraham holds the bound and kneeling Isaac, as he so often held him, by the hair, his own head thrown back, his eyes looking up toward the heavens. Or Rembrandt's famous oil, of 1635, in which Abraham looks puzzled, confused, maybe even a little dazed, his huge hand covering Isaac's face, whether to blindfold him or to smother him we don't know. The angel, who has grabbed Abraham's right hand with his own, looks as if he were about to smack him with his left, though it is more likely that he is simply pointing to the heavenly source of his words. Abraham has dropped his knife, but Rembrandt leaves it suspended in mid-flight, painted, like Abraham's face and every bit of Isaac, in light, its tip still pointed where it was pointed when it was in Abraham's hand, toward Isaac's naked neck.

Twenty years later, in an etching, Rembrandt imagined a much quieter scene, a psychological foil to the oil's high drama. He gathered the movement of muscles, arms, angel, and knife and turned them into feeling. Abraham looks utterly defeated, torn and grieving inside and out, but he is calm, his hand gently wrapped around Isaac's head, his fingers again covering Isaac's eyes but now barely making contact. Here the angel seems to be comforting Abraham as much as restraining him, comforting him just as Abraham tries to comfort Isaac, who is on his knees, bent over one of Abraham's, his hands at his sides. Abraham has the knife in his hand, but he holds it, firmly and deliberately, at a distance, its tip turned safely away from Isaac, on its way out of the painting's frame. Still, Abraham looks ancient—shrunken and ghostlike—as if he were ill or about to be, and it is hard to imagine him providing Isaac with much comfort. This is not the Abraham of the church fathers, or of Luther, let alone the Abraham of John Calvin, who repeatedly calls God's test torture and goes to great lengths to describe Abraham's anguish and grief, yet who nonetheless insists that he remained completely composed and tranquil. Nor is it the Abraham of the rabbis who imagined a dry-eyed Abraham looking forward to the sacrifice or, after God stopped him, praying for permission to go through with it.

Then there was Isaac. Most Christian exegetes working with words imagined him as knowing and willing, quiet if not completely silent, and above all else not suffering. There are so many examples of visual art in which he is portrayed that way that I hardly know where to start. How about the Isaac in the twelfth-century mosaic on the north wall of the cathedral in Monreale, Italy. Granted, he does not look comfortable. Well clad, just like his dad, in Roman garb, he is perched on his back on the edge of a high altar, his hands bound behind him. Only Abraham's firm grip on his hair keeps him from tumbling to the ground. But the awkwardness of the pose only makes the look of calm on Isaac's face all the more striking. Or the Isaac in the thirteenth-century Gothic picture Bible known as the Crusader Bible, where the boy crouches with his bound hands clasped in front of him in prayer, as nonchalant about the surprising turn of events as is his father.

In the lavishly illustrated fourteenth-century edition of Guyart des Moulins's Bible Historiale, Isaac is on his knees, head bowed slightly, hands again clasped in prayer. Abraham appears somewhat taken aback by the arrival of the angel, who has a stern look on his face and a firm grip on the tip of Abraham's knife, but Isaac's face reveals little or no emotion. His poise is all the more remarkable in Donatello's sculpture, for Abraham's knife has already met Isaac's flesh and there is no angel on the scene. Abraham is distressed, his features somehow both marble and in motion, yet Isaac's face is perfectly still. If he is anything but fully accepting of his fate, we can't see it in his astonishingly lifelike face. In Simon Bening's sixteenth-century book border, painted bright in tempera and gold on parchment, Isaac's head is bowed and he looks lost in his prayers, while Abraham, standing behind him, prepares, like a logger, to swing a long sword down on his neck. In Cigoli's oil, Isaac is back up on the altar, nude now except for a shroud across his waist, his left leg extended to the ground, his right leg crossed under it. His head is cocked, his arm pinned behind his back, and his whole body again held in balance by Abraham's grip. The knife is on its way, yet he is at peace. In Jacopo da Empoli's oil, by contrast, there is tension in his cheeks and eyes, and his eyes roll heavenward in uneasy supplication. But his body still speaks of acceptance, with a knee resting on the altar, his head cocked upward, his arms bound loosely where, in a crucifixion, nails might be. A few years later, one of Empoli's students, Felice Ficherelli, painted Isaac nearly flat on his back, his wrists bound, his hands crossed. Yet his raised arms look to me like the arms of a young man stretching as he wakes from an afternoon nap. And then, in Rembrandt's late etching, Isaac is back on his knees, his arms at his side, muscles tense but not straining.

In all those images, and hundreds of others (in Christian art alone), you can find those Isaacs. But despite so many models to learn from and imitate, and endless talk about Isaac's quiet acceptance of his fate, not every artist imagined him that way. The wide-eyed Isaac in the York Psalter (a twelfth-century illuminated edition of Jerome's revision of his own Latin translation of the book of Psalms) looks more than a little alarmed, especially when you compare the expression on his face to the expression in the story's first scene. His hands, uncharacteristically, are unbound, and it seems no more likely that he was praying than trying to push his father away. In Berruguete's sculpture, Isaac's hands are bound high and tight behind his back; his arm and chest muscles strain against his bonds; his mouth is open as if he were crying out in pain or calling for help. In Del Sarto's oils, his mouth is still. It is his eyes that express his alarm, all the more because he is looking not up to the heavens but out of the frame at us, as if we might be able to help him, or at least explain what in the world his father is doing.

In Titian's action-packed and colorful oil, which if you were not familiar with you might assume was the creation of Disney, we look up, from below, at a small boy, already kneeling atop the altar, lorded over by a Hercules-like Abraham, whose huge biceps, forearms, and wrists push down on his head, as if he were trying to hold him underwater. In Caravaggio, the ram looks willing, but Isaac is in obvious distress, held down by the force of Abraham's arm, by the grip of Abraham's hand on his face and around his neck, and by the thumb pressed into his jaw. Isaac's open mouth looks like that of a dying or dead fish, and his eyes are dark and dull. In Pedro Orrente's *Sacrifice,* another baroque oil, the muscles in Isaac's arms, chest, even abdomen, are all bulging. The veins in his neck alone belie acceptance. Looking away (Abraham is always looking away), Abraham pins his head to a slab of stone with the tail of a red blindfold. In Rembrandt's oil, Isaac looks only slightly less miserable, the muscles in his upper body taut, his neck bent back, his face smothered, and the back of his head pressed into the wood of the altar by Abraham's huge hand.

I don't know what those painters intended to show or say about Abraham's state of mind or Isaac's emotions, let alone what viewers saw. I don't know how much or in exactly what ways those images were shaped by their moment in art history, the conventions, the expectations, the cost or status of colors, the works artists imitated or reacted against, the creative avenues opened up or closed off by new materials and techniques, the internal logic of forms. I don't know how much my vision has been shaped by my sensibilities, my ideas, my desires, my place, and my time. Today there are art historians who look at Lorenzo Ghiberti's magnificent bronze relief, designed for a competition in Florence in the very first years of the fifteenth century, and see mixed feelings in Abraham's pose: his torso backing away from Isaac as his arm thrusts at him with the knife. And yet I, who would like nothing more than to see mixed feelings, see nothing but resolve: the contrast between the flex of Abraham's body and the movement of arm and knife a somewhat awkward attempt to represent the body's natural movement, Abraham putting his weight behind the knife blow.

The winner's panel was to adorn the east door of the Baptistery. The competition came down to Ghiberti and Filippo Brunelleschi. Ghiberti won, and afterward he boasted that even the men he had defeated ("without any exception") conceded that his work was the finest. Many scholars believe he made better use of the quatrefoil frame, and the materially minded note that he shrewdly reduced the weight of his relief (it was seven kilos lighter than Brunelleschi's), increasing its appeal to judges calculating the cost of each in bronze, which was then ten times more expensive than marble. Still, I can't help think that the classical order and Gothic elegance of Ghiberti's relief—Abraham's fierce determination, Isaac's hard-bodied, stoic acceptance—also contributed to his victory. Brunelleschi's panel was messier, less harmonious, more natural. Notwithstanding the orderly horizontal and vertical lines, the scene fills the frame only haphazardly, and there is no mistaking Abraham's confusion and the fear, if not agony, in Isaac's face.

It is possible that Brunelleschi, like Caravaggio two centuries later and many others in the years in between, could not imagine the scene without imagining that Isaac had suffered. It is possible that some artists and sculptors realized that Isaac could have suffered some without overshadowing the sacrifice to come. It is possible that his suffering, or at least his struggling, solved a formal problem that arose when a painter or sculptor set out to portray a narrative that takes place over three days. How do you generate drama or add to the suspense? In words, the suspense builds in the movement from command, to response, to preparation, to journey, to the ditching of the servants, to Isaac's question about the lamb. Ghiberti shows us the last moment of that movement. The angel is on his way, but not yet there. He is racing to beat the knife. But in many of the images the angel arrives ahead of us, with a hand (a hand that is not mentioned in the Bible) locked on Abraham's arm or knife. We know that Isaac is safe the moment we set eyes on him (though I must admit that in Brunelleschi it is a really close call). But Isaac can't see the angel—he never can. He doesn't know he is safe, and the tension in many of the images resides in his not knowing.

What I can say is that when I look at those paintings and sculptures, I see familiar scenes in fresh ways. Christian commentators said that Isaac hadn't suffered, and so it is not surprising that in their writings they did not show him suffering. Many rabbis suggested that he had. Yet they rarely showed him in any real pain or distress. Crusade chroniclers told stories of martyrs who considered themselves Isaac's heirs, but it was the martyrs, not Abraham and Isaac, whose gruesome deaths they described. Even in the stories in which it was said or implied that Isaac had died, it might be more accurate to say he fainted or, like a cartoon character, had the wind knocked out of him. One minute he's down and out cold; the next he springs back to life, recites the benediction for the dead, and races off to the Garden of Eden or the academy of Shem. Compare the Isaac of Caravaggio, Donatello, Berruguete, or Brunelleschi to the Isaac in the fifteenth-century Second Nuremberg Haggadah, where he is falling headfirst, his arms outstretched in front of him, "from the Garden God planted for our protection." Drawn or etched simply, he looks like a yeshiva student playing Superman at recess.

It is not that rabbis consciously downplayed suffering. Their commentary, like the story itself, left readers free to imagine it. And there are places—whether in Abraham's or Isaac's words or simply in their tears—where they evoke it. But the rabbis didn't force you to dwell on it. For most of them, Isaac's suffering, like his blood and ashes, was an abstraction. They pondered its meaning and significance, not the experience itself. Some of those oil paintings and sculptures forced me back to the experience. There isn't blood in any of them, nor even a hint that the sacrifice was carried out. All are highly stylized. Most are utterly unreal. Nonetheless, the best of them break the spell cast by dreamy discussions of theology and philosophy and grammar and theories of interpretation and the derivation and meaning of words. Whatever the intent or outlook of the artist, I look at some of those paintings and say to myself: My heavens. This is a story about a father who is about to sacrifice his son.

~~~

I guess with so many people celebrating from such a comfortable distance, without seeming to reckon, really reckon, the cost, I simply wanted someone to acknowledge that it hurt. I wanted someone to say or show that a father could not set out to sacrifice a son, could not nearly sacrifice a son, without causing real pain and suffering, leaving wounds. In a few of the English mystery plays, popular dramas drawn from Bible stories, Abraham and Isaac say as much themselves.

The mysteries grew out of the liturgical drama of the medieval church, which itself had roots in dramatic hymns. Like liturgical plays, the earliest versions of each of the mysteries were written by clerics. Unlike them, they were written in the vernacular and performed out of doors, on major feast days (including Corpus Christi and Whitsunday) and at festivals and fairs. Some performances were overseen by local officials and performed by play masters, one at a time, on stationary stages. Others were overseen by craft guilds and performed by craftsmen, either singularly or in cycles that ran from Creation to the Last Judgment and lasted all day or even several days. A different guild—the barbers did Abraham and Isaac in Chester, the papermakers and bookbinders did it in York—would be responsible for each Bible story, or "pageant." Players would perform on a "pageant wagon," which could be rolled around town for multiple performances in a single day.

Whether stationary or processional, amateur or semiprofessional, the sets, staging, props, and costumes were all elaborate and inventive. The wagons often had two or three tiers. The ground might serve as a fourth. The lowest level might represent hell, but sometimes hell was up on the stage, a huge dragon's mouth. Many angels managed to fly. Public records point to performances in the late fourteenth century, though it is unlikely that those were the first. The earliest extant manuscripts are dated closer to the end of the fifteenth, by which time they were a popular form of theater all over Europe. In England they remained popular through the middle of the sixteenth century, when Queen Elizabeth banned them and every other form of religious drama.

There are six surviving Abraham-and-Isaac scripts, more of them than of any other single Bible story. Yet anyone taking a cursory look might well wonder what the plays add to the archive of interpretation and revision, to the things people have said about and done with the story. On the surface there isn't a more predictable representation of traditional Christian themes: of God's testing and the trials that mark earthly life; of obedience and the often painful demands of faith; of the drama of God's promise to Abraham and the threat to that promise posed by Abraham's sword; and running through all that, the prefiguration of the birth, life, death, and resurrection of Christ. Even someone who reads only the opening and closing pages will get it, for the last words in each play go to a learned man, who takes the stage to sum up the play's meaning and significance. In the Brome play it is a "Doctor," who prescribes keeping, as best we can, God's commandments. He advises women, especially, not to make the mistake, when their children are taken away, "to grouch against God." Whatever God sends, the doctor says, whether wealth or woe, remains true, for as the story of Abraham and Isaac shows, if you keep a good heart and serve him faithfully, he'll take care of you: "Now Jesus that weareth the crown of thorn" brings "us all to heaven-bliss!"

The learned man in the Chester play picks up where the Brome doctor left off, reminding us that the drama we just witnessed signified "Jesus, sacrificed to win mankind's grace." "By Abraham," he understood "the father of heaven," who undid the devil's work with his son's blood. By Isaac, "Jesus," who was obedient, always, to his father, and on account of that obedience managed "death to confound."

The point of the plays could not be clearer, but reading them, what I have to remember is that these plays weren't read quickly or skimmed. Once they were written or revised (and they were revised with abandon), they weren't read at all. They were seen and heard, which made them, like frescoes, tile floors, manuscript illustrations, stained glass windows, sculptures, and decorative lamps—and also like sermons and dramatic hymns—books for those who could not read. And while a play's typological truths and moral lessons could and often were revealed by a learned man in a few lines at the end (just as they had been revealed in a few lines of the Epistle to the Hebrews or a long paragraph in *City of God*), the plays themselves were "books" of hundreds of lines of carefully composed dramatic verse, in which an old man and a young boy (except in the York play, where Isaac is the young man of so much Jewish exegesis) say (and do) things to each other, to themselves, to their audience, and to God.

The Brome play opens with Abraham out in his field, singing Isaac's praise. The boy is not only his beloved son but also his sweetest, and Abraham prays for his good health and long life. God, looking down, decides to test him. An angel conveys his command. Abraham says that he "never loved anything so much" on earth. But God he loves much more. He's sorry, but he'll do it. The angel assures him: So long as you do God's work, you will have no reason to worry.

Abraham calls for Isaac, who is busy praying. Whatever you ask, Isaac says, I'll do with "glad cheer." But it is not long (the stage is small) before they arrive and Isaac notices that his father looks dreadful. Abraham tells him not to worry. But Isaac worries. He wants to know why his father's sword is drawn. He wants to know where the beast is. Abraham asks him to stop talking. Your words, he says, are breaking my heart. Isaac wants to know if he is to be harmed. Abraham says he can't tell him. Not yet. But Isaac wants to know.

"I must kill thee," Abraham says at last.

"Kill me, father?" Why? If I've done something wrong a rod should do. But "with your sharp sword kill me not," for "I am but a child."

Abraham says he's sorry, but it is not up to him.

Isaac wishes his mother were there. "She would kneel for me on both her knees," he says. But she isn't, so Isaac prays that his father will change his mind.

Abraham tells him he must do it. Otherwise, he'll offend God. He's afraid to do that.

"And is it God's will that I should be slain?" Isaac asks.

"Yes," Abraham says. That's what makes it so hard.

Isaac gets it and says he will never complain about God's will. Sure, God might have sent him a better ending. But what will be will be. He tells his father not to grieve. That he has other children. That he will soon forget him. He insists that they should do the Lord's bidding and asks only that Abraham pray for him after he's gone and tell his mother he has left for another country.

Reading those lines and all the others, I see what so many readers before me have seen. I see the role of typology, which is everywhere, not just in the spoken words but also the stage directions, costumes, makeup, and props. A bearded and ancient Abraham looks like God the Father. A nearly nude Isaac sometimes rides the donkey and always carries a bundle of wood tied into a cross. I see the tension between the story's allegorical meanings and its literal meanings. I see why some critics believe the former limits the latter, inhibiting the development of sophisticated dramatic structures, characters, plots, and themes. I see the clash of ideals (such as obedience, acceptance of earthly suffering, and faith) and day-to-day niceties and desires (such as a reluctance to sacrifice one's child), a clash medieval writers could not get enough of. I see the sentimentality. But what holds my attention is something else: the way the story changes when playwrights, without ever drawing our attention away from Abraham and Isaac, slow it down, set the plot in time, the time it takes to recite all those lines.

The Brome Isaac is willing, but he throws his father off with his questions and unwittingly torments him with his good nature. He asks to be forgiven for his sins. He asks to be blessed. He asks Abraham to cover his eyes and give his best wishes to his mother. And he repeatedly asks Abraham to do it and get it over with. The delay, he says, is killing him.

Yet when Abraham asks him, a second time, to stop talking—just to stand for one last kiss—Isaac doesn't understand the request. We have only a little time left, he says.

Your meek words scare me, Abraham says. He asks Isaac to kiss him once more, but Isaac tells him to go ahead.

Not yet, Abraham says. I must bind you.

Just go ahead and do it, Isaac says. I won't hinder you. He is sorry to die but can't bear the waiting. He reminds Abraham not to tell his mother, and then he himself bids her farewell.

Abraham is in tears.

Isaac apologizes for upsetting him and asks for mercy.

Enough, Abraham says. He assures Isaac that he has done nothing wrong. He'd rather die himself, if only God wanted him for an offering.

Stop, Isaac says. Mourn no more. Your weeping hurts as much as the thought of my own death. Afraid of the sword, he asks Abraham to cover his eyes and lay him facedown. He cries out to God, asking him to receive him.

The time has come, and Abraham wants to do God's will. But he can't. "Oh! Father of heaven, what shall I do?"

What are you waiting for? Isaac asks again.

"Now, heart," Abraham cries, "why wouldest thou not break in three?" He raises his sword. The angel snatches it away and thanks Abraham on God's behalf. Abraham tells Isaac to get up, shares the good news, and kisses him. But Isaac, assuming Abraham is still stalling, begs him to kill him. Abraham explains that he doesn't have to. Isaac doesn't believe him, but he comes to and explains his salvation to the ram: "Thou shall this day die for me, in the worship of the Holy Trinity."

God still commands and controls, but Abraham has been transformed by Isaac's distress. In the play's opening scene, he is merely a symbol of obedience, coldly weighing his love for his son against his fear and love of God. By the story's climax, he is a character, a man whose heart is broken, a father who thinks he has no choice but to sacrifice his son.

The author of a third play, the Northampton play, added Sarah to the script, and it is Abraham's exchanges with her, actual and imagined, that give his character its depth. No sooner does Abraham respond to God's angel—"Here I am" and "His will be done"—than his thoughts turn to his wife. He knows she is not going to like the idea of his leaving with Isaac, and she doesn't, relenting only when he argues, as so many of the Abrahams of first-millennium *midrashim* had argued, that it was time for Isaac to learn how to worship God.

Off they go, but Abraham isn't free of her. As soon as he tells Isaac of God's plan, Isaac asks him what his mother will think of it. There is no need to tell her, Abraham says, but Isaac is not so sure. He wishes she were with them, as she had wanted to be. Abraham reminds him that she can't always have her way. He loves him as much as she does. But every time the boy speaks, he evokes her, reminding his father how much she loves to hold him close and kiss him, how much she will miss him, how much he hopes he will bid her farewell for him, and how important it is that he discard his clothes in a way that ensures that she will never see them.

The angel stops him. Abraham thanks God. The test caused him great distress, he says, but he is grateful nonetheless. Then without pause he tells Isaac to dress, quickly, and to say nothing to his mother. Please. Not a word.

The moment they arrive home, Abraham invites Sarah out for a walk, and once alone he fills her in. Where was your mind? she asks. On God, he says, and he tries to explain, but his explanation doesn't square with what we have just seen. We saw his mind on her, and she represented not simply woman's nature but also the part of himself that doubted that he should go through with it. In the end, she concedes that he had no choice—what God wants, God will get—but as a depiction of a type of Mary, her performance is not persuasive. And though Abraham spins his own experience as faith, his words come off as little more than retrospective gloss. In the scenes we've just observed, obedience is what moved him up that mountain.

By the end of a fourth play, the Towneley, even that obedience, bare-bones but still dependable, is strained. Audiences would not have guessed it would be. When God first called, Abraham was almost murderously enthusiastic: "Both wife and child," he had said, "if he bid kill." But for reasons that aren't clear, he never tells Isaac that the sacrifice was God's idea, and so Isaac, though obedient, asks all the questions I imagine that Abraham would have asked of God. He is ready to go where Abraham goes, to do what he wants done, but he wants to know why. He begs for mercy. He wonders, if he has trespassed, whether a good beating might not suffice. The increasing urgency of his questions and the brutal economy of Abraham's answers wreak artful havoc on the play's poetry, especially its carefully metered and measured eight-syllable English lines.

Isaac!
    What, sir?
        Good son, be still!
Father!
    What, son?
        Think on thy get [offspring]!

What have I done?
  Truly, no ill.
And shall be slain?
  So have I het [promised].
Sir! What may help?
  Certes, no skill [For sure, there's nothing].
I ask mercy.
   That may not let.
  When I am dead, and closed in clay.
Who shall then be your son?

Abraham can't stand it. Who could? But he doesn't let on to Isaac. He turns away from him and up to the heavens and says, "Ah! Lord, that I should abide this day!"

"Who shall do what I used to do?" Isaac asks.

Abraham asks him to be quiet. But he can't.

What have I done, father, what have I said?
Truly, no kind of ill to me.
And thus, guiltless, shall be arrayed?
Now, good son, let such words be!"
I love you.
  So do I thee.
Father!
  What, son?

Isaac cries out for his mother. Abraham tells him to stop. It won't help in the way you imagine it would, he says. Then he turns away again, this time to the audience, his eyes filled with tears, which he doesn't want Isaac to see. He wishes more than anything the boy were unkind. But he's not. He's perfect. He'd die for him if he could. "To slay him, thus, I think great sin." He'll never be out of my mind. What shall I say to his mother? he asks. He fears her reaction.

All the while Isaac lies, still as can be, on the altar.

Only after God tells the angel to stop him and the angel is on his way does Abraham try to pull himself together. The crying only makes it worse, he says. The angel rushes in, wrestles him to the ground, and tells him to stop. Who says? Abraham asks. But once persuaded that the angel speaks for God, Abraham thanks him, in a few words, and excuses himself: "To speak with thee have I no space." He needs to talk to his son.

He tells Isaac that he's been saved.

"Sir! Shall I live?" Isaac asks.

Yes, Abraham says. You've escaped "a full hard, grace—thou should have been both burnt and broken."

"But, father, shall I not be slain?" Isaac asks.

"No," Abraham says.

"Then am I glad! Good sir, put up your sword again."

Abraham tells him not to be afraid.

"Is all forgiven?" Isaac asks.

Yes, Abraham says, for certain.

"For feard, sir, was I nearhand mad."

The Towneley play ends there. The manuscript's final pages are missing. We don't know if a learned man took the stage to help clear up the confusion, answer some of Isaac's questions, help dry Abraham's tears. He might have noted that in keeping God's command to himself, Abraham bore the full burden of his faith. Or that typology works by contrast as well as identity: the bewildered Isaac, lying still on the altar, reminds us of Jesus, not knowing why his father has forsaken him. But if Abraham, about to break under the pressure, seems somewhat less than God, it is because he still needed to be completed, perfected by him. The learned man might then have pointed out that God's testing had increased Abraham's love for Isaac. Or that God's ways are not always comprehensible. There is often no explanation for suffering. Or that grace often moves in tandem with obedience, but not always in ways that we can see. He may, finally, have brought the play back to its beginning, the very beginning, noting how Abraham's obedience and stoic faith were just the kind of obedience and faith that it would take to repair the rift created by Adam.

No way to know. Nor, as the play ends with Isaac reporting that he had been nearly mad with fear, do we know whether or not, before the doctor arrived, there would have been a short scene like the scene in the Brome play that comes right after the angel stays Abraham's hand. There, Isaac grabs the ram and is about to blow on the fire to raise the flames when he hesitates and asks:

But, father, while I stoop down low,
Ye will not kill me with your sword, I trust?

Abraham tells him not to worry.

Isaac says he won't, but he still wishes that Abraham would put the sword in its sheath. It frightens him terribly.

Abraham offers the ram. God rewards them, and Abraham is overjoyed, proud that they have obeyed God without complaint. Isaac, however, refuses to join in the celebration.

I was never so afraid before
As I have been at yon hill.
But, by my faith, father, I swear
I will nevermore come there,
But it be against my will!

He never wanted to do anything as much as he now wanted to go home to his mother.

The rabbis were not unaware of the toll the near sacrifice might have taken. They invariably referred to Isaac's fear, and they often traced his blindness in old age back to that fateful day. Some attributed it to the tears (of angels, of Abraham) that had fallen into his eyes. Others, to the blinding light of the heavens. But nowhere in first-millennium Jewish, Christian, or Islamic literature is there so subtle or sensitive an attempt to imagine Isaac moments after the sacrifice, a boy who is afraid to bend down in front of his father and swears never to leave home alone with him again. Abraham's obedience, we are reminded in several plays, helped to repair the rift between God and man caused by Adam's sin. But it also caused a new rift between father and son.

At the risk of repeating myself, I must say that I do not know why some of these plays open up the story in the ways that they do. The form, the time that a playwright took to develop character and plot, certainly contributed, but the form alone, the movement from traditional exegesis to play, from page to stage, can't explain it. Despite hundreds of lines of dialogue and a leisurely pace, some of the mystery plays are mechanical, static, and wholly unbelievable. Neither typology nor the moral lessons of history required so much art.

Nor can I hear the actors' voices, read their body language, or see the expressions on their faces, the light and look in their eyes, infer meaning from the pace and timing with which they delivered their lines. There is subtle humor and even farce, or at least ample opportunity for farce, in many of the mystery plays, and I would not be surprised to learn that some of the scenes or exchanges that I find most poignant on the page were sometimes played for laughs on the stage. One is the moment I just mentioned in the Brome play, after the danger seems to have passed. My sense is that the playwright found a simple way to demonstrate Isaac's complete loss of trust. But I can picture two actors hamming it up, making light of the boy's reluctance to bend down (to feed the fire's flames) so long as his father stood above him with his sword drawn. Likewise, in the Northampton play, there is an exchange I feel sure was intended to bring down the house: Abraham tells Isaac he's to be sacrificed. Isaac asks him if his mother knows of his plans. Abraham blurts out, "She? Mary! Son, Christ forbid?" And that's just one of many lines in the Northampton play that makes me suspect that audiences walked away thinking less about obedience or faith than about women, how they were always getting in (or threatening to get in) men's way.

What's more, and this I feel sure of: Just because a playwright (or painter or sculptor) imagined Abraham's anguish or Isaac's invisible wounds or strains between the two of them doesn't mean they disliked the story, thought the test was regrettable, shared my discomfort with Abraham's response, wished Abraham had protested or that the story had unfolded in some other way. Quite the contrary: they may have concluded that pain and suffering, isolation and anguish, are the price that people pay for their faith. What distinguished the authors of a few of the mystery plays was the sensitivity with which they entered the scene and then found the dialogue to dramatize, to give life to, any number of vast abstractions.

Their art was enhanced by a sort of double vision, or comfort with two contradictory ideas: the near sacrifice was horrible, the sacrifice was sublime. That comfort will not strike those familiar with images of the crucifixion (or with passion plays, stories, and songs) as exceptional. Artists did not shy away from explicit substantiation of Jesus's suffering. "With what rapture," Methodist hymnist Charles Wesley wrote in the middle of the eighteenth century, "with what rapture / Gaze we on those glorious scars!" But befitting the shadow of things to come, the warm-up, most Christian representations of Abraham and Isaac were tamer, and I can't help thinking that one reason for one of the big differences between stories and images of the near sacrifice of Isaac and stories and images of the crucifixion of Christ is as simple as this: Jesus's father allowed it to happen; some say he even willed it. Yet however painful it was for him to watch, God himself didn't actually do the deed. He didn't lead his son to Golgotha. He didn't nail him to the cross. Abraham, by contrast, was commanded to do it, set out to do it, and was about to it. He was about to do it himself.

No one struggled harder to understand how horrible madness, a father setting out to kill his son, could be holy than Søren Kierkegaard, the early nineteenth-century Danish philosopher, whose now-canonical essay, *Fear and Trembling,* part fictional reenactment, part philosophical meditation, part cultural criticism, and part cri de coeur, at once celebrates Abraham and explicitly asks— actually, it insists—that those who would celebrate also acknowledge the "monstrous paradoxes" that follow from his faith:

Abraham had to give up Isaac to have him, to get him back.

Abraham had to believe that he could both give him up (sacrifice him) and get him back (resurrection), a belief that was "absurd," beyond reason, beyond even thought: "Faith begins," Kierkegaard wrote, "precisely where thought leaves off."

Abraham had to place himself, one man, above the community (the universal with which Hegel and others believed that all individuals ought to strive to be in harmony), above the norms, duties, and laws (that we should love our children more than ourselves, that we should not kill) that ought to shape our lives. Faith—the sacrifice of Isaac—required the suspension of the ethical in the name of something higher, Abraham's singular relationship to God.

Crow about Abraham's faith all you want, Kierkegaard said. But recognize that it transformed murder into a holy act, infanticide into sacrifice, well pleasing to God. "So let us either forget all about

Abraham or learn how to be horrified at the monstrous paradox which is the significance of his life."

It was difficult and it was dazzling, right from the start, when Kierkegaard's pseudonym, Johannes de Silentio, wishing he had been there with Abraham in order to better understand him, imagined four different scenarios. In the first, Abraham tries to explain it all to Isaac, but Isaac doesn't understand. He protests and then begs for his life. In frustration, Abraham throws him down, grabs him by the throat, and says: " 'Foolish boy. Do you believe I am your father? I am an idolater. Do you believe this is God's command? No, it is my own desire.' Isaac trembled, and cried out to God. 'If I have no father on earth, then be Thou my father.' But below his breath Abraham said to himself: 'Lord in heaven, I thank Thee; it is after all better that he believe I am a monster than that he lose faith in Thee.' "

In the second, Abraham travels with his head down, goes through all the motions, raises the knife, sees the ram, and sacrifices it instead. He returns home and grows old. Isaac thrives, but Abraham's "eye was darkened, he saw joy no more."

In the third, Abraham thinks of Hagar and Ishmael along the way, and afterward returns again and again to the mountain, alone, asking God's forgiveness for forgetting his duty to his son. He can't understand why it was a sin to offer God the best he had, but if it was a sin, he could not understand why he would ever be forgiven.

In the fourth, Abraham appears calm on the outside, but the muscles in his hand, clenched in anguish, give him away. Isaac loses his faith. They return home and say nothing to anyone about what transpired, ever.

Again and again, de Silentio returns to the scene, but he can't get inside it. Only when he starts to unpack Abraham's faith, distinguishing it from mere obedience, and especially resignation (the Abraham of the mystery plays, who does what he thinks he has no choice but to do, all the while assuming that all is lost, at least in this life and world), does de Silentio make any progress at all. What moved Abraham, what made him the "knight of faith," was the movement beyond resignation, the combination of obedience and hope:

> All along he had faith, he believed that God would not demand Isaac of him, while still he was willing to offer him if that was indeed what was demanded. He believed on the strength of the absurd, for there could be no question of human calculation, and it was indeed absurd that God who demanded this of him should in the next instant withdraw the demand. He climbed the mountain, even in that moment when the knife gleamed he believed—that God would not demand Isaac. Certainly he was surprised by the outcome, but by means of a double movement he had come back to his original position and therefore received Isaac more joyfully than the first time. Let us go further. We let Isaac actually be sacrificed. Abraham had faith. His faith was not that he should be happy sometime in the hereafter, but that he should find blessed happiness here in this world. God could give him a new Isaac, bring the sacrificial offer back to life.

I marvel at the precision and the passion with which Kierkegaard explores the movement of Abraham's faith. So many before him just threw the word out there and assumed that their audience knew what it meant. His distinction between faith and resignation, and later between a tragic hero's sacrifice in the public interest (Agamemnon) and Abraham's purely private undertaking, makes sense to me. Yet for all of Kierkegaard's philosophical fireworks, and the equally explosive power of his prose, the rhythm and repetition, the marvelous range of literary, historical, and theological reference, the grounding of every abstraction in some vivid example, Kierkegaard's interpretation of the story, his idea of what moved Abraham, was less a dramatic departure than an elaboration of a line of thought at least as old as the Gospels. His narrator's speech in praise of Abraham echoes—literally—the Epistle to the Hebrews, and his subsequent analysis of obedience, resignation, and hope owes every kind of debt to Luther, right down to his astonishment and awe, his repeated confession that he not only couldn't have done what Abraham did. He couldn't even understand him.

"I have said however that we cannot comprehend this trial," Luther wrote, "but we can observe and imagine it from afar."

"Abraham I cannot understand," Kierkegaard wrote; "in a way all I can learn from him is to be amazed."

Kierkegaard's idea that faith justifies the suspension of the ethical was also an idea with a long history. Augustine, writing in defense of Hebrew Scripture and Jewish history in the face of Faustus the Manichean's slanders, noted that Faustus didn't bother to try to use the sacrifice to smear Abraham. Everyone knew that Abraham's deed, which would have been considered unnatural and even mad if it had been his own idea, became, by God's command, a model of submissiveness and faith. But Augustine was writing around 400 CE, defending biblical characters who he imagined had lived in an age when what was right was largely defined by God's commands and revealed law. He was not defining the relationship between faith and ethics in his own time, let alone Kierkegaard's nineteenth century.

I can see (the text makes it plain) that Kierkegaard was sticking it to Hegel and perhaps the Danish clergymen whose theology and Sunday sermons were influenced by Hegel. One and all, he thought, they failed to see the contradiction between their identification of the ethical as the highest stage of individual development and their talk of faith. If there was nothing higher than the ethical, and if the individual, acting as an individual against the ethical, was always (as Hegel suggests) in a state of sin or temptation to sin, Abraham shouldn't be celebrated: "He should really be remitted to some lower court for trial and be exposed as a murderer."

Kierkegaard was also sticking it to Kant, who saw the essential harmony of reason and religion, our ethical and spiritual lives. Kant had used God's command to Abraham to argue that even if God were to speak to a man, that man could never be sure that the voice was God's. The infinite is simply beyond our apprehension. But in some instances, Kant says, we can know when a voice we hear is not God's. And one of those instances is when that voice commands us to do something that reason tells us is wrong.

That logic made no sense to Kierkegaard. Or it made sense only if it was true that each man was supposed to determine his relationship to God by way of his relationship to other human beings. If that was the case, God would be nothing but an empty vessel, which men fill with categorical imperatives, moral obligations, and duties. God's role or function would be purely symbolic, even decorative. To have faith in him would mean nothing.

Kierkegaard thought it was the other way around. A man's relation to other men ought to be determined by his relationship to God, a God for whom all things are possible, including making himself known and heard. "God is God for me because he speaks to me," Luther had said. Part of Abraham's terrible trial was, and part of the terrible loneliness of faith is, the knowing and not knowing, the certainty that lies so close to doubt, the proximity of the sacrifice that would be holy to the temptation to sacrifice that would be sin.

I can see that Kierkegaard was arguing with Hegel and Kant, and (reading his essay alongside his journals) I can also see that he was arguing with himself, trying to make sense of, justify, and explain his own choices, his own faith, his own duty, his own sacrifices, especially his decision not to marry Regine Olsen, a woman he seems to have truly loved. Sometimes he wondered if, in breaking off the engagement, he had demonstrated his own lack of faith, the faith that it would have taken to leap into marriage, fatherhood, and family. Other times, he wondered if he had sacrificed Regine, or himself, or both, sacrificed worldly pleasure and reward to something higher, whether philosophy, theology, writing, or God. Or conversely, if in breaking off the engagement, he, like Abraham, had leapt into the absurd. He broke off the engagement and yet he continued to imagine, absurdly, that somehow, later in life, he would end up with her.

I can see where he is going, but I can't go there with him. Marriage is sacrifice, often compounded by children. Not marrying is sacrifice too. Most commitments involve both embracing and letting go. But to the degree that Kierkegaard turned to philosophy to help make sense of his own life, he failed to see that to acknowledge that every choice calls for sacrifice, and every long-term commitment is a leap of faith, is decidedly not to say that all sacrifices are equal. To obey God when he tells you to sacrifice worldly pleasure for philosophy or religion is not the same as obeying when he tells you to sacrifice your child, however similar the chemistry and mechanics of the faith that feeds each instance of obedience.

As for Kant, it is complicated. He wanted ethics and law grounded in reason, always coming from within. Judaism, he thought, was little more than the sum of its cold, spiritless, externally imposed rituals and laws, a mindless form of heteronomy perfectly exemplified by Abraham's mute acquiescence to God's command. The man knew nothing about the richness of the legal tradition or the philosophical tradition or the variety and fluidity, the heart and soul, of the interpretive tradition I've been tracking here. Nevertheless, Kant's conviction that religion and reason, divine commandments and ethics, were in harmony had resonance in age-old Jewish thought and practice, and in the centuries since his death, his influence on Jews and Judaism has been considerable. There was no place for Judaism, as he understood it, in the universe of human reason he imagined. Yet when he proposes what Abraham should have said to God—"That I ought not to kill my good son is quite certain. But that you, this apparition, are God—of that I am not certain, and never can be, not even if this voice rings down to me from (visible) heaven"—Kant sounds more than a little like a rabbi, including at least a few rabbis long before his enlightened time.

Kierkegaard's understanding of Abraham's faith is wholly familiar to me. It is as old as the Gospels. It is electric Luther. His ideas about the suspension of the ethical alarm me. His effort to understand the story from Isaac's point of view is attenuated. Yet I keep going back to his essay, and not simply because I can't resist mind-bending philosophy when it comes in lyrical prose.

No one goes—or seems to go—to greater lengths to celebrate Abraham's faith. Yet no one before him went to greater lengths, with such empathy or imagination, to resist the lazy understanding and idealization and celebration of that faith, the bombastic but ever-so-easy evocation of testing, of obedience, of a father's willingness to give up a child he cherished and could not replace. No one was as dismissive of commentators who cheapened the story, who drained it of all its drama and significance, by saying that God didn't mean it, that it was just a test, the outcome of which was never in doubt. Or as dismissive of the storytellers who rushed Abraham from command to deliverance and reward as if he were traveling on a winged horse as opposed to an ass. No one looked down with such scorn on those who shirked the hard work of recalling that the journey was three days, of trying to imagine Abraham's thoughts and feelings along the way, his anguish, his desperation, his loneliness, his fear and trembling, the temptation to stall on the one hand and to hurry and get it over with on the other, to turn back, to scream, to run away, to cry, to curse one's bad luck, and most of all to give up, to give up.

Abraham arouses Kierkegaard's admiration, and at the same time he appalls him. ("He who has explained this riddle," he wrote in a notebook, "has explained my life.") I don't share his particular admiration of Abraham, or what sometimes seems to be his longing for the kind of faith he ascribes to him, or any other faith that trumps the ethical, any more than I am moved by the moral lessons of the mystery plays, or the theology of so many of the great drawings and sculptures and paintings. I have my own ideas about Abraham and my own ideas about the story. But if it is to be a story of that kind of faith (the faith of the author of Hebrews, of Augustine, of Luther, and of so many others whose ideas of faith they shaped), I prefer Kierkegaard's adult version to all those that read like lazy children's stories. I prefer, and even take some solace in, the versions that deliberately and painstakingly show the beginning and middle of the story before they show the end, and even at the end, those that account for the cost as well as the reward.

I can spend a lot of time with Kierkegaard, and for that matter Kant, without thinking much about where the story came from and what it meant at the time. Kant plucked it out of Scripture to make a point about the proper relationship, in theory, between divine revelation and human reason. The relationship between the two in ancient Near Eastern history was beyond his purview. Kierkegaard argued that faith like Abraham's trumped reason, transforming murder into a holy act. If it ever occurred to him that in Abraham's time—or the time the story was written—child sacrifice might not have needed to be transformed, might have been perceived as a holy act in the first place, he didn't let on.

Kierkegaard thought as hard as anyone about Abraham's experience. But in his mind, that experience existed outside of history. He brought it into his own time. Abraham might well have returned from Moriah just a few days before he put pen to paper. There is nothing wrong with reading a sacred story that way, and anyone who thinks there is is bound to be frustrated. That is how ancient interpreters read Scripture. In fact, that's how ancient interpreters transformed an anthology of ancient literature into Scripture, and that's also how many church fathers and rabbis of late antiquity read it, and that's how generation after generation of Islamic interpreters read the sacred books of the Christians and Jews as well as their own. That's how many if not most people read sacred history and, to be honest, secular history too. We remake it, shape it to our needs, our interests, and our desires. I call attention to it here simply to draw a contrast between all of them—between most of us—and the readers and writers who in the seventeenth and eighteenth and nineteenth centuries believed there was another way, a better way, to read. Their first questions weren't theological (Why does God test the righteous?), philosophical (Does reason create God or God create reason?), ethical (Should Abraham have protested? Did he have a responsibility to tell Sarah and Isaac what he was up to?), typological (What does the story tell us about the life, death, and resurrection of Christ?), or even practical (If God pulls the strings, why not rail against him when misfortune strikes?) so much as historical: Who wrote the Bible? When? What did it mean to the authors and their earliest readers? What does it tell us about the world in which they lived?

"What took them so long?" people ask me. "Nothing, really," I reply. Those questions didn't arrive, full-blown, in the eighteenth century, with the rise of rationalism and empiricism and the great leaps forward in the sciences that we call the Enlightenment. Or even a century earlier with the Dutch philosopher Baruch Spinoza, whose work contributed so much to both the Enlightenment and modern biblical scholarship. For centuries some readers—Muslim, Jewish, and Christian—had been asking questions about the plain sense of the text, and some of those questions led them to questions about the author's meaning and intent. But what readers did when they got there, whether they pursued those questions or ducked them, depended on what they wanted to know.

Think about it: No one was closer to the origins of the words than the writers who first composed or recorded them. However inspired they felt, wherever they thought their inspiration had come from, they knew something that people coming after them didn't necessarily know about how and why particular parts of the anthology had come to be. Some of the early editors and redactors must have known too. Time passed and Second Temple sages began to attribute the anthology, in whole or part, to Moses. The moment they did, questions arose. It was some of those questions (about repetition, about seeming contradictions, about strange word choices, about anachronism, about seemingly ungodly behavior, about the things God didn't seem to know, even about the name of God) that had moved the rabbis of late antiquity to midrash in the first place. They asked difficult questions and they came up with elaborate answers. Some of those answers took the form of explanations: God tested Abraham to demonstrate his fear of God, not to gauge it; Moses used "Elohim" to signify God's justice and "YHWH" to signify his "mercy," or Elohim to signify any one of his several attributes and YHWH to signify his essence. Some took the form of stories. We may see some of those explanations and stories as far-fetched, but if a person's primary concern was what the text, literally or figuratively, meant to them, how they might explain it to their students and congregation, how it might help them get close to God, questions about authorship were largely beside the point. They still are. Those who wanted to believe, believed. Martin Luther frequently paused to speculate about the relationship between the author's intent and the text's meaning, about what the author was thinking and feeling when he wrote a particular passage, why he included this insight or detail or excluded that. Luther simply assumed that Moses was the author. Those who didn't want to believe, didn't. And those who wanted to believe but had doubts ended up somewhere in between.

Back in the twelfth century, Abraham Ibn Ezra had called Isaac Ibn Yashush, a fellow Jew in Muslim Spain, "Isaac the blunderer" for asking how Moses could have known anything about the kings of Israel and Judah. Yet Ibn Ezra's own reading, his close attention to the meaning of words, Hebrew words, in the context of the words around them, surely anticipated the critical study of the Bible. It also left him with questions of his own. Why, he wondered, did the author, writing about the patriarchal age, write a line like "at that time the Canaanites were in the land" when the Canaanites were still in the land when Moses died on the east side of the Jordan. Similarly, why did Moses begin his valedictory address, "These are the words that Moses addressed to all Israel on the other (east) side of the Jordan," as if the writer were on the west side when he was writing? Moses never made it to the west side, the Promised Land. Why, for that matter, did Moses refer to himself in the third person and to people and places and things that didn't exist in his day, including, in Genesis 22, a mountain Jews referred to as Zion? Moses wrote: "as is said to this day, 'on the mount of the Lord there is sight' "—clearly evoking (in Ibn Ezra's mind) the mountain on which Jerusalem and its Temple were built, the place where God sees or is seen. But Moses couldn't have known about Zion. Ibn Ezra suspected that those who read carefully would "recognize the truth." But he didn't advocate broadcasting it far and wide: "He who understands," he wrote, "will keep silent."

That was wishful thinking. Those who study, and from their study think they know things others do not, are often inclined to speak. As the centuries passed, more and more readers were swept up in the enthusiasm for the plain sense and original meaning of Scripture. And in the heightened interest in the history of the early church (and religion more generally) that the enthusiasm for the plain sense of Scripture sparked. And in the thirst for knowledge of ancient languages, including Hebrew, that the study of both the plain sense and its context in church history contributed to. And in great leaps forward in astronomy, physics, and biology, and in the rise of rationalism and empiricism in philosophy. In the midst of all that ferment, what some people wanted to study and speak about, in the same way that they studied and spoke about other works of ancient literature, was the origins of the Bible.

Theories multiplied like Israelites in biblical genealogies. Some readers tried to square new findings with old traditions. One fourteenth-century interpreter, identifying what he considered unmistakable similarities between the prose style of Moses and later biblical writers, concluded that the prophets had completed a project that Moses had begun. Several sixteenth-century scholars, by contrast, credited Moses with all five of the books attributed to him. Scribes coming along after him, they believed, had simply edited them, updating here and there. Other readers were prepared to jettison tradition. Thomas Hobbes was among those who, in the seventeenth century, argued that the evidence pointed to an author, an original author, some time after Moses, though Hobbes himself couldn't say with any certainly how long after.

In the middle of the seventeenth century, Spinoza gathered the evidence of previous commentators and added evidence of his own—all the anachronisms (including references to the future that had to have come from the pen of a writer working later), the repeated use of the phrase "to this day," and the sentences that simple common sense suggests Moses didn't write: Would Moses have told the story of his own death? Would the humblest man who ever lived have described himself as the humblest man who ever lived? It is clear "as the sun at noon," Spinoza concluded, that the Torah of Moses was written by someone "who lived long after Moses."

Questions about authorship invariably irritated those who believed that every word came directly from the mouth of God. They still do. But that wasn't their only purpose, and in many ways they were the least potent part of the challenge Spinoza posed to traditional ways of reading the Bible. He and those who shared his assumptions believed that the text, which the ancients and so many after them had assumed was intentionally cryptic, was simply distant, the product of a different place and time. Its relevance lay not in eternal and universal meanings and truths but rather in the meanings it authors originally meant to impart. The interpreter's job was not to iron out or explain away wrinkles, contradictions, duplications, obvious errors of fact, difficult passages or dubious characters, but rather to try to understand them all as objects of history. To do that, interpreters needed to cast aside the distracting, often mystifying, commentary of the rabbis and priests and turn their attention to the words on the page, learn all they could about who wrote them, compiled them, and arranged them, and how they went about doing all that. Knowing something about the authors and their editors, or at least the world in which they worked, was essential to knowing what Spinoza most wanted to know: what the words actually meant.

Those assumptions turned traditional assumptions—especially of scriptural inscrutability, perfection, and timelessness, assumptions about the reading of sacred texts that many Jews, Christians, and Muslims shared—on their heads. The Jews of Amsterdam censured him, and after the fact Protestants and Catholics condemned him too. Others were ostracized for lesser critical crimes. Richard Simon, a French priest and Hebraist whose aim, in the late seventeenth century, was to rebut Spinoza, tried to persuade his readers that Moses had indeed written the laws. Later, the prophets, guided by the spirit of God, had merely organized and polished them. Simon was expelled from the church and most copies of his book were burned.

But neither the questions nor the intellectual ferment behind them could be contained, and in eighteenth- and nineteenth-century Germany, a small but determined group of scholars, some amateurs, some academic, even a clergyman here and here, turned their attention to Hebrew Bible stories (starting with the story of Creation itself, and then the Flood) that seemed to be told two or more times (doublets and triplets). They moved from an analysis of the differences between the two versions—one that was hard to miss was the name of God—to an analysis of other passages and parts that seemed to be written in different styles or voices or from dramatically different points of view. Then they used those differences to develop theories, some competing, some complementary, about the "documents" they believed the Bible was made of, when those documents were written, and what they revealed about the history of ancient Israel.

If you know the name of just one of those scholars, it is probably Julius Wellhausen, a professor of Old Testament history, Oriental languages, and theology at Greifswald until 1882, when he dropped theology from his teaching portfolio, having concluded that his scientific approach to Scripture, "despite all caution" on his part, rendered his students unfit for the Protestant clergy. Four years earlier he had published his *History of Israel*, in which he synthesized several centuries of "higher criticism."

Wellhausen imagined that the Five Books of Moses actually comprised four different documents, written over the course of several centuries, beginning a few hundred years after Moses. J was the writer whose God was called YHWH, and YHWH looks and often acts a lot like the gods of old: he walks around in the Garden of Eden; after he curses Adam and Eve, he clothes them. Religion in J's time was a cult of nature and fertility, its festivals predominantly agricultural. E's God was Elohim, and he wrote just after J. His faith was also primitive, but in his pages, where God often appears in dreams and visions, there are hints of elevation, of the spirit to come. D wrote in the age of the prophets, the height of Israelite spirituality and ethics. Festivals marking firstfruits, the barley harvest, the wheat harvest, and the ingathering, were now and forever after linked to the history of Israel and its God. P came last, and everywhere his pen touched papyrus or parchment, he revealed a priestly concern with temple cult and ritual, sin and guilt, sacrifice and law. The divorce of the religion of Israel from nature, the common man, and perhaps reality itself, was complete. Judaism, a mature but dry, legalist, spiritless faith, came not in the beginning, with Abraham, Isaac, and Jacob, or later with the revelation at Sinai, the conquest of Canaan, the establishment of the monarchy, or even the building of Solomon's Temple, but with the priestly redaction of the Torah and the rise of the rabbis at the end.

Like the documents it analyzed, like every work of history and literature, Wellhausen's work was replete with traces of the world in which it was made, nineteenth-century Europe. Its evolutionary framework was of its age, as was its denigration of Judaism. In the years since, some scholars have challenged specific conclusions and others have challenged his whole approach. There has been debate about the number of sources (soon there were several Js and Es and Ds and also a K and L and S and either several Ps or a P and an H, the latter contributing what many considered a distinct Holiness Code in Leviticus). There have been debates about the dating of sources: an Abraham cycle that was written in Israel in the time of David or Solomon bears a very different relationship to the underlying history than an Abraham cycle written during the Babylonian exile or after it in an archaic form and style. A theory that D preceded H who preceded P provides one picture of the history. A theory that the three writers, who expressed dramatically different views on fundamental questions of theology and law, were contemporaries, quite another. There have been debates about the very nature of the sources, with some insisting that Wellhausen's documents are themselves collages of smaller documents, perhaps even fragments. The key to understanding the Bible's relation to history, they say, or if not history then at least oral tradition, is the study of the smallest units of composition within it. "Form" critics focus on the genre of each unit of composition, whether genealogy, law, prophecy, etiology, saga, legend, or song. "Tradition" critics focus on the shared understandings of the past that linked one portion of the text (one or more story, or entire story cycles, or legal codes, or collections of rituals, or chapters of history) to a particular community, whether a family, a tribe, a priestly circle, a king and his court, a political or religious reform movement, a cult, a city or city-state, or an entire nation.

The debates continue to this day. For many biblical scholars the documentary hypothesis, modified here, supplemented there, remains the point of departure. And even those who consider the idea of a handful of documents written by a handful of writers to be as quaint as the idea of Moses taking dictation in the desert would acknowledge the many lasting contributions of the documentary school and all the other early biblical scholarship—including one of the ideas at the heart of the whole enterprise: the idea that the

Bible is a book that was written and revised by men over the course of several centuries, men with particular passions and interests in particular places at particular times, a book with a past, a past that is worth trying to imagine even if it is a past that we may not (as history) ever know.

To put it another way: In the beginning, all Scripture was local. To some that idea is obvious, unremarkable, even trite. To others it is utterly appalling. It sullies the sacred by dragging it down from the heavens and into the muck. Yet from where I stand, it looks to me as if the rise of biblical scholarship simply and rather dramatically enlarged the sacred and the heavens, creating a whole new galaxy in the universe of narrative, interpretation, and analysis, with practitioners, approaches, perspectives, and methods as numerous as a galaxy's stars. The fear was that scholarship would break Scripture's spell. But scholars cast spells of their own, and for every connection between the word of God and the words on the pages that scholars severed, there were countless other connections between the words and the world that they established or repaired.

Naturally, I was curious to see what scholars had to say about the story of Abraham and Isaac, starting with what they had to say about who wrote it.

For a long time the critical consensus was that it was E, the Elohist, a writer who left his signature first and foremost in the divine name: there's the Elohim (God) who puts Abraham to the test; the Elohim who tells Abraham where to go and whose chosen place Abraham goes to; the Elohim who (Abraham assures Isaac) will see to the sheep; and Abraham's fear of Elohim, which God comes to know. Supporting evidence includes the messenger of God, a figure scholars associated with E. Beersheba, a place scholars associated with E. And all the parallels in setting, plot, character, and theme that link the story of the near sacrifice to the story of the expulsion of Hagar and near death of Ishmael, which immediately precedes it and which scholars were sure was an E story.

Was there any doubt? By the source critics' own criteria, there was room for it. After all, the messenger who saves Isaac—unlike the messenger who saves Ishmael—is an angel of YHWH (the Lord), and after Abraham sacrifices the ram Abraham calls the place "YHWH-Yireh—as is said to this day, 'On the mount of YHWH there is sight.'" And that same messenger of YHWH delivers the second address, and YHWH himself swears Abraham's reward. That makes five YHWHs in all, one for every Elohim.

And yet so sure were the early source critics that the story of Abraham and Isaac was an E story, the debate among them was not about who wrote it but how all those Yahwehs got into an E story.

The fourth and fifth YHWHs were easily dispatched. Just about everyone assumed that the second angelic address was "secondary," meaning that it was tacked on later. The first three were more troublesome, but one way or another they were explained away too: Some imagined an older layer of tradition appropriated by E. Some imagined an E story revised by a post-Elohist editor. Some imagined two parallel (perhaps regional) traditions, a northern E tradition and a southern J tradition, combined after the fall of the northern kingdom, Israel, by the author who combined J and E or later by R, the redactor. Some imagined two sharply divergent traditions, a sacrifice and a near sacrifice, combined in a similar way.

When, in the second half of the twentieth century, a few scholars had the temerity to challenge the attribution of the core of the story to E, they made note of the debate about the divine name but quickly moved beyond it. However and whenever the Elohims and the Yahwehs got there, the final version is a J story in its vocabulary and its phrasing, J in its particular sense of God's testing and Abraham's fear of God, J in its concern for God's promise and provenance, and J in its inimitable style.

Some of the champions of J are among the revisionists who doubt that there was an independent E source, as opposed to, say, an E editor of various earlier sources. Be that as it may, they insist that J was the author of the story of the near sacrifice. They don't deny the echoes in form and content of the story of Hagar and Ishmael. But they argue that there are many plausible explanations for those echoes, the most obvious of which is this: J wrote that story too.

I took all this in from a considerable distance, and with a certain mischievous pleasure. That pleasure increased as time passed and I realized that even the boldest scholars of the documentary school—the ones who are sure that J was from Judah and E from

Israel and P (coming before, not after, D) was an Aaroneid priest in the court of King Hezekiah (appalled by JE's elevation of Moses and his lack of respect for their ancestor Aaron in the story of the Golden Calf) and D (the author of the entire history from Moses to the fall of Judah) a priest (like E) of Shiloh (probably Jeremiah, contemptuous of the northern kingdom and kind to Josiah) and R another Aaroneid priest, probably Ezra—even they are circumspect when it comes to the story of the near sacrifice.

Still, I couldn't help wondering if, after more than a century of scholarship, there were anything (just one thing, about authorship, composition, and dating) upon which everyone who gave or gives any thought to such matters agrees.

Early on there was widespread agreement that the story was among the earliest Hebrew Bible stories, perhaps written or recorded as early as the tenth century BCE. But before long, some scholars, including some of the same people who challenged the attribution to E, turned the chronology upside down, arguing that it, along with many of the other J stories in Genesis, was a late one, masquerading as an ancient story, late in style, late in reference to places, people, things, late (a lot like Deuteronomy) in outlook, perhaps as late as the Persian period, which began in 539 BCE when Cyrus defeated the neo-Babylonians and Israelite and Judean exiles began to return to Zion and rebuild the Temple.

Similarly, there was once agreement that God's second address, through his angel, was written long after the rest. Some considered it an awkward addition, clumsily appending God's earlier and oft-repeated promises to a story that stood perfectly well on its own. Others thought it a profound and subtle commentary on the story of the near sacrifice, the very earliest commentary, which not only knit God's test into the complete cycle of stories about God's promise and God's providence, but also raised it to a higher theological plane: If God's initial call, his choice of Abraham, could fairly be called arbitrary (What, one might ask, did he do to deserve God's blessing?), after Moriah it could be called arbitrary no more. From then on, God's promise, Israel's chosenness, was firmly grounded in Abraham's deeds, and those deeds and human agency itself had an obvious place in God's plan.

Eventually that consensus also broke down. Prominent scholars, while in complete agreement with the "earliest commentary" arguments about purpose and profundity of the second angelic address, have come to see it as essential to the rest of the story as God's command, Abraham's response, the angel's retraction, and the ram.

That leaves just one small but not insignificant area of agreement.

There are, as I have said, scholars who think that J wrote the story. And, though I have not had reason to mention them, there are scholars who think it possible that J was a woman, a writer in the court of Solomon's son, Rehoboam.

But I've yet to find a scholar who believes both that J was a woman and that J wrote the version we know. Which means that everyone who has weighed in believes that the story was written by a man.

But what was he trying to say?

Something about child sacrifice, it has long been assumed.

Evidence of the practice comes not just from the myriad reports and references in the Hebrew Bible but also from Canaanite literature (much of which was uncovered in the early twentieth century in the ancient port city of Ugarit), from Greek and Roman history and literature, from archaeology (especially studies of Carthaginian burial grounds, cremation urns, and bones of infants that seem to have been burned white), from suggestive ancient Near Eastern inscriptions and even a few suggestive works of art.

None of that evidence is conclusive. The vast majority of the literary evidence is polemical, people accusing other people of sacrificing children, and the physical evidence, including the most damning of it, the human remains in Carthage and other neo-Phoenician cities and colonies in North Africa, has been the subject of ongoing debate. Some anthropologists are certain that the bones are the remains of sacrificed children. Others suspect that they are third-trimester fetuses and perinates. Still, many scholars believe that the weight of the evidence suggests that the practice was not entirely a figment of the polemical imagination. A king, in a moment of public crisis, might sacrifice a child in the hope of appeasing an angry God and thereby saving a city. A warrior with his back to the wall might sacrifice in the hope of drawing God into battle on his side. And just about anyone, grateful for a bountiful harvest or healthy herd or brood, might have been moved to give back some of what God had bestowed.

But what was the story trying to say about the practice?

The spectrum of respectable opinion has been wide.

At one end are those who, yesterday and today, believe that the story was a polemic against it—its critical moment not when God asked or when Abraham set out but when God said stop and Abraham obeyed. In the telling, the author put God and the very first Hebrews on the side of the angels (and later the prophets) in the effort to eradicate the scourge of human sacrifice from the ancient Near East. At the other end are those who believe something approaching the opposite: that the story is a narrative expression of an old and essential element of Israelite theology, God's claim to every firstborn son. "You shall give Me the first-born among your sons," God says in Exodus 22. It was a matter of consecration and donation. Like the firstfruits of the field and the firstborn of the flock, the firstborn son belonged to him. He didn't always take what was his. (In all but that one of the several instances in the Torah where God lays claim, he quickly and neatly adds unmistakable instructions for redemption.) But he could and there were times when he did.

In between the extremes are the historical and tradition-minded critics who imagine that the story signaled the transition from one moment or ideal to the other, preserving the memory of a change in cult practice, perhaps even an actual event that prompted the change, early in the second millennium BCE, the age of Abraham, Isaac, and Jacob. And the form critics who, while agreeing that the story preserved a memory, believe it preserved the memory not of an event but of a story—perhaps pre-Israelite or non-Israelite oral tradition—a story (etiological) that explains the origins of something. It is possible that it originally explained the origins of a cult site or place-name, but more likely the combination of place and practice, perhaps answering the question "Why was it that at this particular place it became permissible, or even desirable, to substitute an animal for the firstborn son?"

But what place? As far as anyone knows, neither Moriah nor YHWH-Yireh was the name of an actual place. Those inclined to see layers of older tradition behind the story imagined a Canaanite cult site and story. Others imagine Judean or Israelite sites (some propose Jeruel, some El-Roi). In either case, the original name of the place was lost when a later writer or editor came up with the story's final place-names. Others still, digging deep into the roots of words, exploring associations based in meaning and associations based in sound, mapping Abraham's movement around Canaan, calculating distances, conclude, as many rabbis concluded centuries before, that the site of the near sacrifice, the place where the Lord saw, was always understood to be Jerusalem. Which is why when the author of Chronicles got around to the building of the Temple, he wrote: "Then Solomon began to build the House of the Lord in Jerusalem on Mount Moriah."

The scholars who have assumed that the story was originally about sacrifice, one way or another, have dominated the debate, but there are others who believe that they may well be mistaking the story's plot for its meaning. By the time the story was redacted, and perhaps even by the time the version we know was written, prophecy and law had eliminated child sacrifice. Readers understood it was detestable to God and his people. The practice was no longer at issue.

What was at issue, they say—after the Assyrians overran Israel in late eighth century BCE, or while the Babylonians threatened Judah in the early sixth, or after the Babylonians captured Jerusalem in 586, razing the Temple and carrying many Judeans off into exile, or even after the first exiles began to return from captivity a half century later, when the population was sparse, the boundaries uncertain, the Temple rebuilding project faltering, the great nation seemingly small and weak and forever at the mercy of great empires—was God's promise.

Wherever it came from, these scholars insist, whatever it once looked like, the story we know can only be understood in the context of that promise and the threats to it, which means in the context of the entire Abraham cycle. It begins with God's first call and command (give up your past) and God's promise (I will bless you) and proceeds from there, ever so slowly, characterized by confusion about both the promise and the plan, by questions about who was going to get what and when, by uncertainty and doubt, by snares and detours, by heartaches, grave threats, and near death. Nothing is for certain. Nothing comes easy—without testing, without trial, without degradation.

Imagined from the perspective of Abraham and Isaac over the course of three days, the story might be said to distill to its essence and recapitulate all the Abraham stories that come before it. The God who calls and promises is also the God who seems capable of going back on his promises, the God who gives life is also the God who can withhold life and even take it away. It is harrowing, but in the end that God, the one and only, shows mercy to and rewards those who fear him. God returns Isaac to Abraham and then reaffirms his promise: because you had done this, Israel would be delivered. Israel would be redeemed.

And what about the "this," the thing that Abraham has done,

the command he has obeyed, the aborted sacrifice at the heart of the plot? The scholars who read the story that way would say that if, somehow, we could ask the author what he was thinking, he'd likely take the question in stride, maybe even shrug. He wouldn't deny the monumental place of sacrifice in the imagination of many ancient Israelites, or the possibility that tradition and form critics were right when they say there were older versions of the story and older layers of meanings that the author may not have been conscious of. But, hard as it might be to believe, he would say: I was not thinking about child sacrifice one way or another. I was thinking about Abraham's future and looking for something hard, really hard, for him to do.

Among the scholars inclined to see the story deeply embedded in the entire Abraham cycle are those who considered themselves critics of the Bible as literature. The literary critics acknowledge and make use of the findings of the source critics, the tradition critics, the form critics, and all the others critics who identify and study the sources and documents from which they think the Bible was made.

And they make use of the findings of the redaction critics, who study the art of the editors who cut and spliced and wove and joined and sometimes wrote the parts together.

And the textual critics, who study the differences—variants— among all the extant versions of the redacted text, variations across languages and time, variants in different languages at the same time, and variants in the same language at the same time. Sometimes those differences are huge, including entire sections of Jeremiah, Job, and Daniel. And sometimes they are small. The late-antique and medieval rabbis went to great lengths to explain the significance of the word "behind" (*ahar*) in the line "Abraham looked up and saw a ram behind." Today scholars believe that *ahar* was a transcription error: in the ancient text the word was *ehad,* meaning "a" or "one" ram: Abraham looked up and saw "a" ram.

And they make use of the findings of linguists and philologists and anthropologists and archaeologists and historians of the ancient Near East, who identify all the parallels between the stories, covenants, vassal treaties, languages, laws, rituals, social practices, and even the gods of ancient Israel and all the peoples (the Canaanites, Egyptians, Hittites, Phoenicians, Assyrians, Mesopotamians, and Persians) among whom so many ancient Israelites were born, lived, and died.

The literary critics of the Bible learn from and acknowledge the work of all those scholars. But their own work is grounded in their conviction that no matter how many people had a hand in it, how long it was in the making, how many earlier forms it took, how much of it was borrowed from neighbors, how many different kinds of imperatives shaped it, how often and how dramatically transcription, translation, and exegesis transformed words and meaning, the final product (which happens to be the only version of most of it that for many years now anyone has actually set eyes on) is, in addition to everything else, and perhaps above all else, a work of literature.

The literary critics are too tactful to point out that much of the evidence offered in the brief against divine or Mosaic authorship displays a dismaying innocence of the history of literature, from the ancient Greeks to the whole gamut of modern and postmodern writers. What if Moses were a precursor of Dickinson or Joyce or Beckett or Faulkner or Woolf? What if God were a writer who couldn't stop revising?

There is no point. Few of the literary critics attribute the books to God or Moses.

But where other scholars see doublets and triplets, they see the clever development of plot, character, and theme.

Where others see inconsistency and contradiction (and in that contradiction evidence of competing traditions and schools and circles and courts), the literary critics see multiple points of view, artful appropriation and juxtaposition, and every kind of ambiguity.

Where others look behind the text in the hope of finding oral tradition, political and theological orientation, and historical facts, the literary critics look right at it and find carefully composed poetry and lyrical prose.

Where others see fractures and fragments, pieces and parts, smudges and crooked seams, J and E and D and H and P and G, literary critics see the Teaching of Moses and the Holy Scriptures— remarkably coherent works of ancient literature, literature without which it is simply impossible to imagine or understand the literature, to say nothing of the graphic art, music, religion, and politics, of the past two thousand years.

All that and, what's more, they have great taste. To a man, they have had nothing but the highest praise for my story:

"The most perfectly formed and polished of all the patriarchal stories"—Gerhard von Rad

"The profoundest recorded experience in all the history of the patriarchs and the telling of it soars to comparable literary heights."—E. A. Speiser

"One of the peaks of ancient narrative."—Everett Fox

"A masterpiece of biblical literature."—Robert Alter

"A masterpiece of economy, psychology, and artistic subtlety."—Jack Miles (not only a former Jesuit seminarian but also a biographer of God)

One of the pioneers of the literary approach, a German philologist and critic named Erich Auerbach, set the tone. Living in exile in Istanbul in the early 1940s (after the Nazis forced him out of his post at Marburg), Auerbach went to work on a sweeping study of (nothing less than) the representation of reality in Western literature. In his opening chapter, he uses the story to demonstrate how ancient Hebrew writers harnessed the awesome literary power of the unseen and the unsaid.

Think about it: we don't know where God was when he called

out to Abraham or where Abraham was when he answered, "Here I am." That one Hebrew word (*hi-ne-ni*) at once reveals, with characteristic concision, Abraham's attention and readiness, while it completely conceals his physical location, where he actually was. We don't know when they spoke. Was it the afternoon or the evening before the morning Abraham rose early, or in the middle of the night? We don't know Isaac's age, or the ages of the two servants or even their names. We don't know anything about the lay of the land they all passed through on the first two days. In fact, we know nothing at all about those days, not even the weather. Did a bright sun and clear sky mock Abraham's distress, or did dark clouds and sand-whipping winds make for a perfect harmony between what he saw and what he felt? We don't know. We don't even know if Abraham was distressed. We don't know anything about what he was feeling or thinking, and we know next to nothing about what Isaac was feeling or thinking. We don't know what Sarah knew or even where she was. Only through the eyes of artists, working later, can most of us begin to picture the scene of the sacrifice, the altar, or the knife.

In short, we are told or shown only what we absolutely need to know to follow the action. Everything else, Auerbach writes, is "left in obscurity; the decisive points of the narrative alone are emphasized, what lies between is nonexistent; time and place are undefined . . . thoughts and feelings remain unexpressed, are only suggested by the silence and the fragmentary speech; the whole, permeated with the most unrelieved suspense . . . and directed toward a single goal, remains mysterious and 'fraught with background.'"

Auerbach's analysis of Genesis 22 comes in a close comparison of the biblical style to "the genius of the Homeric style" as it is displayed in chapter 19 of the *Odyssey*, a chapter in which every element of plot, character, and theme is set in the foreground, every scene is fully illuminated, every connection made explicit, every thought is expressed, and every act takes place in the story's present, right in front of our eyes, and is fully explained. And while I can imagine some less-enamored critic spinning all of Auerbach's talk of background as a backhanded compliment ("what is memorable about your writing is what you didn't write"), he doesn't mean it that way. He warns us not to mistake the skeletal structure—the withholding of detail, description, and dialogue, especially detail and dialogue that reveals interiors—for evidence of a primitive stage in the evolution of storytelling. Rather, he sees it as evidence of a sophisticated sense of memory, thought, emotion, and action, all set squarely in the flow of time—so sophisticated that unlike Homer, whose stories can be analyzed but resist interpretation and allegory, biblical literature cries out for interpretation. In fact, Auerbach argues, it must be interpreted or transformed by allegory to be fully understood and explained.

Not every critic accepts all of Auerbach's premises. Or considers Hebrew Scripture so singular. Or shares his estimate and appreciation of its literary value. But many do, and the point is that before Auerbach, most critics would have found the idea that the literature of the ancient Israelites could be spoken of in the same breath as the *Iliad* and the *Odyssey* laughable.

How could I not appreciate Auerbach and all those who have followed in his footsteps? But the truth is that I was smitten by scores
of biblical scholars, and I (just like the literary critics themselves)
have learned from loads of them. I have learned from those who
study the parts, the fragments and supplements, as well as those
who, studying the final product, never give the parts a thought.
From those who study law, ritual, and theology as well as those
who study narrative, poetry, and song. From those who study huge
themes as they developed over centuries and those who study parts
of speech, tenses, prefixes, suffixes, word roots, letters, and vowels
in a particular text or at a particular moment in time. From those
who believe that the interpretive tradition—the vast body of literature that Scripture gave rise to—is one thing, and modern biblical
scholarship quite another. (The story that Abraham smashed his
father's idols, narrowly escaped death by fire at the hands of an idol-
worshipping tyrant, and left home to separate himself from those
who refused to heed the word of the one true God is tradition. The
idea that the historical Abraham was part of a great migration early
in the second millennium and that the stories about him were written early in the first millennium BCE to help legitimize monarchy,
empire, and the centrality of Jerusalem to both is scholarship.) And
I have learned from the scholars who believe that when it comes
to the Hebrew Bible, a book that took shape over centuries and

contains within its pages most of what we know about its context, there is (more than) a little rabbi in every biblical scholar.

In time, scholars began to study the interpretive tradition with the same energy, intensity, and rigor they studied Scripture. Needless to say, I have learned from them too, and it has been my good fortune that one of the first to turn his attention to Abraham and Isaac, Shalom Spiegel, a professor of Bible, medieval Hebrew poetry, and midrash at the Jewish Theological Seminary, was blessed by a slew of muses. Born in Romania and educated in Vienna, Spiegel came to New York by way of Haifa in 1929. Two decades later (at about the same time, coincidentally, that Erich Auerbach published *Mimesis*), he was asked to contribute an essay to a volume that was to be published in honor of a fellow seminarian, the librarian and historian Alexander Marx. Spiegel contributed a critical edition of a previously unpublished twelfth-century poem, Rabbi Ephraim's *Akedah,* and an introduction to the same, *Me-aggadot ha-akedah,* the legends of the *Akedah,* which in Judah Goldin's inspired translation is called *The Last Trial: On the Legends and Lore of the Command to Abraham to Offer Isaac as a Sacrifice: The Akedah.*

Spiegel's original Hebrew subtitle, "A Liturgy by Rabbi Ephraim of Bonn about the Slaughter of Isaac and His Resurrection," revealed exactly which "legends" Spiegel was most interested in. Drawing upon a stunning range of sources (from Scripture and other ancient literature to the earliest understandings of it in law, ritual, and liturgy to the latest biblical scholarship), he examines a series of moments and interlocking themes, starting with the rabbis' questions about Isaac's whereabouts at the end of the story and concluding with questions about God's second call from heaven. In between, he looks closely at all the *midrashim* that leave the impression that Abraham actually sacrificed Isaac—or that makes it clear that many ancient and medieval rabbis imagined that he had.

The pleasure Spiegel took in the excavation of versions and variants is palpable. To tag after him as he chases an explanation (for Isaac's absence), or a motif (Abraham begging God to let him do it), or a recurring image (Isaac's blood or ashes), or an association (Temple sacrifice, synagogue prayer), or an obscure, fleeting, forgotten, and perhaps (Spiegel suggests) sometimes even suppressed reference, hint, or slip back toward its first trace, seeming to exhaust every possibility before darting off in an entirely different direction with the same or some intimately related end in sight, is literally thrilling. Unlike the rabbis (who rarely even tried), Spiegel somehow manages to make the most abrupt and artificial transitions in his narrative and analysis seem smooth and natural. Just like them (or their editors), he was never satisfied with a single way of seeing, saying, understanding, or explaining, when two or more were at hand. When we are through, we grasp not only the early association of the binding of Isaac and the deliverance of Passover but the likelihood of an even earlier connection between the rituals of Passover and the rituals intended to provide people with protection and deliverance from the demons and destroyers who wreaked havoc after dark in the first full moon of spring. We grasp not only the later association of the binding and Rosh Hashanah (atonement for all owing to the merit of the fathers, the Akedah Merit) but the reason why, in the nineteenth century, in the midst of the Jewish enlightenment, some scholars insisted that the whole of idea of the Akedah Merit was a corruption by way of Christianity.

When Spiegel is through, what began as an introduction to a poem is at once an imaginatively organized and richly annotated history of midrash, a penetrating midrash on midrash, and an unforgettable work of art, at once solemn and playful, passionate and wise, dripping with lament and yet maybe not entirely despairing, chock-full of learning yet unfailingly lyrical, a prose poem that pays homage, in its word choices, its sentence structure, and its irrepressible inquisitiveness, not just about the substance of his sources but also about their sound.

Spiegel devotes his longest chapter to the relationship between the story of Abraham and Isaac and the story of God and Jesus.

He touches upon but he doesn't dwell on the question of which came first. That is partly because he is confident that key pieces of the Christian story predated Christianity. It is also because he is confident that the lines of influence ran more than one way: "Is this to say that the Christians learned their lessons from Judaism and the Jews picked up nothing from their Christian surroundings? Not at all! Beliefs and opinions float from place to place and pass over from one religion to another wittingly and unwittingly. There are conceptions like the Akedah Merit that start out at first to act as influence and end up being influenced themselves." But it is mostly because he believes that the roots of both Jewish and Christian stories lay deep in the pagan world. The Canaanites, for example, also appear to have had stories about the death and rebirth of gods and the sons of gods.

Common origins didn't necessarily mean common destiny, and Spiegel identifies crucial differences between the two sets of stories: the Satan who tried to stop Abraham, unlike the devil, had no autonomy; he was always under the control of God. The merit of the binding of Isaac, unlike salvation through Christ, was not literally derived from the deeds of one man, or even two. It was the merit of all the fathers and sons that encouraged God to show mercy to their descendants. What's more, Jewish atonement was not permanently fixed. God always wanted more. Good deeds had to keep coming. The biggest difference of all, in Spiegel's telling, was that the remnants of paganism, the heritage of idolatry, "which in Judaism remained peripheral," grew to become dominant in Christianity. The ancient Israelites worked slowly and hesitantly and often with mixed feelings to suppress or sublimate or transform the ideal of human sacrifice. Then Christian Jews came along and put a bloody human sacrifice at the center of their faith.

But, Spiegel insists, for Jews no less than for Christians, the weight of the past, all that blood and all those ashes, all the deaths and resurrections, were not easily thrown off. The pull of habit, of tradition, was strong. "The ancient pagan demand for the actual sacrifice of children was not uprooted from the world, nor perhaps from the heart either." Persecution alone kept the ideal alive, the fire burning, the sacrificial knife honed.

It is not until several pages before the end of his essay (67 pages in Hebrew; 135 in English) that Spiegel first mentions Rabbi Ephraim of Bonn's *Akedah*, the 105-line poem all those pages were intended to introduce. Ephraim, writing several decades after the Second Crusade, drew on a thousand years of midrash and may also have made an original contribution to it when he provided what appears to be a new answer to an old question, "Why the second address from heaven?"

Some said that Abraham had interrupted God's first address (when he looked up, spotted, and sacrificed the ram). Others said that Abraham had demanded to hear from God himself, not one of his angels. Others said, more simply, that God had had more to say.

Rabbi Ephraim imagined an entirely different scenario:

He made haste, he pinned him down with his knees,
He made his two arms strong.
With steady hands he slaughtered him according to the
*   rite,*
Full rite was the slaughter.

Down upon him fell the resurrecting dew, and he revived.
The father seized him then to slaughter him once more.
Scripture, bear witness! Well-grounded is the fact:

*And the Lord called Abraham, even a second time from
    heaven.*

*The ministering angels cried out, terrified:
Even animal victims, were they ever slaughtered twice?*

Where, Spiegel wondered, did Ephraim get the idea that Abraham had nearly slaughtered Isaac twice? He had just shown that ancient midrash was full of evidence that Abraham had been eager to do it, and full of hints that he had done it—once. But Spiegel suspected that the idea that Abraham had tried again was born closer to home. Scattered among the chronicles of the Rhineland martyrs, he found accounts of men and women who had evoked Abraham as they slaughtered their children. And he found accounts of men and women who had sung the *Alenu* as fires burned around them, just as Isaac, in some midrash, sang amid his flames. And he found accounts of brides and bridegrooms who had gone to their deaths "together," as Abraham and Isaac had walked together and in some commentary even built the altar together, like a Jewish father building a wedding canopy for his son. And he found accounts of children who, like Isaac, had lost blood from wounds. But it was another motif altogether that helped him make sense of Ephraim's poem: accounts of men and women who, figuratively speaking, had twice sacrificed their lives to God.

One chronicle of the massacre at Mainz records an incident in which crusaders discovered, among piles of corpses, Jews who had somehow survived their wounds. Renounce your faith, they said to them, and you'll be saved. The wounded hadn't the strength to speak. Instead, they raised a finger toward the heavens. The crusaders finished them off. There were similar stories in the chronicles of the massacres at Mehr and Elnere, instances where attackers had left people for dead, returned to find them alive, and then killed them again. In one, a man who had killed his wife and three sons before stabbing himself survived his wounds. Crusaders converged upon him and asked if, now, he would convert. When he said no, they dug a grave. He buried his wife and sons and then lay down himself. They buried him alive, but still he didn't die. They dug him up and asked again. Again he refused. So they put him in the grave a second time.

"The boundaries between midrash and reality get blurred," Spiegel observes. The idea that Abraham had tried twice may have had its origins in those accounts. But it also may have had its origins in Rabbi Ephraim's own personal experience. He was born in 1133, thirty-seven years after the First Crusade. In the early days of the Second Crusade, his father sought refuge for his family in Wolkenburg, under the protection of the bishop of Cologne. Spiegel imagines them and their neighbors huddled there, waiting for the "fury of those who had gone wild with destruction of the Jews" to die down. They would have recalled that it had been fifty years since the last great slaughter, and they might have told stories of all those who had "sprayed their own blood and the blood of their dear children, and underwent many an Akedah, and built altars, and prepared sacrifices." Ephraim was thirteen at the time. Later he wrote poems about the martyrs, and a memoir, full of facts he had gathered about the decrees and persecutions of his own time. "Perhaps," Spiegel wrote, "from what his ears had picked up while he was still of a tender age, fear-ridden and impressionable, years later when the commentator and poet tried to resolve the difficulties in the biblical Akedah narrative, there rose to the surface, from the hidden recesses of his soul: 'The father seized him then to slaughter him once more. Scripture bear witness! Well grounded is the fact': if not in Scripture, then in the experience of the Jews in the Middle Ages."

And then again in the experience of the Jews in the middle of the twentieth century.

Spiegel never mentions it, never even hints at it, not even in those final pages, pages filled with pained Jewish responses to persecution and gruesome death in the Rhineland, but he wrote in the immediate aftermath of persecution and death in Germany, Poland, Belarus, Lithuania, Latvia, and Estonia the likes of which not even the Jews had ever known. Which is to say he wrote a history of the stories of Isaac's death and resurrection just as evidence for the latest chapter of that history began to accumulate. Even before the outcome of the war was clear, before the camps were liberated, before the last ghetto was razed, before the death marches and mass executions were halted, victims and witnesses had begun to make the connection between the Shoah, the catastrophe in Europe, and the Olah, the holocaust demanded of the very first Jews.

Among them was a prisoner in Auschwitz, a father there with his son. It was the eve of Rosh Hashanah, 1944, and the Nazi commander had ordered a selection. The teenagers above a certain height, large enough and strong enough to work, would live. The rest of the group, of sixteen hundred, would go to the gas. Under such circumstances, the father of a younger or shorter boy had just one hope. He could try to bribe a *kapo* to pull a boy from the group condemned to die. Since that *kapo* himself would be held accountable if the numbers didn't add up, for every boy he pulled he would have to find a substitute from among the boys who, for the time being, had been spared.

The father approached a rabbi, a distinguished Hungarian scholar of Jewish law. The father had some money stashed away, and he wanted to know if, under the circumstances, it would be permissible for him to offer that kind of bribe: "May I save his life at the expense of another?" The rabbi wouldn't answer him. He said he couldn't. To do so would require consultation with other rabbis and perhaps an appeal to a higher authority. It was complicated. He didn't even have his books. He urged the man not to ask again. The father persisted. The rabbi remained mum. The father concluded that he had done all that was required of him. He had asked a rabbi, and the rabbi's refusal to answer was his answer:

it could not possibly be lawful for him to offer the bribe. If it were, the rabbi surely would have told him so, allowing him to redeem his son, his only one. So the father did nothing, and he passed the next day, the rabbi remembered, in a kind of euphoria, joyful that he had had the privilege of "giving his only son's life in obedience" to God. "He prayed that his act might be as acceptable in the sight of the Almighty as Abraham's binding of Isaac," which also happened on Rosh Hashanah and which we are reminded of in our "Torah reading and prayers."

That story would be too good for a sermon to be true—if there weren't so much evidence that others saw it the same way. Here's Rabbi Simhah Elberg: "I think that Isaac, the eternal Jew, was never taken down from the Akedah. Mount Moriah has always been transferred from one land to the other," from Spain to France, from France to Germany, from Germany to Poland. Elberg had studied in Warsaw and was back there, from Paris, for his sister's wedding when the Nazis invaded. He managed to flee. The rest of his family died in the camps. "The Akedah of Treblinka was to the people what the Akedah of Isaac was to a single individual. Both sanctified our history, our existence. Treblinka is the culmination of Mount Moriah. The Akedah-of-Isaac nation has survived the test. The wretched voices of millions have been ripped forth from the flaming red fires." Elberg looked ahead to redemption, but he warned that it had yet to come, not even with the exodus of hundreds of thousands to the land of Israel. The nation remained in limbo, somewhere between exile and redemption.

"The Akedah of Isaac, of multitudes upon multitudes of the children of Israel, was created in our generation before our very eyes," wrote Reuven Katz, a rabbi who had studied in Belarus, Lithuania, and Vilna and led congregations elsewhere in Eastern Europe before he emigrated to Petah Tikvah in the early 1930s. "It has killed six million brothers and sisters without any pity for the beauty of Jacob. More than a million children and babies among them. Since the destruction of the Temple, Israel has had no Olah (burnt) offering of so many Akedahs, dying in the purity of sanctification of God and land." Yet Katz believed the community had stayed true to God and, like Isaac, would be reborn: "The people of Israel have earned a country and a life of sovereignty and freedom, with the promise of 'Unto thy seed will I give this land.'" Just as the ashes and blood had once led to freedom from bondage, so the latest sacrifice would lead to the Promised Land. "The blood itself is absolution of Israel. The blood of the holy ones and heroes who brought Israel freedom and the country itself. The blood of the righteous functions as the desired conciliation for the sin of the generation."

But what was the sin? There was no agreement. Some said assimilation. Some said neglect of Torah. Some said it was one or more of the age's "isms": secularism, socialism, humanism, nationalism, scientific Judaism, and other forms of Reform. Some said it was Zionism. Some said it was opposition to Zionism, or simply finding peace in exile. Some said, as the authors of the Crusade chronicles had said, that it was the sins of generations past. What made the present so much more frightening was not just the magnitude but the agent. In antiquity, Abraham, Moses, and Jeremiah had led the way, even to the altar. "Today," Rabbi Elberg wrote, "Hitler has spoken in the name of God. For us, that is the bitterest punishment of all."

Others accepted the analogy but rejected the idea that the Jews had done anything wrong. History, they said, showed that the Jews did not need to sin to suffer and die for their God. It started with Abraham and Isaac, said Kalonymus Kalman Shapira, the Hasidic rabbi of Piaseczno, Poland, in a lesson he taught in a secret synagogue in the Warsaw Ghetto. When Abraham demonstrated his desire to bind, and Isaac his desire to be bound, they inaugurated "a form of worship that requires total self-sacrifice for God and the Jewish people." Shapira spoke those words in early October 1940, one year to the day after his only son succumbed to injuries he had sustained in the German bombing of the city, which also took the lives of Shapira's daughter-in-law and sister-in-law. His own wife had died shortly before the war. His mother died soon after his son, of grief. Shapira's only daughter would be sent from Warsaw to Treblinka in 1942. The rabbi himself was the last to go, deported to a work camp at the time of the ghetto uprising, and then shot to death in late 1943. He left three years of Torah commentaries back in Warsaw, buried in a milk carton. A construction worker found them after the war.

God's angel stopped Abraham's sacrifice, Shapira said, and for that reason every murder of an innocent Jew by a gentile is "in absolute antithesis to the *Akedah*." Yet it is an antithesis that "actually consummates" it. The *Akedah*s of Warsaw, Treblinka, Auschwitz, Bergen-Belsen, Dachau, Babi Yar—of all the blood-soaked lands of Eastern Europe—were simply the latest and by far the greatest instances of consummation, of Jewish self-sacrifice, of suffering and dying to sanctify God's name. The Torah does not say "God tested Abraham." It says "After these events, God tested Abraham." Why? "Because," Shapira said, all these events, "all murdered Jews, comprise the final act of the *Akedah*. Their martyrdom turns God's wrath away from the Jewish people, and so the murdered ones die for all the Jewish people, in an act that rises to the level of the *chesed* (loving-kindness) of Abraham."

The predictability of that response did nothing to lessen its sting. It was a way of thinking that was at least a thousand years old at the time of the Crusades, and it was fed by ideas about the relationship between sin and suffering, blood and absolution, that were much older than that. What's more, old as it was, it was not static, some rusty relic dragged out of storage in the aftermath of disaster and then again on days of remembrance. It was still vital and in flux in the early decades of the twentieth century, employed by a variety of people in a variety of ways, the secular no less than the religious, nowhere more than in Palestine, where Jewish pioneers and subsequent waves of Jewish settlers, many of them chased out of their homes and homelands by pogroms and other forms of persecution in Europe, faced hostility from their new neighbors.

"We are all bound here," Yitzhak Lamdan wrote, in a poem he called "Upon the Altar." Lamdan had come from the Ukraine in 1920, part of Zionism's third wave. Six years later he published "Masada," the poem for which he is best known, an epic that takes its title from the name of the hilltop desert fortress where, according to Josephus, a thousand Jewish rebels under siege committed mass suicide rather than surrender. Masada fell to the Romans in 73 CE, three years after the fall of Jerusalem. Now, after nearly nineteen hundred years in exile, Jews were returning, and Lamdan was prepared for more of the same: "We are all bound here, and with our own hands we brought wood here." This time there was no question about where the lamb was or whether the sacrifice would be accepted. "Therefore let us silently stretch out our necks over the altar."

"Hah, it's not me," Lamdan wrote, in another poem, playing on the coincidence of his name and that of his subject:

another Isaac was there.
The fire was different, and different was the binding.

I knew where I was being led from the start,
Not for testing's sake did God command the one who
*   led me.*
I loved to walk and walk, and I didn't ask for a ram.

Many writers of Lamdan's generation imagined themselves as the sacrificed sons or (as they grew older and had children of their own) the fathers of sacrificed sons or even the sons of sacrificed mothers and fathers in a life-and-death struggle for a national homeland and a future for the Jewish people. Some celebrated the sacrifice, or at least saw it as necessary, as Natan Alterman did in a poem in which Abraham is a little Polish boy sleeping, upright, on his stone front steps. The boy's murdered parents and younger sister urge him to "come home," but he is afraid to move. Enemies still threaten. The night is full of daggers and blood. He cries out. His mother cries back: "I am glad! Were it not for the knife in my breast / My heart would break in two." Here the sacrifice comes first, and it is only when God calls—when the ancient thunder comes from on high—and says, "Do not fear," and then promises to make the boy mighty and "bless those who bless you" and "curse those who curse you"—that the boy is willing to go forth to the new nation: "For the command that thundered to Avram the father / Still thunders to Avram the lad."

Others resigned themselves to what they took to be the inevitability of sacrifice, a resignation famously dramatized in the diatribe of Amichai, one of the characters in *Days of Ziklag*, S. Yizhar's thousand-page novel of Israel's war for independence. Amichai is a soldier, part of a small squad struggling to hold a remote desert outpost under enemy siege. At one point he says he hates "our father Abraham for going to bind Isaac." He wants to know "what right" he has "over Isaac." If Abraham wants to offer a sacrifice, "let him bind himself." He hates "the God who sent him." He hates that Isaac is "nothing" but the "object of a test" between "Abraham and his God." He hates the "sanctification of God in the *Aqedah*." He hates the killing of the sons as "a test of love!" He hates the world that stands still and does not cry out: "Villains, why must the sons die?" He hates all that, and yet in the end Amichai concedes that there is "no evading the *Aqedah*." It "only seems you could leave everything and run." But you cannot: "This is what life is like. . . . If you're not ready to be killed and kill—there'll be no good in the world. No justice, no love, no beauty."

Some distinguished between passive and active martyrdom, elevating the latter, the militant martyr. Others denied the value of the distinction: "The Aqedah too," Zalman Shazar, a poet, journalist, Labor Zionist, and later the third president of Israel, wrote in the early 1940s, "when it occurs out of free choice, is an expression of supreme heroism, and it is no less active than standing at the gate with a gun in one's hand." But either way, Abraham and Isaac were alive and on the scene—even before the arrival of news and refugees from Hitler's Europe or, just a few years later, the invasion of Arab armies that began hours after the new state of Israel declared its independence.

Yet if the turn to the story of the near sacrifice and the history of martyrdom to explain the Holocaust was wholly predictable, the vehemence with which that reading of the story and that explanation of Jewish catastrophe were contested was not. Today, many people are likely to find the dissenting views commonplace. That's because after more than half a century of relentless reconsideration, reinterpretation, and recasting—reinterpretation and recasting that has come in waves, taken every imaginable shape and form, and shows no sign of abating—for many people it has become commonplace. Views that for ages were unorthodox have become part of the mainstream. But it is useful to remember that in the context of the life of the story, they have not been mainstream or commonplace for long.

Some argued that the analogy between the binding and the Holocaust failed, on the simplest level, as analogy.

For starters, God commanded Abraham to sacrifice Isaac. He didn't command the murder of Jews. The idea that he did, that Hitler and his soldiers were doing God's work, was abhorrent, contemptible, not the least of which because it echoed the apologetics of all those who, whether they welcomed the final solution or regretted it, said that genocide was punishment for deicide and the continuing rejection of Christ. Or those who put it more subtly but no less repulsively: a divine reminder of Christ's sufferings. The whereabouts of God, the God of history—whether he stood by and watched the whole thing unfold, or he went into hiding, or (as some writers said) he was dead—were irrelevant. The murder of six million Jews and millions of others was wholly the work of men.

Second, Abraham set out, in response to a divine command, to sacrifice a son he loved. The Jews of Europe didn't set out to sacrifice their children or themselves. They were murdered. By people who hated them.

Third, the angel of God said stop, and Abraham stopped. He didn't sacrifice Isaac. Neither God nor anyone else stopped the Nazis. They killed for years.

Most of the writers who rejected the analogy entertained the details only long enough to sweep them aside. That's because they rejected the very idea of it. There was, they said, no useful analogy. The attempt to exterminate the Jews of Europe, all the Jews of Europe, simply because they were Jews, stood alone as a catastrophe in kind and degree. Pinchas Peli, a scholar of Hebrew literature and Jewish studies and a widely read essayist, worked his way through one possible biblical precedent after another—from Cain and Abel to Job—before concluding that none would suffice. "The Shoah stands out in its uniqueness in Jewish history and the history of Jewish martyrdom," he wrote. "The sacrifice of Isaac, with all its mystery and all the variety of interpretations given it, will always remain a world apart from the Shoah." The philosopher Emil Fackenheim reminded his audience in a series of lectures, later published as *God's Presence in History,* that the Rhineland martyrs, like most Jewish martyrs in history, had chosen to die rather than to convert. The crusaders had killed them because of their faith. The victims of the Holocaust weren't given a choice. Hitler killed them in an attempt to exterminate "a race."

Fackenheim believed that those who likened the binding and the Holocaust misunderstood both—and Jewish theology to boot. Jews don't die for God or to glorify God. They live for God. In fact, Fackenheim argues, the imperative to live is among the most important lessons of the Shoah, an imperative he imagines in the form of a 614th commandment: Thou shall survive as Jews, thou shall not contribute to Hitler's project by dying, by giving up, by cursing God (however much we have to wrestle with his angels), let alone by abandoning him. What Fackenheim calls the "commanding voice of Auschwitz" demands the end of the exaltation of martyrdom. Jews are "forbidden to hand Hitler yet another, posthumous victory," he writes. "They are commanded to survive as Jews, lest the Jewish people perish." They are commanded to remember the victims, "lest their memory perish. They are forbidden to despair of man and his world, and to escape into either cynicism or otherworldliness." And finally they are "forbidden to despair of the God of Israel, lest Judaism perish." Fackenheim concedes that a secularist can't make himself believe or be commanded to believe. And that the Holocaust might well force believers into an entirely new relationship with God. But "one possibility," he insists, is "wholly unthinkable: A Jew may not respond to Hitler's attempt to destroy Judaism by himself cooperating in its destruction."

Elie Wiesel, who survived slave labor, a death march that took the lives of thousands, the loss of his mother and one of his sisters to the gas chambers of Auschwitz, and of his father (who was with him almost all the way to the end) to dysentery, starvation, exhaustion, and several brutal beatings in Buchenwald, insists that the notion that Jews died to sanctify God, just like the idea that Isaac died on Mount Moriah, is contrary to both the spirit and the letter of Scripture, a confusion of Christian and Jewish stories. "In Jewish tradition man cannot use death as a means of glorifying God," he writes. "Had he killed his son, Abraham would have become the forefather of a people—but not the Jewish people." Fackenheim advocated the end of martyrdom. Reading Wiesel alone, you might think that it never existed: "For the Jew, all truth must spring from life, never from death. To us, crucifixion represents not a step forward but a step backward: at the top of Moriah, the living remains alive, thus marking the end of an era of ritual murder. To invoke the Akedah is tantamount to calling for mercy—whereas from the beginning Golgotha has served as pretext for countless massacres of sons and fathers cut down together by sword and fire in the name of a word that considered itself synonymous with love."

Wiesel, like many writing before him and many writing after, prefers to ponder Abraham's small victories: his argument on behalf of the innocent of Sodom, his insistence (in midrash) that God himself rescind the command, his refusal (in midrash) to leave the altar before he had given God a piece of his mind. Nor is he alone in noting that Jews are more inclined to commemorate good days, days of liberation, exodus, revelation, deliverance—Passover, Shavuot, Purim, Hanukkah—than the many disasters. The commemoration of the latter are bunched into one, Tishah b'Av. Wiesel doesn't deny, he would be last to deny, that the story of Abraham and Isaac seems to contain in its small frame so much Jewish destiny. Or that it has repeatedly been employed to describe and explain one catastrophe after another. But, he insists, the story doesn't end with catastrophe. It ends with Isaac, still alive. Isaac is a hero not for suffering, not for almost dying, but for surviving. "Suffering, in Jewish tradition, confers no privileges. It all depends on what one makes of that suffering. Isaac knew how to transform it into prayer and love rather than into rancor and malediction." His reward, in Wiesel's mind: "The Temple was built on Moriah. Not on Sinai."

Once again, change came with catastrophe. It came in waves.

Sometimes it came quietly and unobtrusively, as it did when commentators carried bits of biblical scholarship out into the wider world. Back in the 1860s, Abraham Geiger, a German rabbi, a scholar, and a founder of Reform Judaism, was among those who had argued that the story's meaning was simple and clear: "Lay not thy hand upon the lad." That was the "true worship" of God. Geiger's interpretation infuriated his former Bonn University classmate and friend Sampson Raphael Hirsch, a founder of Modern Orthodox Judaism. Hirsch charged that Geiger, "in his raving madness," had turned the moment on Moriah—Abraham and Isaac's "free will surrender of their own beings," the very height of Jewish spirituality—into its opposite, a trite epiphany. A century later, Geiger's interpretation was everywhere: in Bible commentaries, catechisms, sermons, popular histories and encyclopedias of religion, guides to religious literacy, and Bible stories for children. In *The Story of the Jew,* one of my Hebrew school textbooks, published in 1964, the story is characterized as a "bitter cry" against the pagan practice of child sacrifice. Abraham demonstrated his ("and the Jews'") heroic willingness to accept God and his law, and God made known that "He could not accept human blood." Nearly fifty years later, in his book on the city of Jerusalem, James Carroll, a former priest and prolific writer, put it precisely the same way: "The point of the story is that on the holy mountain God intervened to end human sacrifice."

Sometimes it came in riotous song, including a burst of up-tempo sixteen-bar electric blues, with Robert (ben Abraham) Zimmerman, a.k.a. Bob Dylan, belting out the lyrics above Mike Bloomfield's slide guitar, Al Kooper's piano, and Sam Lay's drums. Between verses, Dylan blew on a whistle that mimicked a siren, and the cacophony of sounds expressed Dylan's so-it-goes cynicism at least as much as the street slang and sarcasm of his words:

> *Oh God said to Abraham, "Kill me a son"*
> *Abe says, "Man, you must be puttin' me on"*
> *God say, "No." Abe say, "What?"*
> *God say, "You can do what you want Abe, but*
> *The next time you see me comin' you better run"*
> *Well Abe says, "Where do you want this killin' done?"*
> *God says, "Out on Highway 61"*

Dylan's Abraham is, briefly, a sixties rebel, but note that neither the angel of God nor any other form of deliverance is on its way. Sacrifice becomes killing in a setting that is less Genesis than the end of days.

Sometimes it came when commentators concluded that God would not have tested Abraham in that way, not even to teach him that he abhorred child sacrifice. One was G. Henton Davies, a distinguished Baptist minister and Oxford Old Testament scholar. In a commentary on Genesis commissioned in the late 1960s by the educational arm of the Southern Baptist Convention, Davies surveyed a wide range of traditional interpretation and modern scholarship before concluding that God would not have asked so cruel a sacrifice of anyone but himself. What happened was that Abraham, afraid that his love for Isaac, his inability to imagine his life without him, had compromised his connection to God, decided to give him back. The ram was the savior, but God did not stop a sacrifice he had set in motion. Rather, he saved Abraham from his own obsession and his own misunderstanding of God.

Not everyone could or would so cavalierly discard the story's first line. And surely, others said, God tests us. The question is how he wanted Abraham to respond. Change came when commentators began to answer that question by arguing that Abraham (and Dylan) got him wrong. God had actually wanted Abraham to argue, protest, even resist. He had *expected* Abraham to say, "You must be putting me on." And while any number of comedians played the gap between expectation and response for a laugh—Woody Allen's God asks Abraham how he could do such a thing and then interrupts his answer. "Never mind what I said," the Lord spake. "Doth thou listen to every crazy idea that comes thy way?"—most commentators portrayed it as tragedy. It was a test, and Abraham failed. The proof: he lived for another seventy-five years and prospered, but God never spoke to him again.

Change came when exegetes explicitly took on earlier exegetes, none more than Kierkegaard, as if that tortured soul had not suffered enough. Jean-Paul Sartre and Martin Buber, following Kant, parted ways with him at Abraham's first "Here I am." "If I hear voices," Sartre asked in 1945, "what proof is there that they come from heaven and not from hell, or from my own subconsciousness, or some pathological condition? What proof is there that they are intended for me?" When we prepare to suspend the ethical, Buber warned in the early 1950s, we had better be sure we have been "addressed by the Absolute" and not "one of his apes." "Ever and ever again, men are commanded from out of the darkness to sacrifice their Isaac."

The French philosopher Emmanuel Lévinas was more patient, sticking with Abraham for the entire length of the three-day journey. He imagines the determination it must have taken to get from tent to mountaintop. But in light of that determination, the gathering momentum, the fear and the trembling, the sheer force of Abraham's faith, Lévinas is certain that the critical moment in the story is not God's initial command, or Abraham's response, or even the angel's retraction. It is when Abraham puts down the knife.

Unlike the painters, who to a man picture Abraham's head turned away from his son, his gaze fixed on God's angel or the heavens, Lévinas imagines Abraham looking right at Isaac, face-to-face, and what he sees shows him that he should not kill him. Where Kierkegaard went wrong was in thinking that our singular relationship with God somehow exists independently of (and above) our singular relationship with others, our responsibilities to others, when in fact our relationship with others (in this case, Isaac lying on that altar) ought to mediate our relationship with God.

The story, Lévinas argues, is not about the suspension of the ethical, but rather its birth: "That Abraham obeyed the first voice is astonishing: that he had sufficient distance with respect to that obedience to hear the second voice—that is essential."

Others gave Abraham even more credit than that. Some saw in his painstaking preparations and roundabout route (why else would the journey have taken him three days?) a subtle form of resistance. He was stalling, a tried-and-true "weapon of the weak." But all along he was confident that if he gave God enough time, he would come to his senses. All along he had faith that God would not stand idly by while he violated his law. Claire Elise Katz, an American philosopher as wily as any late-antique rabbi, does not go quite that far, but her Abraham still discovers the ethical before God's angel says a word: he looks at Isaac's face, sees the difference between right and wrong in his eyes, and drops the knife. That (not Abraham's desire to strangle Isaac!) was why the angel said, "Don't lay a hand on him." The knife posed no danger. His hands were all he had left. Neither God nor his angel needed to stop the sacrifice. Abraham had stopped it himself.

Omri Boehm, another extraordinarily resourceful young philosopher, whose analysis of Genesis 22 is grounded in his reading of Maimonides and Ibn Kaspi as well as Kant, employs source criticism (who wrote what, when, and why) to argue that the idea of an ethical Abraham was not simply a figment of the late twentieth-century imagination. Rather, it had ancient roots. The original story, Boehm believes, comprised verses 1 through 10, followed immediately by verses 13 and 14. Verses 11 and 12 were added later, probably by the same writer who added verses 15–19, the angel's second address. If you skip from the end of verse 10 to the beginning of verse 13, you will see what Boehm means: just as Abraham is about to sacrifice Isaac, he looks up, sees the ram in the thicket, and decides to sacrifice it instead of Isaac. All his own doing. God doesn't say anything. He does not have to.

Jack Miles contributed a forward to Boehm's book, and he appreciates it for the same reasons I do: Boehm's fearless elevation, perhaps even excavation, of a religious model of disobedience to an "unlawful command." But Miles's own retelling of the story, in *God: A Biography,* is somewhat more open-ended.

Miles sees the binding as the climax of a protracted power struggle, a struggle with many dimensions but control of human reproduction at its heart. Who was calling the shots? God, the creator and destroyer who repeatedly promised Abraham offspring but took forever to deliver? Or Abraham, the man who (while waiting) handed his wife over to a pharaoh; fathered a child with Hagar; laughed when God said that he would soon father a second child with his ninety-year-old wife; spoke up for Ishmael even after God had informed him that Isaac was on his way; gave Sarah to a second man, this one a king; and made the case for sparing the sinning cities of the plain? No accident, Miles believes, that the thunderclap of a command to sacrifice came so soon after Abraham's brief on behalf of the Sodomites. God demanded deference. Evidently, the sacrifice of his foreskin was not enough.

Abraham calls his bluff. He sets out but never says he will do it. He tells his servants that he and Isaac will be back. He tells Isaac that God will provide the lamb. As we read, we have no way of knowing whether he is on his way to sacrifice his son or just playing a high-stakes game of chicken, instructing God, pleading with him, cajoling. Abraham goes through all the murderous motions before God stops him and declares victory—"Now I know that you fear God, for you have not withheld your son"—and "for the seventh and final time, promises Abraham abundant offspring." But, Miles writes, "it is as much God who concedes defeat as Abraham," for Abraham's obedience has "actually been far more ambiguous than God chooses to believe. He has not, after all, slain his son, and perhaps he would never have done so."

~~~

All that, and yet in it—and in untold variations—there was very little aid or comfort for Isaac. No matter why God asked, or how he hoped Abraham would respond, or what Abraham was thinking, or who ultimately stayed Abraham's hand, the boy remains in the shadows, an afterthought, wounded even when Abraham doesn't touch him, left only with scars and the memory of one immortal line.

Change came when commentators, many of them in Israel in the 1960s, began to identify with Isaac's experience as a victim and to launch their critique of the story from his point of view. Theirs were not the dorky, willing Isaacs of ancient and late-antique commentary and narrative. Nor were they the militant and heroic Isaacs of the pioneers and second and third waves of Jewish settlers in Palestine. Nor the often weary but stoic Isaacs of the War for Independence— all of whom had only yesterday (and sometimes still) revered their fathers (at least on paper) and accepted the role even when they did not celebrate it. No, these were unwilling Isaacs, furious at their fathers, at all the fathers, who in the name of God or land or state could not stop sacrificing their sons.

The sacrificing father in "The Way of the Wind," a stark and chilling short story Amos Oz published in 1965, is Shimshon Sheinbaum.

Sheinbaum is an intense, driven, and ruthlessly self-disciplined Labor Zionist, utterly sure of himself and his every belief, conviction, even instinct. He walks up to an open window and knows instantly where the wind is coming from, and when and how it will arrive. Although he is a patriarch of the labor movement, a movement intent on making not only a new nation but also new kind of Jewish man, late in life he himself has no heir. So he "conquers" Raya Greenspan, a woman thirty-three years his junior, and three months after their wedding, a son, Gideon, is born. But Gideon, however beloved, turns out to be "something of a disappointment." He is, in his father's eyes, weak, bewildered, vacillating, sniveling, lovesick, slow, the author of sentimental poems and cruel parodies, "not the stuff on which dynasties are founded" but rather a perfect representative of a whole generation, exuding "an air of shallow despair, of nihilism, of cynical mockery. They can't love wholeheartedly and they can't hate wholeheartedly, either. No enthusiasm, and no loathing."

When Gideon announces his intention to join the paratroopers, his father assumes it is one more of the boy's bad jokes. But he is serious, and though his mother refuses to give her permission (an only child seeking assignment to a combat unit needed both parents' consent), Sheinbaum goes over her head and gets an exception to the rule. Redemption would come on Independence Day, when Gideon's unit was scheduled to perform in an air show, jumping in front of family, friends, and neighbors and landing on the soil of his very own kibbutz. His father can't wait.

The day comes. Gideon jumps. But the wind takes an unexpected turn and blows him off course. His chute gets caught in power lines, and though spectators believe he will survive the fall, he is afraid to let go. He dies hanging on those lines, electrocuted, crucified upside down on the cross of his father's ideology, obsessions, virility, dreams, and desires.

.   .   .

It is not supposed to be that way. Sons are supposed to bury fathers, not fathers sons. Moshe Berfel, the protagonist of Yariv Ben-Aharon's 1966 novel *The Battle,* worries that the burying fathers, endlessly sacrificing sons "on the altar of war," were engaged in a futile effort to evade their own death sentences. "Should not a father die for his ideals?" Berfel asks. "Is it not my duty to bury him before he buries me? I mean, before his ideals are realized?" Two years later, in a symposium that took place on Kibbutz Givat Haviva, the poet and essayist Eli Alon argued that honesty requires that we, all of us, evaluate our ideals and our very lives not just from the point of view of Isaac, but "from the point of view of the dead Isaac, from the point of view of the dead." If we do, he said, "we'll be surprised to discover that many of the slogans and values that seem necessary to us, in order 'to give meaning to our lives,' and for which we were ready to die, will suddenly seem to us vanity and folly."

The poet and playwright Hanoch Levin took Alon's call literally, or felt the same impulse at the same time. The perspective of the dead Isaac is exactly what a few audiences got in his wickedly satirical cabaret piece *The Queen of the Bath.* (Golda Meir is the queen.) In one scene, Levin's Abraham is frail and deeply apologetic: God wants it, he tells Isaac. What can I do? Levin's Isaac, edgy and articulate, tries to reassure him, and urges him to go ahead and do it, if that's what God wants. It is not a big deal, he says, the slaughter of one kid, just a kid. They go back and forth in that way, until, finally, the angel calls out. Unfortunately, Abraham is hard-of-hearing. It is Isaac who hears God's voice, and now, with their roles reversed, he must persuade his father not to kill him. The scene ends with Isaac wondering what will happen if God calls out to other fathers, commanding them not to sacrifice their sons, but none of them can hear.

The next thing we know, Isaac is in his grave, singing a song as

Abraham buries him. The dead Isaac rejects the idea that there was anything honorable about his father's obedience to God's whim:

Father dear, when you stand over my grave,
Old and tired and forlorn here,
And you see how they bury my body in the earth
And you stand over me, father dear,

Don't stand then so proud,
. . .

And don't say you've made a sacrifice,
For the one who sacrificed was me here,
And don't say other high-flown words
For I am very low now, father dear.

Father dear, when you stand over my grave
Old and tired and forlorn here,
And you see how they bury my body in the earth—
Then you beg my pardon, father dear.

In 1970, Levin's play was stillborn. Shortly before opening night, the censorship board demanded the removal of two scenes, including the exchange between Abraham and Isaac, which it considered offensive to the fathers of soldiers. The theater appealed and won, but many of those in the audience for the initial performances were indeed offended, and religious members of the Tel Aviv city council put pressure on the theater to shut down the show. Actors began to fear for their safety, and the show closed after nineteen nights. But Isaac continued to speak, and over the next two decades, a period marked by a surprise Arab attack and traumatic war in 1973, the continued occupation of East Jerusalem, the West Bank, the Gaza Strip, the Golan Heights, and (until 1979) Sinai, the invasion of Lebanon in 1982, the Sabra and Shatila massacres, the rise of the antiwar movement and the First Intifada, Isaac's point of view informed almost every discussion and debate. So strong and so widespread was the identification with him that a whole generation of writers and artists became known as "the generation of Isaac."

Not that there haven't been times when patience with him has worn thin. How, writers wondered, after all these years, could he be so naive? How could he go marching off to Mount Moriah, fooled again? How, with only rare exceptions (Leonard Cohen's Isaac, who threatens to kill to stop senseless sacrifice, was one) could he not protest? How could he forget that he and his Arab brother faced the exact same threat?

In a poem first published in 1982, Yitzhak Laor calls his namesake an idiot—"This Idiot, Isaac." Yet Laor saves his bitterest words for Abraham, whom he likens to Amalek, Israel's ancient archenemy. Recall Moses's warning, in his farewell address: "Remember what Amalek did to you on your journey, after you left Egypt—how, undeterred by fear of God, he surprised you on the march, when you were famished and weary, and cut down all the stragglers in your rear. Therefore, when the Lord your God grants you safety from all your enemies around you, in the land that the Lord your God is giving you as a hereditary portion, you shall blot out the memory of Amalek from under heaven. Do not forget!"

Now the poet warns the patriarch:

> To pity the offering? . . . The ass?
> Thus to surrender? From the Negev to Mount Moriah to
>   be sacrificed?
> To trust a father like that? Let him kill him first. Let him
>   slam his father
> his only father Abraham
> in jail in the poorhouse in the cellar of the house just so

he will not slay.
Remember what your father did to your brother Ishmael.

At least one poet, the magnificent Yehuda Amichai, did pity the offering, the actual offering, in a poem he published the following year. Amichai's protest is less explosive than Laor's, more sardonic than furious. But it is every bit as subversive of the story's traditional meanings. In Amichai's hands, the binding becomes a simple stunt or photo op. The shofar, blown for thousands of Rosh Hashanahs to remind God to remember Abraham and (in remembering) to contain his wrath, becomes a bugle or party horn. And the substitution of the ram for Isaac, for so long and to this day widely understood as a giant step toward civilization, a reason for religious pride, becomes just another form of barbarism. While all around him rabbis, priests, clerics, and laypeople continued to ask, and argue about, whose sacrifice was the greatest and why, Amichai concludes that

> *The real hero of the sacrifice was the ram*
> *Who had no idea about the conspiracy of the others.*
> *He apparently volunteered to die in place of Isaac.*
> *I want to sing a memorial song about the ram,*
> *His curly wool and human eyes,*
> *The horns, so calm in his living head.*
> *When he was slaughtered they made* shofars *of them,*
> *To sound the blast of their war*
> *Or the blast of their coarse joy. . . .*

Fifteen years later, Amichai imagined that Abraham had "had three sons" and he riffed on the root meaning of each boy's name. Ishmael was saved by his mother, Hagar. Isaac was saved by God's angel. But Yivkeh, a third son, we've never heard of "because he was the youngest" and, "much-loved," "wasn't saved by anyone." When he was small

his father called him affectionately Yivkeh will cry
my little cutie-pie. But he sacrificed him on an altar.
And in the Bible it is written, "the ram," but it was
  Yivkeh.
Yishmael never heard again of God his entire life.
Yitzhak never laughed again his entire life.
And Sarah laughed only once and never again.
Abraham had three sons.
He will listen, he will laugh, he will cry.
Yishmael (Let God listen), Yitzhakel (Let God laugh),
  Yivkehel (Let God Cry).

Here the ram survives, and there is no hero of the *Akedah*.

I am not sure any writer has returned to Mount Moriah as often as A. B. Yehoshua. He seems as unable as Kierkegaard's de Silentio to stay away. Yet unlike Silentio, who as a child found the story beautiful and grew to admire it more and more, Yehoshua found it intolerable from the first. He thought God's command was an outrage. No God worthy of worshipping would make such a demand. He thought Abraham's willingness was an outrage. It made no moral sense whatsoever. Yet Yehoshua understood that the story was the bedrock of God's blessing, the linchpin of the covenant, the reason, on the Day of Judgment and every other day that justice and mercy hangs in the balance, that God suppresses his wrath.

Secular himself, it naturally occurred to Yehoshua to see what would happen if he took God out of it—as the instigator of the sacrifice, the first cause. He imagines Abraham as an old man, with Isaac coming of age, remembering how, when he was Isaac's age, he had mocked his father's gods and ultimately left his father's house. What if Isaac came to mock his God, the God to whom he had devoted his life, and sacrificed so much? It was through Isaac that the covenant would be passed. What if he rebelled, continuing the line but not the covenant?

So Abraham took Isaac up. Bound him. Raised the knife, and then dropped it. He told Isaac: "God stopped me, and saved your life." From that moment on, whatever else he thought of Him, Isaac would believe that he owed his life to God.

Yehoshua took God out. He calls what remained the "knife game," a game in which fathers bound their sons, their futures, the future of their nation, to their ideals and their faith by submitting them to life-threatening dangers and then saving them at the last moment. But, Yehoshua quickly concluded, that was not enough. The game was too dangerous. Who knew where the knife would ultimately fall? And what kind of damage would be done, so long as the game—ending in Isaac's deliverance—could be idealized, held up as the metaphor for all of Israel's experience, for all of Jewish experience, used as evidence that no matter how bad things got, how many lives were lost, how much suffering there was, God would ultimately come through.

Yehoshua had conveyed that danger and damage, the near-death happening over and over, in *Early in the Summer of 1970*, a nightmarish early novella. It is the story of a Bible teacher, several years past retirement age and under pressure to retire, but unwilling to, because of the war. He insists that he can't leave the school and students now that they—all the teachers, all the fathers—are sending them to their deaths. The head of the school doesn't see the connection. But the old man just keeps showing up for class, until the day the head pulls him out to inform him that his son, the old man's only son, has been killed in action in the Jordan Valley. In a daze, the father travels to Jerusalem to recover his son's body, but there's been some mistake. The body in Jerusalem is not that of his son, and when he travels east into the valley, toward the river, it is not his son again and again. Along the way, he prepares the speech he'll deliver at graduation to students about to leave school for the army: "On the face of it, your disappearance is nothing, is meaningless, futile. Because historically speaking, however stubborn you are, your death will again be but a weary repetition in a slightly different setting. Another tinge of hills, new contours of desert, a new species of shrub, astounding types of weapons. But the blood is the same, and the pain so familiar"

Two decades later, Yehoshua published *Mr. Mani,* the story of one family over several generations, from the middle of the nineteenth century to the end of the twentieth. Yehoshua tells the story backward, which means that the novel begins at the end and ends at the beginning, begins with a mysterious suicide and ends with a mysterious sacrifice, or more precisely a father confessing— to a rabbi—to the sacrifice (on the steps of the Dome of the Rock, the Temple Mount, Mount Moriah) of a wayward son, a son with a dangerous (in the father's mind) obsession: reuniting the sons of Ishmael and Isaac. The danger is not simply that the boy has elevated the value of peace among different people in a particular place, Palestine, above the value of his distinct religious tradition, but also that as he struggles to remind the Ishmaelites of what they have forgotten (that they are actually Jews, or were once Jews), the young man has himself forgotten that he is a Jew.

It is a disorienting novel, a distressing novel, a difficult novel (the story is told in five conversations we hear only one side of), and often an enigmatic novel, an epic large parts of which we are left to imagine for ourselves. Critics and other readers do not even agree who ultimately wields the sacrificial knife, the Jewish father in hot pursuit of his son or the Muslims guarding the shrine. Yet from beginning to end it is an extraordinary evocation, at once utterly fantastic and utterly realistic, of the powerful sway that our ancestors hold over us, whether or not we know who they were or what on earth they have to do with who we are. Yehoshua traces the Manis all the way back to Moriah not to celebrate ritual or obedience or faith or sacrifice to (or for) God or country (in war after war "of no choice"), but to try to break its spell or at least loosen its grip, to undo the costly inheritance once and for all. But I can't imagine who would know better than he—a novelist who has enacted the binding in the hope of eradicating it, killed Isaac in the hope of saving his children—just how difficult a task that is going to be.

27

And then there is Sarah. I left her for last simply to try to convey a sense of the way the waves of commentary came. If one of the first was generated by revulsion (revulsion against genocide and the blind obedience to authority that was widely believed to have contributed to it, revulsion against the interpretation of that genocide as martyrdom), that wave broke among many others, as one postwar social movement after another generated challenges to one form of authority after another and each new challenge gave rise to new questions, or new answers to old ones. Yet it was only with the feminist movement, when the authority of men—divine and human—over women was added to the list, and when women began to enter the rabbinate and ministry and the academy in ever-increasing numbers and increasing numbers of women poets and fiction writers began to make their voices heard, that the ancient question—Where was Sarah?—was raised anew. In the late second millennium, as in the early first, Sarah came last.

Writers turning to her have had a lot to work with. She is as clearly defined a biblical character as Isaac is indistinct, as active in defense of her interests as he is passive, as strong as he is weak. So strong and so decisive that though the poet Eleanor Wilner's Sarah (a late second-wave feminist, right down to her perfectly correct consciousness of caste and class) may be a bit of a stretch, the gist of her initial response to God would not have surprised third- and fourth-century rabbis and priests. God said, "Go," and she said, "No." Abraham was asleep in his tent. She stepped out of hers and stood between "the desert and the distant sky." Then, speaking in a soft voice, words "the canon does not record," she told God she wouldn't be chosen, and if she could help it, neither would her son. In light of God's promise, the sacrifice was a sham or a sin. "Shame," she said to him, who must have known she would choose Isaac: "What use have I for History—an arrow already bent when it is fired from the bow?"

She wakes Isaac and tells him what she knows. She plans to leave, before Abraham wakes, to track down Hagar, whom she ("drunk with pride") cast out. She gives Isaac a choice: to come with her or go with Abraham, to choose or be chosen. He's confused, uncertain how he'll greet Ishmael, wondering what, if he's not chosen, he will be. She tells him he must choose. He wants to know what will happen if they go. "I don't know," she says. "But it is written what will happen if you stay."

We don't find out what Isaac decided. Or maybe we do, if Scripture accurately records it. But in other poems, and sermons, and songs, and commentary, Sarah doesn't leave the choice to Isaac. Sometimes, she and Isaac flee. Sometimes, she prevents Abraham from leaving, as the rabbis worried (and Satan hoped) she would. Sometimes she goes after them and stops them before they reach Moriah. In one novel, she follows them all the way to the mountaintop, where she finds Isaac piling wood on the altar and Abraham "standing to one side, an absent look in his eyes." Sarah urges Isaac to run, but before he can, Abraham scoops him up into his arms. She appeals to God, making her case as a party to the covenant, as a convert to his idea of justice, and most of all as a mother. Then she spots the ram and cries out, "Abraham, Abraham, look at the ram behind you." Afterward Abraham claims he did not hear her. What he heard, he says, was the voice of God. Sarah tactfully concludes that she and God must have cried out together.

Sarah has been written into the story in every which way. In one recently discovered midrash, a midrash attributed, with fitting license, to Rashi's sister, it is all a bad dream of Sarah's, a working out of the trauma of leaving her home and her father's house, of wandering endlessly, of being handed over to lecherous men in Egypt and Gerar, of having Isaac taken out of her arms for circumcision. In another, more recent take, a Colorado rabbi audaciously explains the old mystery of Sarah's absence, or whereabouts, not just in chapter 22, but for all the years between the weaning of Isaac, in Beersheba, and her death, in Hebron (when Abraham still resided in Beersheba and clearly was not with her when she died). It turns out that she, alarmed by Abraham's increasingly bizarre behavior, had decided to leave him shortly after Isaac was born. Hagar's banishment was nothing but a ruse, the first step in a scheme that ultimately allowed the two of them to get away with their sons. Afterward they arranged an early form of joint custody with the boys' father.

Other readers, writers, critics, and scholars, while generally sympathetic to the spirit and intent of those who wrote Sarah into the story, have devoted their own efforts not to adding Sarah to the biblical story but rather to exploring what her exclusion from it tells us about ideas about men and women in the world that made the Bible and the world the Bible made. Among the first was the philosopher Carol Ochs who, in a brief essay written in the late 1970s, touches upon a wide range of responses (rabbinical, historical, psychoanalytical, and philosophical) before concluding that at the heart of the story and the entire cycle of Abraham stories was the conflict between matriarchy and patriarchy. In the former, a man's primary allegiance was to offspring and blood relatives. In the latter, to an abstraction, the voice of God. Abraham has to prove himself, especially after he had argued with God about Sodom, prove that he has left the old tradition behind. "God demands that he denounce the most fundamental tenet of the matriarchal religion and kill his own child," Ochs wrote. "Abraham passes the test and is pronounced fit to be the father of a new, patriarchal religion."

Two decades later, the anthropologist Carol Delaney surveyed an even wider range of readings, Jewish, Christian, and Muslim, en route to her own. She agrees with Ochs (and the scholars who had weighed in after her, most notably Nancy Jay) that the struggle for power at the heart of the story was not between Abraham and God but between Abraham and God on one side and Sarah on the other. Delaney agrees that the story conveyed a powerful message about the outcome of that struggle, about who was in charge. But in her mind its essence was what it said about why Abraham was in charge, what it said about the intellectual underpinning, in particular ideas about reproduction, of male power. Patriarchy, she argues, was built upon the idea that men are the Gods on earth, creating human life when they plant the seed. Women merely provide the womb, the soil in which the seed grows. Delaney is dubious about much of the evidence used to support the idea that child sacrifice was widespread in the ancient Near East. But whether it was or wasn't, she believes that the story had less to do with idealizing or prohibiting it than with answering another set of questions entirely, then and long afterward: Whom does Isaac belong to? Whose seed is he? Who gets to decide whether he lives or dies? The legacy of the earliest answers to those questions of power and authority, Delaney argues, has been century after century of child sacrifice through child abuse, poverty, inequality, and war.

I don't think that Sarah would have agreed that Isaac belonged to Abraham. That is why she had to be left out of the story. There would have been a wicked fight. Abraham himself suggests as much in Alicia Ostriker's poem "The Story of Abraham," a parody in which the covenant takes the form of an eye chart, with the command to sacrifice coming (right after the command to circumcise—"a mark of absolute / Distinction, it would only hurt for a minute") in the fine and blurry print at the bottom. When Abraham hesitates, saying he needs to talk "some of this out" with his wife, the print suddenly turns bold:

> NO WAY. THIS IS BETWEEN US MEN.
> AND IF YOU HAPPEN TO BE THINKING
> ABOUT LOOPHOLES
> FORGET IT, MAN. It said they preferred
> Not to use strong arm techniques. It said
> I'd already signed on.

Right up to that moment, Ostriker reminds us, in an essay titled "Out of My Sight," Sarah has played a pivotal role in the story cycle. It is she who twice saves Abraham's life by pretending to be his sister. It is she who comes up with the idea of the coupling that produces Ishmael. It is she who gives birth to Isaac, and after Isaac was born, it is she who insists upon the banishment of Hagar and Ishmael. But with Ishmael out of Isaac's way, Sarah is no longer essential to the story, and with God's big test ahead, she may well have been an impediment to the fulfillment of God's grand plan. Neither Sarah's absence from Genesis 22 nor her death in the first line of Genesis 23 was an accident. Like Rebekah and Miriam and any number of other strong biblical women who follow, she has to be silenced and removed from the scene. And in Ostriker's analysis, nothing could be more telling or sobering than the words (in the traditional Hebrew version of the text, and maintained in the Septuagint, the King James Bible, and the Jewish Publication Society translation until its most recent, 1985, revision) with which Abraham twice asks the Hittites for land to bury his wife: "I am a stranger and a sojourner with you: give me a posses-sion of a burying-place with you, that I may bury my dead out of my sight."

The biblical scholar Phyllis Trible is no less frustrated by Sarah's absence. But she is less impressed than Ostriker and other feminist critics by Sarah's role in the previous chapters. Trible wants her in the story of the near sacrifice, but for a different reason. God tested Abraham, she argues, to see if he could let go of Isaac, let go of the human attachment most precious to him, let go of every-thing but God. But Abraham had already left his native land, his father's house, and his father. He had twice handed Sarah over to other men. He had risen early to see Hagar and Ishmael off. He has nothing to prove. It is Sarah who has repeatedly failed God's tests. It is she who needs to be encouraged to detach, to disavow her idolatrous worship of Isaac, and in doing so to find God. "The dynamic of the entire saga," Trible writes, "from its genealogical preface on, requires that Sarah be featured in the climactic scene, that she learn the meaning of obedience to God, that she find libera-tion from possessiveness, that she free Isaac from maternal ties, and that she emerge a solitary individual, non-attached, the model of faithfulness." In the spirit of the Syriac songwriters fifteen hundred years before her, Trible wants Sarah in the story not as a mother desperately clinging to her only son but as a woman fully prepared for God's test—Here I am—and thus completely worthy of God's blessing.

Others don't want Sarah in the story on those terms, and some don't want her in it at all. Among the latter is Wendy Zierler, a profes-sor of modern Hebrew literature, who recently went searching for a feminist reading of the *Akedah* and found it in the juxtaposition of Genesis 22 and Deuteronomy 6: "And you shall love the Lord your God with all your heart and all your being and with all your might." What Trible sees as Abraham's "liberation from possessive-ness" en route to proximity to God and some great future, Zierler sees as costly detachment from and even the sacrifice of the people closest to him, the living sands and stars. Abraham passes God's test but ends up all alone. Zierler wants Sarah to remain outside the story as an alternative to Abraham's attachment to God by fear and awe. She wants Sarah as a "model of love," love of family and neighbors as well as (and as a form of) love of God. Zierler notes that the very next time the word "love" appears in the Bible, at the very end of Genesis 24, when Abraham's servant brings Rebekah to Isaac, Sarah is there: "And Isaac brought her into the tent of his mother Sarah and took Rebekah as his wife. And he loved her, and Isaac was consoled after his mother's death." "Even after her death," Zierler writes, "Sarah is the one who keeps the notion of love alive in the text."

All that was left was the funeral, which the Israeli poet Benjamin Galai, early among those to write from Sarah's point of view, evokes in his rewriting of the opening of Genesis 23, *Hayei Sarah*:

And the life of Sarah
was
a hundred years, twenty years, seven years.
    . . .
The years of Sarah's life.

And she died—
But really,
Her candle had gone out many days, many before
Her last resting place was dust.
And the coffin she lay in was made of all the years,
The memory of wood cleft on another mount,
On another mount, in the Land of Moriah.

Sarah rested, but not always, even today, in peace. In the sea of sympathy, there has also been criticism, including criticism for her treatment of Hagar, which has occasionally been laced with the old but still chilling thought that the near sacrifice was punishment or payback, an instance of Sarah reaping what she sowed. In Shin Shifrah's "Hagar," an Israeli mother tries to allay her daughter's fear of the Arab other:

> *Do not fear, my daughter,*
> *Hagar,*
> *Only the name is strange,*
> *A storm in the desert*
> *A dry throat,*
> *Do not fear*
> *Hagar*
> *Because the destiny of Hagar*
> *Is waiting in ambush at the entrance*
> *To Sarai's*
> *Tent.*

Criticism has also come from Isaac, whose complaint is sometimes that his mother cooperated with his father ("Butcher me and bring my flesh back to my mother," one of Hanoch Levin's angry Isaacs commands Abraham) and sometimes simply that she failed to protest. In Israel, even the question "Where was Sarah?," which since the 1970s has so often been the starting point for sympathetic storytelling and analysis, has occasionally been turned against her, against all the mothers, as it is in a poem Yehudit Kafri published in 1988. Kafri's narrator wonders why Sarah depended on a God so tyrannical to protect Isaac, and why (as Abraham saddled the donkey) she herself did not say, "Do not raise your hand against the boy," and finally (if Abraham had ignored her):

> *Why did she not stand*
> *In the middle of the road*

And whisper through pursed lips:
You will not pass through this way
As long as I live!

I understand where Kafri and the others are coming from, but I am old-fashioned enough to believe in authors and to hold them responsible for who is and who is not in their stories. It was not Sarah's fault she wasn't there. I am more inclined to put her in and give her the chance to deliver those very lines or, as so many have tried to do, to explore the meaning of her absence. Or the cause of her death. You may recall that some rabbis imagined her dying of shock when she learned where Abraham and Isaac had gone. Others, her dying of joy when she learned that Isaac had been spared. My favorite interpretation suggests a third possibility. It comes from Rabbi Kalonymus Shapira, who found himself having to explain Sarah's death to fellow worshippers and students in the Warsaw Ghetto in early November 1939, one month after a German bomb took the life of his son. "The Torah," he said, "may also be telling us" that Sarah "died in order to show God that a Jew should not be expected to suffer unlimited levels of anguish. Even though a person, with the mercy of God, survives and escapes death, nevertheless elements of his capability, his mind, and his spirit are forever broken, and as a result of his ordeal, lost to him. In the final analysis, what difference does it make, whether all of me or part of me is killed?"

If all else fails, as it so often does, I would try to find one more way to express sadness and regret, as Eli Alon does in a poem he published in 1989:

In the beginning there was this story:
a father
his son
the God
and the sacrificial knife.

Sarai? Where is Sarai?
A small footnote
in an dreamed-up land
nothing but a springboard to
the Father
the God
taking over the stage.

What Sarai? Where is Sarai?
Have we ever had a mother
to protect us
to have mercy?
. . .
And when a son is born to us
What we will give him? What is there in our hearts
Besides that knife?

Alon's final question begins with an echo of Isaiah and ends with a shout-out (part tribute, and perhaps also part rebuke) to Haim Gouri, whose poem "Heritage" is a quietly devastating expression of resignation and fate, first published in 1960. Gouri was a young man, but his Abraham is old and the day is late. The ram arrives last, to answer the boy's question. Abraham sees the angel. The knife slips from his hand, and he turns to go. Isaac sees only his father's back. But the story doesn't end there. Recall Yehoshua's worry about the knife game. Look again at Rembrandt's oil.

Isaac, as the story goes, was not sacrificed.
He lived for many years,
Saw what pleasure had to offer, until his eyesight dimmed.

But he bequeathed that hour to his offspring.
They are born
With a knife in their hearts.

Sarah was not there, in that poem, but half a century later, toward the end of his ninth decade, Gouri closed a cycle of new poems with the haunting cry "if only," if only she had been, the nagging thought that perhaps "everything could have been different on that Mountain, / if we had only listened to her voice."

28

The author of Ecclesiastes was exaggerating when he said there is nothing new under the sun. Either that, or he was a writer who prized sound more than precision, and he realized that it was more elegant to say that there is nothing new than to say that there is nothing new that doesn't have some old in it. For all the innovation, the careful analysis and the wild and crazy speculation, the clever application of critical theory and biblical criticism, the subtle and not-so-subtle subversion in poems and stories and songs, the measured criticism and boundless fury, the recasting of collective religious experience as secular national experience, family drama, even individual trauma and angst—for all that, the "new" more often than not had "occurred long before." Changes in context could be enormous. Changes in the meaning of words in the minds of writers and readers could be enormous. Changes in the uses to which words were put could be enormous. Changes in a particular commentary's currency could be enormous. Antecedents might be near. Or far. Or both, a chain extending back to antiquity. The new may be fully cognizant of the old. Or completely oblivious. All that I know for sure is that the day it is written or spoken, all commentary is modern commentary. And all commentary is rooted in the past, in tradition, often more than one.

. . .

The new didn't come out of nowhere, or all at once, or once and for all. It didn't extinguish or (always or everywhere) even displace the old, for history is not half a superhighway with all the cars and trucks traveling in the same direction at roughly the same speed. Nor is it a raging river or swollen stream, nor an arrow or straight line of any kind, nor even a stampede. At every moment, there were people on the shoulder, along the bank, above or below or to one side of the line, outside the fray; at every moment there were people who went about their religious lives in blissful innocence or studied ignorance of the ferment going on all around them. And at every moment there were people who paid close attention and in one way or another pushed back, or even stepped back, making history— like tradition—much more of a conversation, a conversation in time and across time, a dialogue, a dialectic, a debate, an argument, sometimes even a bit of a brawl.

What that means is that there have been, and there still are, commentators, Muslim, Christian, and Jewish, who insist that God didn't ask, wouldn't ask, and there have been, and still are, commentators who insist that he most certainly did. Among the latter were dozens of Southern Baptist ministers and church newspaper editors who, in 1969, were outraged by G. H. Davies's commentary on Genesis, commissioned for them by the Baptist Convention's educational board. They had many objections, but they were particularly incensed by Davies's interpretation of Genesis 22 (he had said that the sacrifice was Abraham's idea, not God's), which they believed "clouded a clear divine directive," and, like the historical scholarship that infected the whole volume, would only undermine Baptist belief in the literal truth and infallibility of the Bible. Davies was not without his defenders. Nonetheless, at the national convention the following year, messengers voted overwhelmingly to withdraw the volume, destroy all unsold copies, and find another writer to revise it. Two years later the revision appeared. Its author assured readers that today God certainly would not ask a man to sacrifice a son. In fact, from Abraham's day on, God's people could point to Mount Moriah as evidence that he didn't want human sacrifice. But Scripture got history right: the command had come from God.

What that means is that there are some who say that God should not have asked and there are others who reply that there is no "should" independent of God. Who could blame the latter for quoting the remarkable Kalonymus Shapira, who, in one more of his Warsaw sermons, had expressed that reply so trenchantly: The nations of the world, he said, even the best of them, believe that "truth exists in and of itself, and that God commanded the truth because the truth can be nothing but true." The Jewish people, on the other hand, believe that all the "truth that exists in the world" is true only "because God commanded it so, and wanted it so." When God commanded Abraham to sacrifice his son, "the binding of Isaac became the truth, and if He had not later commanded Abraham not to harm him, then the truth would have been to slaughter him."

More than half a century later, Seyyed Hossein Nasr, a distinguished scholar of Islam, in conversation about the story with a handful of Jews and Christians, seemed puzzled by all the hand-wringing, the fretting about God asking and Abraham obeying. Some clergymen and women even wondered how they could believe in such a God and celebrate such a man. Abraham, Nasr countered, was a friend of God, imbued with his spirit and presence, as close to God as a human could be. Isaac—or Ishmael—was a prophet who willingly chose to participate. We can't ask how we can believe in a God who asked for such a thing without asking "Where do we get our ethical norms? If we have a source of ethical knowledge that is independent of God, then we are not living in the biblical or Qur'anic world."

That means there are some who, teaching the Old Testament to Christian children, omit the near sacrifice altogether, skipping from

Isaac's birth to his marriage, or who tell the story quickly and talk a lot about Abraham's love of God. And there are others who explain it bluntly, asking kids to "try to imagine going out and killing" a beloved pet dog or cat "with a knife because some voice" in their head told them to. It would be very scary and might even seem impossible, but "God wants to see that we trust Him all the way," the way "Abraham trusted God enough to kill his only son." Another writer explains that because of Abraham's trust and his willingness, God was willing to sacrifice his son on that same hill and to let his son's blood wash away the sins of ordinary women and men. But only the sins of those who reached out to him, who let Jesus into their hearts: "This morning," he told them, "you are on the top of the hill. The lamb is there waiting to take your place. God is waiting to save you. The Holy Spirit is whispering into your ear to get saved. Will you this morning? Or will you burn in the fire of hell someday because you said no to God?"

There are some readers who diagnose Abraham as depressed or accuse him of abuse (a reenactor of his own childhood trauma) and there are others who insist that those who do say less about Abraham than their own lack of historical and religious imagination. Among the latter is Jon Levenson, a prolific scholar of Jewish studies and ancient Hebrew literature, with a deep and abiding passion for the theology of the Hebrew Bible. Levenson is a mild-mannered professor and public lecturer, fond of puns ("there was lots of sects in Ancient Israel") and wisecracks with a critical edge ("Some say that after returning from Moriah, Abraham and Isaac never spoke again. Show me where they spoke before.") But in response to commentators whom he believes have abused Abraham, he can wield a fearsome pen. The mistake Abraham's critics make, he argues, is to think of the patriarch as they would think of a father today who sets out to sacrifice a child. That father would be acting in flagrant disregard—in Jewish tradition alone—for the provisions for substitution in Exodus; the prohibition of child sacrifice in Leviticus and Deuteronomy; and the Talmud's elevation of law over oracle and prophecy. To diagnosis that father as deranged or abusive, Levenson acknowledges, would be fair, "but it is a symptom of acute myopia and mind-numbing parochialism to think that this must also have been the case in a society that practiced sacrifice (even, on occasion and for a while, child-sacrifice) and did not confuse it with murder."

That means that there are writers who are furious at their fathers, at all the fathers. Remember Yitzhak Laor, who in the aftermath of Israel's first war in Lebanon had likened Abraham to the Amalekites and warned all the Isaacs to watch out for him. And there are others, including Laor a decade later, who remember their fathers as hardworking and comforting to them when they were sick and when, with military service looming, they were afraid to die. If there is a crime now, it is not against a people. Nor is it the attempted sacrifice of a son. It is much more mundane, but painful all the same: a father's inability to understand his son's experience, especially in war, and his inability to see that however much he would like to protect him—

> *I won't let them take you, my son*
> *I am the ram*
> *I am the angel*
> *I am your father*

—he can't.

That means that there are still some who imagine that Abraham killed Isaac, including the biblical scholars who believe or suspect that the story was an E sacrifice story (verses 1–10 and 15–

19) transformed into an aborted sacrifice story by a later editor or redactor, perhaps with the simple addition of verses 11–14 and the phrase "a second time" in verse 15. Take those lines out and you will read a sacrifice story too. Like so many readers before them, the scholars who hold this view note Isaac's absence at the end of the story. Source criticism provides them with another intriguing clue. As Richard Elliott Friedman puts it, "Isaac never again appears as a character in E."

And there are others—many others—who are as sure as they are sure of anything that Abraham stopped and sacrificed a ram instead. One is the father of a twenty-eight-year-old Iraqi who in the early years of the second Iraq war was accused of collaborating with U.S. forces. The young man was said to have provided the information, tragically inaccurate, that resulted in a botched raid. Civilians were killed. The young man's tribe was humiliated. Villagers, fearing insult and retribution from the tribe of the victims, gave the father an ultimatum: "Close the door" on the matter, they said, or we'll kill your entire family. Otherwise an outsider would close it for them, sparking a long and bloody cycle of violence. The father and another son did the deed. Not long afterward, Anthony Shadid, the indefatigable Lebanese-born American journalist, sat with the father. He spoke quietly, with tears in his eyes. "I have the heart of a father and he's my son," he said. "Even the prophet Abraham didn't have to kill his son."

That means that there are some who struggle to make sense of what they take to be the baffling contradiction between Abraham's eloquent questions after God revealed his plan to destroy Sodom (first he asks if he'll punish the innocent along with the guilty, then he asks if he won't spare the guilty on account of the innocent) and his abject silence after God commanded him to sacrifice his son. And there are those who insist there is no contradiction at all. In the first instance, God confided in Abraham and perhaps sought his counsel. In the second, God commanded him to do something. In the first, Abraham raised questions of justice in the context of sin. In the second, he understood that Isaac's innocence was imperative: the victim was supposed to be without blemish. In the first instance, Abraham argued and God listened. In the second, Abraham did exactly what God had asked him to do—he served God—even when doing so meant, in the words of the Israeli scientist and philosopher Yeshayahu Leibowitz, separating that service from "all human needs, feelings, and values, even from the great historical ends," the nation God had promised him. As Leibowitz sees it, the sequence of events made perfect sense, for it is the service to God, not the ethical argument, on which Judaism stands: "The highest symbol of Jewish faith is the stance of Abraham on Mount Moriah, where all human values were annulled and overridden by fear and love of God."

There are Catholic and Protestant clergy, theologians, and scholars who speak and write against the idealization of senseless sacrifice, the fixation on pain and suffering, the reveling in violence and bloodshed. And there are ministers and priests who deliver sermons (depending on the denomination, on Holy Thursday, Good Friday, Easter Vigil, or the third Sunday of Pentecost in the first year of the lectionary cycle or the second Sunday of Lent in the second year) about the purity of Abraham's heart, the primacy of his faith, and the magnificence of the sacrifice that his sacrifice led to: "The image of Isaac carrying the wood of the sacrifice tips us off that this story points beyond itself to a future sacrifice beyond all comprehension. The ram caught in the thicket is not the true substitute, and the true sacrifice does not take place upon Moriah. It is the Lamb, not the ram, God's Son, not Abraham's, that is offered. Like Isaac, he carried the wood of the sacrifice up the slope of Mt. Calvary. But unlike Isaac, he did so freely, knowing what that sacrifice would cost him. And his sacrifice accomplishes what no animal sacrifice could possibly accomplish—the eternal salvation of all willing to accept this free gift of love."

What that means is that there are Muslim parents who when asked by their children to explain the Festival of the Sacrifice (which comes on the tenth day of the last month of the Islamic calendar, at the height of the Haj, and during which, to this day, millions of Muslims sacrifice a goat, a cow, or a lamb, or arrange for someone to sacrifice one for them—one-third they eat, one-third they share with friends, one-third they give to the poor) quickly change the subject. Or explain that the lamb they have just sacrificed is the same one that will someday lead them to paradise over the knife-blade-narrow al-Sirat Bridge. Or tell them that Abraham knew that God wouldn't make him go through with it—no one he loved so much would hurt him or his son. And there are those who explain that they are commemorating Abraham's willingness to sacrifice what he loved most in the world without any expectation of reward, his demonstration that there was nothing he would not do for Allah.

That means that there are Jewish commentators who argue that Jews don't suffer or die for God, that Jews live for God, that the God of pain and suffering is a false god. And there are Jewish commentators who argue that they most certainly do. For the latter, Rabbi Joseph B. Soloveitchik, one of the twentieth century's seminal Jewish philosophers, Talmud scholars, and teachers of Modern Orthodoxy, is an irresistible authority. Soloveitchik once said that he "recoiled" from all the talk of how "the observance of *mitzvot* is beneficial for digestion, for sound sleep, for family harmony, and for social position." The religious act may end in joy, but it "is fundamentally an experience of suffering." God says: "Offer your sacrifice!" It started with Abraham: "He was not to fool himself in thinking that he'd get another son." Or that he would ever forget Isaac: "Out of your sleep you will call for Yitzchak, and when you wake up you will find your tent desolate and forsaken." Nevertheless, God demanded that sacrifice, and what began on that mountain continued in the great Temples built upon it and then in the synagogue and throughout our religious lives today: "Build an altar, arrange the pieces of wood. Kindle the fire. Take the knife to slaughter your existence for My sake. Thus commands the awesome God. This approach is the basis of prayer. Man surrenders himself to God. He approaches the awesome God and the approach expresses itself in the sacrifice and *Akedah* of oneself."

What that means is that there are mothers who blame God, as a mother does in Chava Cohen-Pinchas's poem "A Request." She's a nursing mother, baby in hand, her arms stretched out like the ram's horn in the bush. She asks God to listen, to make his "Sukkah of mercy / Like the shade of the vine and the fig." She asks him not to test her, not now of all times, not to play hide-and-seek. She calls out to him, as God called to Adam and Eve in the Garden, "*Ayekah*?" But he's not around:

With my short hand I cover my eyes
My voice is lost in a scream
With no Sound

*Where are you (*Ayekah).

And there are mothers, like the mother in Shin Shifrah's "Isaac," who blame themselves:

For me no ram was held in the thicket.
I bound
And I slaughtered.

God did not pay attention.
He laughed.

Not even the notion (seemingly as benign as it has been ubiquitous) that the story was originally a polemic against child sacrifice has gone uncontested. In recent years, Jon Levenson has made the most wide-ranging case against it, arguing that it is a kind of wishful thinking or apology that can't survive a close, critical, and clear-eyed reading of the text in the context of the Hebrew Bible and numerous other ancient Near Eastern sources. God says in Exodus: "You shall give Me the first-born among your sons." "Most fathers," Levenson writes, "did not have to carry out this hideous demand. But some did. Abraham knew it was his turn when he heard God in his own voice, ordering the immolation of Isaac."

At some point in time it became permissible, perhaps even preferable, to substitute an animal for a child. At some point, revealed law proscribed the sacrifice of children. In the seventh and sixth centuries BCE, prophets, usually attributing the practice to the influence of neighbors and their gods but in at least one instance (Ezekiel) attributing it to bad laws given as punishment by God, vehemently condemned it. But the very terms and the vehemence with which Ezekiel and Jeremiah waged war against child sacrifice suggest that the proscription did not take hold overnight.

Even as practice yielded to law and polemic, the religious idea behind it remained strong. So strong that Levenson considers it more precise to say that child sacrifice was not eradicated so much as it was transformed, transformed into rituals of donation (paschal offerings, consecration to the priesthood, circumcision, and prayer) and into narratives: Stories that express the idea that the beloved son belongs to God. Stories that express the idea that God's promise to Israel was grounded in a father's willingness to sacrifice his son. Stories that express the idea that the dire threat to Isaac, and Israel, was inseparable from the blessing, that God's chosen always suffer humiliation before they exult in redemption. And in Levenson's telling, that humiliation and redemption (death and resurrection) of latter-born but beloved sons in conflict with their older brothers did not end with Ishmael and Isaac and Esau and Jacob and Joseph and all his brothers. Rather, it ended up animating the great and long-lasting conflict between at least two more siblings: Judaism ("Tell Pharaoh that Israel is my firstborn son") and Christianity ("This is my beloved son, with whom I am well pleased").

Like just about everyone who has written about Genesis 22 since the publication of *The Last Trial,* Levenson is indebted to Shalom Spiegel. Spiegel, too, had seen child sacrifice behind the story and ancient understandings of it. He, too, had seen the celebration of an eager Abraham and a willing Isaac, of blood and ashes, of death and resurrection, rooted in the transformation or sublimation of practice into ritual and narrative. But whereas Spiegel identifies the practice as pagan and the idealization of it as an atavism that Jews sought to suppress, Levenson sees both practice and idealization as essential to Israelite and rabbinic theology. Whereas Spiegel is among those who imagine that the primary purpose of the story was to attach a great name to a new norm ("abolish human sacrifice, substitute animals instead"), Levenson demurs. God does not command the substitution. The story lacks the kind of phrase that often signals a biblical explanation ("and Abraham offered up the ram as a burnt offering instead of his son, as is done to this day"). And later tradition does not refer back to the incident as the reason for the redemption of the firstborn. Might the story have signaled the *permissibility* of substitution? Perhaps, Levenson says. But only modern distance from and enlightened distaste for the ideal of sacrifice could make it possible for readers to imagine that a story in which God commands Abraham to sacrifice Isaac and then rewards him for his willingness to do so was intended to reveal God's unequivocal opposition to human sacrifice.

.   .   .

It is a challenging and utterly absorbing interpretation. In some places it is simply dazzling. In others, merely profound. But it is not the last word. Heavens willing, that won't come until the end of time. There are others who believe that just because the story wasn't a polemic against or even a straightforward etiology of substitution doesn't mean it was, in the beginning, an explicit idealization of child sacrifice. Stories, they say (and Levenson himself repeatedly shows), work in such complicated ways. It is possible that it was neither a polemic nor celebration, but rather a story about God's care for all those who obey him, penned in a moment of deep despair about Israel's fate. It is also possible that, written or redacted long after the arguments about child sacrifice were settled, it was both a celebration of *and* a polemic against the practice. Israel gets to demonstrate that its God doesn't want it, and Israel also gets to celebrate the idea of it. Remember: there was a lot of talk: endless accounts of this king or that group of wayward people passing children through the fire; passages in Exodus in which God seems to ask for the firstborn; and one instance—the king of Moab, fighting against Israel—in which the sacrifice of a son appears to have been effective. Yet there is not a single instance in the entire Hebrew Bible in which an actual human sacrifice is celebrated.

Idealization is one way of reading the story, but it is just one of many possible ways of reading it, and even in Levenson's own account it is a reading that gets stronger as time goes on. Late Second Temple interpreters and then late-antique rabbis were more enthusiastic than anyone before them—or anyone whose sentiments we are aware of. Their enthusiasm reveals a lot about the theology of rabbinic Judaism, and perhaps, also, the relationship between it and early Christianity, but the later that enthusiasm comes, the less it tells us about earlier readings and meanings and contexts. When evidence comes from a dizzying number of times and places—and when so much of that evidence is difficult to interpret and some of it is difficult to date—it is almost inevitable that even the most critically and historically informed Bible scholars will be reading some of it backward, or at least in several different directions at once. I'd be the very last—the thought would never come to my mind—to fault Levenson for using rabbinic enthusiasm to suggest things about the story's ancient meanings and context. Nor for occasionally getting carried away and interpreting like a great medieval or late-antique rabbi himself, as he does when he says that when God called, "Abraham knew it was his turn."

We don't know that and can't know that from the story or its context. There is no other hint of child sacrifice in Abraham's day or anywhere else in Genesis. That Abraham knew exactly what to do when God called tells us no more than that he knew exactly where to go. God could have shown him one as easily as he showed him the other. Whenever it was written or redacted, whether we read it as actual history, an ancient folktale, or a sacred story, it is set in the imagined age of the Patriarchs, centuries before the appearance of the ritual, literature, archaeology, mythology, and law on which every possible historical argument for the practice or transformation of child sacrifice is based. We'll never know what Abraham was thinking. All we know for sure is what, in a story, he says and does. His silence is one that we, as historians, can't fill.

That means that there are some who can imagine themselves responding to God's call just as Abraham did, just as the poet Uri Zvi Greenberg imagines himself responding, in his impassioned tribute to Jerusalem, "city of the Father's glorious trial," where even on a rainy night, "that fire, kindled at dawn, still burns on the hill":

> *"If God were to command me now, as once He did*
> *My ancient Father—I would surely obey,"*
> *Sing my heart and my flesh on this night of rain,*
> *As the Angels of Peace stand at the head of my sleeping*
> *children!*

What can equal this glory, this wondrous zeal—
Alive since that ancient dawn to this very moment—for
the Mount of Moriah?
The blood of the covenant sings on in the father's fervent
body.
He is prepared to offer his sacrifice on the Temple Mount
at dawn.

And there are others, like Ra'yah Harnik, a poet and (after the first Lebanon war) a grieving mother who, writing just three decades later, in the early 1980s, turns Greenberg's and Abraham's "Here I am" into an equally emphatic "Here I am not":

I will not offer
My first born for sacrifice
Not I

At night God and I
Make reckonings
Who can claim what

I know and am
Grateful
But not my son
And not
for sacrifice

There is no end to it. Not a day goes by when someone, somewhere, doesn't add to it. Not a day. And even now, after all these years, I still haven't had my fill. But it wasn't all the biblical commentary or scholarship or even the ever-widening circle of conversation that initially drew me to the story or prompted me to write about it.

Awkward as it is to admit, I knew next to nothing about any of that when I began.

I came to it from an entirely different direction.

It was early in the third millennium. Dark days. Terror attacks had sparked a global war on terror and there was no end to either war or terror in sight. Wherever I turned, I heard the word "sacrifice." Eulogists praised soldiers for making the ultimate sacrifice. Proponents of staying the course in Iraq in the face of a fierce insurgency and the threat of civil war argued that if we withdrew, our dead would have sacrificed their lives in vain. Opponents called for the repeal of recently enacted tax cuts, and perhaps even a reinstatement of the military draft, to ensure that the sacrifice exacted in two surreally distant conflicts was not borne entirely by a few. Americans accused the parents of Afghani, Pakistani, and Iraqi suicide bombers of sacrificing their children. Afghanis, Pakistanis, and Iraqis accused coalition commanders of doing the same. One American antiwar activist, video camera in hand, stalked pro-war congressmen and prominent political commentators, asking them if they would sacrifice one of their children to retake Falujah, a city they had not heard of before 2004.

I started reading about sacrifice, and then child sacrifice, in history and literature, sacred and profane. I wanted to know who had sacrificed children and when and why. I found a slew of accusations (one group of people accusing another of sacrificing children) and a lively scholarly debate (truly heroic efforts to tease experience out of scant evidence) about which of those accusations were true. I also found the story of Abraham and Isaac, the ground zero of Western child sacrifice stories. Before long I had turned from books and essays *about* the story to the story itself, and then to all the Abraham stories in Genesis, and then to commentary on those stories, starting in antiquity.

It was an unexpected turn, but I was hardly the only one who had taken it. A lot of people were reading, talking, and writing about religion, especially religious extremism. And though the conversation was dominated by talk of Islamic extremism, fair-minded observers couldn't help but notice that here at home it was not only militant Muslims who posed a threat to pluralism, equality, freedom, and secular democracy. Right-wing Christians campaigned against gay rights, women's reproductive rights, sex education, contraception (even when it meant AIDS prevention), stem cell research, climate science, the teaching of evolution, and any number of other ungodly manifestions of the separation of the Christian church and the state. And when they turned their attention from social issues to mosques, madrassas, Qu'ran-carrying magistrates, and sharia law, they confirmed the fears of many, not all of them Muslim, that our wars near and far were at least part crusade. Jews had their extremists too, if just a few, a small minority of a small minority, but some of them—like the religious nationalists in the occupied territories and their allies in Israel proper—were worrisome way out of proportion to their numbers because, I'd like to think, of the tinderbox in which they lived and the roadblock they seemed to pose to Mideast peace. I couldn't help notice that many settlers based their claim to the West Bank on God's covenant with Abraham. Some threatened to die as martyrs before they gave up their land, no matter who, Arab or Jew, tried to take it away.

In the midst of all that, one small but exceedingly loud group of writers insisted that religion itself, not just resurgent fundamentalism, was at the root of all the trouble. Moderate and even liberal religion simply provided cover for the crazies, masking the unreason and the truly deleterious influence of the ideas and beliefs at religion's core. As they did, they ended up legitimating and reinforcing reactionary religious authority. Once you grant texts (or gods) authority, they said, you can't complain when people do things with them that you don't like.

In every indictment, Abraham was named. The charges extended well beyond his mistreatment of Isaac, a few bad days in a distant land a long time ago. Critics considered him culpable for what they took to be the long half-life of his perfect performance on God's gratuitous test: centuries of patriarchy, persecution, and abuse; crusading, jihad, and holy war; blind, deaf, and dumb obedience and faith. Who, they asked, could calculate the damage done by the idea (that we must be prepared to sacrifice what we hold most dear) at the heart of Abraham's devotion? When more sanguine observers objected to all that and maintained that he, the common father of Muslims, Christians, and Jews, was actually the last best hope for interfaith dialogue, reconciliation, and comity, his critics scoffed, pointing out that Abraham's descendants have fought over his inheritance, God's blessing for the ages, much more than they have gathered in peace around his table. What he really was was the father of killing in God's name. (And his apologists: they were the first to invoke the Nuremberg defense.) In every argument, the near sacrifice was introduced as evidence that God is a monster, or a delusion, or at best not so great. That people should give up their faith.

I had nothing in common with and little sympathy for fundamentalists or fanatics of any denomination, least of all for those whose absolute certainty contributed to their turn to violence. I had a host of things in common with even their harshest critics. Some of them were family and close friends. On many days I myself wondered what kind of God would, for no good reason, command a man to sacrifice his son, and why so many people would celebrate, as the patriarch of patriarchs, a man so prepared to obey. There were all sorts of things about Islam, Christianity, and Judaism, past and present, that rubbed me the wrong way, though I would be quick to add that I didn't and don't know remotely enough about any one of them to render a good or fair judgment. The idea of my judging religion, en bloc, was out of the question.

But by that time I did know something about Abraham and the story and, much to my surprise, I found myself inclined to stick up for him and it. I did not expect to persuade everyone to read the story as I read it. I do not now. But I did expect that at least a few would find, as I have found, more than a little consolation, perhaps even reason for hope, in the life of the story. I feel sure that even those who despise the story and dismiss as beside the point all my talk of Abraham as a character, the story as a story, and (most ludicrous of all) the author as an author (let alone an author who got the story wrong), will acknowledge that what people have made of Abraham and the story is much more complicated than the harshest criticism allows.

For one thing, readers have had misgivings from the beginning. If there was ever a time when people paid close attention to the story and were completely comfortable with it, as it was, on the page, a time readers didn't think it in need of repair, there is no record of it. But the devout didn't think they could get rid of it. Or take some wide detour around it. It stood between creation and nation, or salvation. So they asked questions, and answered them with commentary, interpretation, and stories, which in turn generated more questions, and more interpretation, and more stories.

Out of all that, dissenting traditions were born. In the second half of the eighth century BCE, the prophet Micah laid out a long list of things that God might want from him (calves a year old, thousands of rams, myriad streams of oil, his firstborn) before concluding that all he really wanted was for him to "do justice, and to love goodness, and to walk modestly" with his God. A century later Jeremiah went even further, saying that the idea of human sacrifice had never even entered God's mind. Some scholars say Micah paid homage to the ideal of child sacrifice in the very way that he argued that it wasn't what God wanted, and that Jeremiah protested way too much. Both, they say, were rewriting history, God's and Israel's early years. But even if they were, it is telling that they wanted people to believe their revisionist history and theology, and it is also telling that the rabbis who called attention to their words in the Mishnah and Talmud wanted people to believe it too. Just as it is telling that there were rabbis in late antiquity who imagined Abraham stalling, and rabbis who imagined him praying along the way that he wouldn't have to perform the sacrifice, and rabbis who imagined God's angels weeping at the injustice of it all, and rabbis who imagined God's daughter, the Torah, rejecting Abraham as a suitor because he didn't plead with God on behalf of his son.

Abraham has had critics forever. The story has been used as evidence that God abhors human sacrifice for nearly as long. And if martyrdom had not been hotly contested, apologists probably would not have gone to such great lengths to turn it into sacred historical precedent. Any honest appraisal of the merits and demerits of our religious traditions would have to take our interpretative traditions, all those questions and answers, all the things that people have done with what they have inherited, into account.

In fact, I couldn't imagine a better foil for the fiction at the heart of fundamentalism, in all its varieties, than the fluidity, multiplicity, and variety of revelation over time, the thinking and rethinking, the talk and the argument, the writing and rewriting, the vast array and mélange of meanings, the engagement with troubling texts, and the marriage (at times happy, at times troubled, at times both) of tradition and innovation. Nor could I imagine a better way to display that variety and fluidity than to shine some light on the long and protean life of nineteen lines of ancient literature, a story that many (including the vast majority of the people who have taken it into their own hands as if it were a clump of soft clay) believe to be the work of God.

It was then that it first occurred to me to write a brief history of the story, a book about some of the things that people have done with it, Muslims, Christians, and especially Jews, who have returned to it more often and have revised it in more different ways.

No sooner did that thought occur to me than I began to have doubts.

Where would I start? How would I ever get a handle on two thousand years of commentary and two hundred years of scholarship, to say nothing of all the ritual and liturgy and literature and drama and music and art? How would I figure out where to survey and where to take soundings, how to strike a balance between depth and breadth, when I would need to know more than I knew about a commentator's life and times to understand a particular commentary, when I would need to show or tell more to explain? Who would stick with me? How many at this late date would care? I felt a little like Kafka's Abraham: He has faith. He wants to do what he has been called to do, in the right spirit, in the right way, but he simply can't believe that it is he who has been called to do it.

It didn't help—though of course it did—that every single time I mentioned the project to anyone—every time, to anyone—he or she recommended a take on the story I just had to see, watch, listen to, read:

- An illustrated catechism one of my students had saved from Sunday school.
- An essay on the interpretation of dreams in medieval Islamic exegesis.
- A play written by the Calvinist theologian Theodore Beza, who put the devil in the costume of a monk.

· A public radio program on young people who are "losing" their religion. One thirty-three-year-old, who was raised a Muslim but is now an atheist, recalls hearing the story of Abraham when he was in the fifth or sixth grade: "His God tells him to sacrifice his son. Then he takes his son to sacrifice him, and he turns into a goat." And even back then he thought: "That's crazy! Why would this guy do this? Just because he heard a voice in his head, he went to sacrifice his son and it turned into a goat? There's no way that this happened. I wasn't buying it."
· Oratorios of Carissimi and Charpentier.
· A poem of Emily Dickinson.
· The commentary of the Lubavitcher Rebbe, recommended to me by a young Lubavitcher in Bryant Park. He had asked if I wanted to wrap tefillin. I said, "No, thank you," and then asked him if he wanted to talk about the *Akedah*. He lit up and asked: "Do you know why Abraham's sacrifice was the greatest of all sacrifices, greater even than all the martyrdom that came after?"

"Why?" I asked.

Because, he explained at great length, the martyr sacrifices his life in order to preserve his self: his beliefs, his ideals, his understanding of God, all the things he is and lives for. Abraham sacrificed his very self, thereby demonstrating that at the core of one's being lies not that self but the connection to the creator, the spark of divinity within. "Check out *Vayera*," he said, "at chabad.org." Later, I did. The entry is several thousand words, most of which he had recited by heart.
· Goldfaden's opera. Britten's canticle. Stravinsky's sacred ballad.
· The commentary of one imam, also posted on the Web, delivered in a Friday sermon during the Festival of the Sacrifice, recommended to me by another young man as I stood outside a midtown Manhattan mosque. The

prophet's greatness, the young man explained, was his willingness to sacrifice not just his life but his entire self to Allah.

· Agnon's *Only Yesterday*. Mossinsohn's *In the Negev Plains*. Makiya's *The Rock*. Saramago's *Cain*.

· Several recent Rosh Hashanah sermons in which rabbis have hypothesized that Isaac was living with Down syndrome or some other form of developmental disability.

· The drawings, paintings, sculptures, and photographs of Shoshana Heimann, Avraham Ofek, Menashe Kadishman, Natan Nuchi, and Adi Nes.

· "The Parable of the Old Man and the Young," penned by Wilfred Owen, an English poet and, in 1918, a soldier on the western front. Decades before his theme became a regular trope of antiwar protest ("It's always the old to lead us to the war, it's always the young to fall"), Owen's Isaac is a young soldier in the trenches, "bound" by his father "with belts and straps." Abraham stretches forth his knife. The angel says stop, points to the thicket, and commands him to offer the Ram of Pride instead:

> But the old man would not do so, but slew his son,
> And half the seed of Europe, one by one.

Owen's turn came as his unit crossed the Sambre-Oise Canal, at Ors, one week before the armistice ending the war was signed.

· The sculpture of George Segal, commissioned to commemorate the killings at Kent State, which sits in the shadow of the apse wall of the Princeton University Chapel. Sometime before I last visited, a vandal or prankster or found-art exegete placed a condom on Abraham's thigh-high knife.

· Any number of psychoanalytical interpretations, starting with that of Erich Wellisch, who sees in the near sacrifice

Abraham's effort to resolve the Oedipus conflict and overcome the death instinct with love.

· A rap song, a rock band, a clever British sketch comedy skit, countless comic strips (including *Peanuts*), a memoir (*The Last Testament*) attributed to God, and now (I kid you not) a video game called *The Binding of Isaac*. The object of the game is to keep Isaac away from his mentally ill mother, who believes God wants him as a sacrifice.

· The *Encyclopedia of the Bible and Its Reception,* in which the entry on the *Aqedah* is forty columns of fine print.

· A sixteenth- or seventeenth-century Cretan play, in verse.

· Sari Nusseibeh's *What Is a Palestinian State Worth?*

· A pivotal scene in Fatih Akin's *The Edge of Heaven,* in which a Muslim man, long estranged from his father, explains the Festival of the Sacrifice to a Christian friend.

"We have the same story," she says.

He recalls that as a child he was frightened by it. His mother had died young. He asked his father if he would sacrifice him if God asked.

"What did your father answer?" his friend asks.

"He said he would even make God his enemy in order to protect me."

· Avivah Zornberg's *Genesis: The Beginning of Desire.*

· Daniel Mendelsohn's *The Lost.*

· Orhan Pamuk's *The Museum of Innocence.*

· David Grossman's *To the End of the Land.*

· Yael Feldman's *Glory and Agony.*

· Chinua Achebe's *Things Fall Apart.*

I started writing. My doubts lingered. I wasn't the only one who had them.

My mother, heretofore the most loyal and indulgent fan of my work, repeatedly asked my wife and siblings why I was writing about "that" story, and she made no effort to hide her distress from me. Isaac's line alone ("the saddest line in all literature," she once said) was more than her heart could bear. It was visceral. Every time she overheard me talking about it, she would grab her head by the hair, as if she were trying to pull it out, and say, "Stop, stop. I hate that story. I can't listen to another word."

A trade book editor, another fan, said he was fascinated by the subject and intrigued by my take on it, but he wondered if I was qualified to write the book. "You have no training or special expertise in any relevant area," he said. "You don't even have the languages you would need."

"It is worse than that," I said to him (and forever afterward to anyone who would listen). "The real problem is not that I am not qualified. It is that I know how much I do not know."

A neighbor of mine, whose observance of Judaism includes the study of a page of Talmud a day, was even more skeptical. "There are limits to interpretation," he said, "boundaries you can't cross." He calls my approach "everyone gets a say" and "anything goes" and he thinks it makes the past a simple projection of the present. What I am doing, he believes, is substituting individual preference ("my story") for received tradition, the authority and collective wisdom of the men who have transmitted Scripture and revelation from generation to generation and together, as a religious community, continue that work today. "Don't surrender to the zeitgeist," he says. "Don't succumb to the rot that all truths are relative, interpretations equally valid, authorial intentions meaningless. Before you know it you'll be saying that the words belong to readers, that writers are merely the first of them, that the author is dead."

I assure him that reports of the death of the author are greatly exaggerated. Not even the rage for sampling, pastiche, homage, collage, impersonation, copying, pasting, mash-up, and flat-out plagiarism that has characterized the early digital age has killed him—or her. He's as alive as he has ever been, maybe more so.

Another neighbor, equally observant, objects (with a wry smile) every time I refer to the story as a story. "It is not a story," he says.

But I was determined or stubborn or foolhardy or simply in thrall with the material. And I thought the time was right. So I plowed ahead, reading and writing and talking (or so it seemed) about nothing else. Still, it did not come easily. Pages accumulated. If I told you how many it took to produce each one of these, you wouldn't believe me. If I showed you, you would worry. By the time I had a rough draft of the whole thing, years had passed and I could not call my history brief.

"How will you know when you're finished?" one friend asks me, about once a week. "When you have read enough?"

"It's hard to know," I say. "There is no end to it."

"Maybe not," he says, "but more does not equal better."

"Time's up," another says. "Put down your pen. Let go of it."

Those two could not be more enthusiastic about the project. Others are less so.

"You really want to celebrate this story?" one friend asks. We talk a lot. Sometimes we argue.

"I am not celebrating," I say. "I am showing what people have done with it."

"What they've done with it? You want to celebrate? You need to get out a little."

"Not everything," I say.

"What then? When?" another friend asks. "Not a day goes by that I don't see a photograph of the gruesome aftermath of a suicide bombing or some other form of religious violence. Haven't we had enough sacrifice? Enough doing in the name of God?"

"You are cherry-picking a meaning," I say.

"It's not as if it is an obscure meaning," he says.

"But it's just one," I say.

"Yes, one. What God asks, you do. What you think God wants, you do. Even kill."

"But we are not stuck with any one meaning," I say. "Not the original meaning, not the literal meaning, not the latest meaning, not the dominant meaning, not the meaning to a historian, not the meaning to a theologian, not the meaning to the most orthodox or the most reformed."

"I think a lot of people have been stuck with one meaning," he says. "Or struck. It is time to move on."

"Would that we could," I say.

"We can," he says. "But even if we couldn't, you are not just acknowledging lineage, deviant genes in our cultural pool. You are full of pride. You're trying to rehabilitate a terrible tradition by excavating and restoring a few rare artifacts."

"Some of those artifacts have become common currency," I say. "Others remain promising possibilities."

"You have drunk the Kool-Aid. Or turned Talmudic. You are so caught up in the minutiae, in the esoteric, in the tiniest twists and turns of text and interpretation, that you've completely lost sight of the big picture."

"Big pictures have their place," I say. "But so do the minutiae. The twists and turns. The give-and-take."

"One doesn't have to be an in-your-face atheist to dislike this story, you know. Or to be alarmed by your fondness for it."

"I want to keep the conversation going. It still—"

"Occasionally it inoculates someone against religion," he says. "That's the only good it does today."

"It still turns readers into writers," I say. "It forces us to think through and beyond what is written, and given. It makes us add and take away."

"Listen to you. Soon you'll be reciting Micah and Jeremiah. You love the story. You defend it as if you wrote it yourself."

And what could I say? I wanted to revise it and have it too.

I did, and I do.

Acknowledgments

~~~~~~~~~~~~~~~~

My greatest debt is to the scribes, translators, commentators, scholars, writers, and artists, only a small fraction of whom I have managed to mention in all these pages, who have wrestled with this story before me. Three scholars I must mention here are David Nirenberg, Barry Walfish, and Steve Whitfield. At the eleventh hour, each of them took the time to read the manuscript and provide essential encouragement, criticism, and suggestions for revision. No one, mentioned or unmentioned, bears any responsibility for my errors and missteps.

Two terrific institutions, one small (Paragraph, the writer's workspace on Fourteenth Street) and one large (the New York Public Library on Fifth Avenue and Forty-Second Street), provided me with a place to work at two critical moments toward the end. Thanks to Lila Cecil, Ally Collier, and Joy Parisi at Paragraph, and Jay Barksdale, Allen Room liaison at the library, for facilitating my residencies, and to so many fellow writers and scholars for fine and fun company during breaks.

My agent, Anne Edelstein, and my editor, Dan Frank, have once again been great readers, critics, and friends. Their support and their patience illuminate the limits of our understanding of both reason and faith. At Schocken Books, I am also grateful to Jillian Verrillo, Lindsey Ross, Muriel Jorgensen, Nicole Pedersen, and so many others whose names I do not know.

Ongoing support from chancellors, provosts, deans, department chairs, and department administrators at Rutgers University, Newark, where I teach history and creative writing, has made my writing life possible. These colleagues have not only tolerated my waywardness but actually cheered me on. Special thanks to David Hosford, Steve Diner, Phil Yeagle, Sallie Kasper, John Gunkel, Jack Lynch, Deborah Williams, Fran Bartkowski, Gary Farney, Clement Price, Christina Strasburger, and finally two dear friends as well as inspired leaders, Jan Lewis and Beryl Satter.

I have been working on this book for a long time, and there are so many others to thank, for so many different kinds of things: Noah Bickart, Barry Bienstock, Omri Boehm, Deb Bohr, Alice Dark, Naomi Danis, Vivian Dietz, Bruce Dorsey, Greg Downs, Dan Ernst, Joy Ernst, Jody Falco, Ruth Feldstein, Richard Gaskins, Rigoberto Gonzales, Rachel Hadas, Ellen Herman, Martha Hodes, Tayari Jones, John Keene, Diane Klein, David Lelyveld, John McGreevy, Jani Masur, Lou Masur, Matthew Moore, Jim Oakes, Jayne Anne Phillips, Aaron Sachs, Bob Sadowsky, Akhil Sharma, Brenda Shaughnessy, Jeffrey Steinman, Ezer Vierba, Sean Wilentz, Jeff Fischer, Eliza McFeely, Karen McFeely, Drake McFeely, Mary McFeely, Bill McFeely, Len Tesler, Wendy Goodman, Sue Weil, Sandy Goodman, Deb Bernstein, Bob Goodman, Jon Mohrer, Jill Mohrer, Jackson Goodman, Samuel Goodman, Jennifer McFeely, Burton Goodman, and most of all my mother, Rachel Lehr. She really did hate the story, but she still would have loved this book.

Notes

~~~~~~

CHAPTER 2

14 the way the opening: Genesis 12:1 and 22:1.

CHAPTER 3

23 "Face to face the Lord": Deuteronomy 5:4–6.

23 someone would revise it: For a lively and concise introduction to the
voluminous literature on biblical origins and authorship, see Richard Elliott Friedman, *Who Wrote the Bible?* (San Francisco, 1997),
and Friedman, *The Bible with Sources Revealed: A New View into
the Five Books of Moses* (San Francisco, 2003). For a sense of how
fluid our understanding of the sources remains, even in the work of
individual scholars committed to one approach or another, compare
both books to the first edition of Friedman, *Who Wrote the Bible?*
(New York, 1987). For a guide to reading the Bible that also provides an engaging introduction to the documentary hypothesis and
source criticism and teems with useful insight and references to recent
scholarship, see James L. Kugel, *How to Read the Bible: A Guide to
Scripture, Then and Now* (New York, 2007). My ideas about inner-
biblical exegesis and revision have been shaped by Kugel, as well as
by Michael Fishbane, *Biblical Interpretation in Ancient Israel* (New
York, 1985), and numerous contributions to the *Jewish Study Bible,*
especially Benjamin D. Sommer, "Inner-Biblical Interpretation," and
the introductions and annotations to Genesis, Exodus, and Deuteronomy, written by Jon D. Levenson, Jeffrey H. Tigay, and Bernard M.
Levinson, respectively, all in Adele Berlin and Marc Zvi Brettler, eds.,
The Jewish Study Bible (New York, 2004). Two other translations
and commentaries are also ragged from daily use: Robert Alter, *The
Five Books of Moses: A Translation with Commentary* (New York,

2004), and Everett Fox, *The Five Books of Moses: A New Translation with Introductions, Commentary, and Notes* (New York, 1995). I have taken my epigraph from Alter.

CHAPTER 4

24 Jubilees: R. H. Charles's translation (1917) is readily available online at http://www.sacred-texts.com/bib/jub/. But see also the translation of O. S. Wintermute, in James H. Charlesworth, ed., *The Old Testament Pseudepigrapha*, 2 vols. (New York, 1983), 2:35–142. My translations come, as noted, from Wintermute; from James C. VanderKam, ed. and trans., *The Book of Jubilees*, 2 vols. (Lovain, Belgium, 1989); and from the more readily available excerpts in James L. Kugel, *Traditions of the Bible: A Guide to the Bible as It Was at the Start of the Common Era* (Cambridge, 1998); Kugel, *How to Read the Bible: A Guide to Scripture, Then and Now* (New York, 2007); and also Kugel, "Exegetical Notes on 4Q225 'Pseudo-Jubilees,'" *Dead Sea Discoveries* 13 (2006): 73–98.

25 she was taken from him: Jubilees 13:10–15.

25 the author of Nehemiah: Nehemiah 9:7–8.

26 Ben Sira: Sirach (Ecclesiasticus) 44:20.

26 book of Judith: Judith 8:26–27.

26 One poet, a contemporary, boasted: Philo the Epic Poet, fragments 1–2, in Eusebius, "Preparation for the Gospel" 9.20.1, reprinted in H. Attridge, "Philo the Epic Poet: A New Translation and Introduction," in Charlesworth, *The Old Testament Pseudepigrapha*, 2:783.

27 "one who loved the Lord": Jubilees 17:17–18, in VanderKam, *The Book of Jubilees*, 2:105.

28 "one who fears the Lord": Jubilees 18:9, in Kugel, "Exegetical Notes."

28 "your first-born son": Jubilees 18:10–11, in Kugel, "Exegetical Notes."

28 instead of his son: See Jubilees 18:12. See also Wintermute, in Charlesworth: "And Prince Mastema was shamed. And Abraham lifted up his eyes and saw a ram was caught in the thicket by his horns. And Abraham went and took the ram and placed it up for a burnt offering instead of his son. . . . It is Mount Zion."

28 "Go in peace": Jubilees 18:16, in Kugel, "Exegetical Notes." See also Wintermute, in Charlesworth: "And all the nations of the earth will bless themselves by your seed because you obeyed my word. And I have made known to all that you are faithful to me in everything that I say to you."

28 We show them: Kugel, "Exegetical Notes."

29 Abraham observed Passover: James C. VanderKam, *The Book of Jubilees,* a volume in the series Guides to Apocrypha and Pseudepigrapha (Sheffield, 2001), 52–53; Shalom Spiegel, *The Last Trial: On the Legends and Lore of the Command to Abraham to Offer Isaac as a Sacrifice: The Akedah* (New York 1967), 51–59 and passim; Jon D. Levenson, *The Death and Resurrection of the Beloved Son: The Transformation of Child Sacrifice in Judaism and Christianity* (New Haven, Conn., 1993), 176–199.

CHAPTER 5

30 Philo: Philo, *On Abraham* 32–37 (Colson, Loeb Classical Library, 289). See *Philo,* 12 vols. (Cambridge, 1929–62). *On Abraham* is in volume 6.

31 "neither bent nor wavered": Philo, *On Abraham* 32.170.

31 would have known the stories: For Leos and Aristodemus, see Pausanias, *Description of Greece,* 1.5.2; Jerome, *Against Jovinianus,* 1.41; and Diodorus Siculus, *Library of History* 17.15, all cited in Shalom Spiegel, *The Last Trial: On the Legends and Lore of the Command to Abraham to Offer Isaac as a Sacrifice: The Akedah* (New York, 1967), 9–12. For Athamas, Phrixus, Helle, and Jason, see Apollonius of Rhodes, *Jason and the Golden Fleece,* trans. Richard Hunter (New York, 1993).

33 Jephthah: Judges 11.

33 king of Moab: Kings 3:27.

35 he risked his life: Josephus, *Jewish Antiquities* 18.8 (Thackeray, LCL, 242); Philo, *On the Embassy to Gaius* (Colson, LCL, 379).

CHAPTER 6

36 Flavius Josephus: Flavius Josephus, *Jewish War, Jewish Antiquities,* and *The Life.* See *Josephus,* 13 vols. (Cambridge, Loeb Classical Library, 1926–65). The story of the near sacrifice is told in *Jewish Antiquities* 1.222–236 (Thackeray, LCL, 242).

37 "find him obedient": Josephus, *Jewish Antiquities* 1.233–234 (Thackeray, LCL, 242).

37 God found "surprising": See Josephus, *Jewish Antiquities* 1.234, in William Whiston's translation, in *The New Complete Works of Josephus,* revised and expanded, translated by William Whiston and commentary by Paul L. Maier (Grand Rapids, Mich., 1999), 68.

37 the rites of sacrifice: Josephus, *Jewish Antiquities* 1.228–231.

38 awash with Jewish blood: See, in addition to Josephus himself, Martin Goodman, *Rome and Jerusalem: The Clash of Ancient Civilizations* (New York, 2007).

39 "how he tested Isaac": Judith 8:26.

39 in mind as well as body: Philo, *On Abraham* 32.172 (Colson, LCL, 289).

39 made his way to the altar: Josephus, *Jewish Antiquities* 1.232.

40 his exact age: Josephus, *Jewish Antiquities* 1.227. Scholars using Jubilees's calendar and chronology to calculate Isaac's age have come up with both fifteen and sixteen. Rabbis would later estimate both twenty-six and what would become the most common rabbinical estimate, thirty-seven. See *Genesis Rabbah* 54:6 and 56:8, in H. Freedman and Maurice Simon, eds. and trans., *Midrash Rabbah*, 10 vols. (New York, 1939, 1983). See also Ibn Ezra on Genesis 22:4 in Abraham Ibn Ezra, *Ibn Ezra's Commentary on the Pentateuch* (New York, 1988), 224–225.

CHAPTER 7

41 Pseudo-Philo: *Liber Antiquitatum Biblicarum (L.A.B.)* 18:5, 32:1–4, and 40:2. See D. J. Harrington, "Pseudo-Philo: A New Translation and Introduction," in James H. Charlesworth, *The Old Testament Pseudepigrapha*, 2 vols. (New York, 1983), 2:297–377, and Howard Jacobson, *A Commentary on Pseudo-Philo's Liber Antiquitatum Biblicarum with Latin Text and English Translation,* 2 vols. (Leiden, 1996).

42 "eternal life and time without measure": Pseudo-Philo, *L.A.B.* 32.3, as quoted in James L. Kugel, *How to Read the Bible: A Guide to Scripture, Then and Now* (New York, 2007), 26, and Kugel, *Traditions of the Bible: A Guide to the Bible as It Was at the Start of the Common Era* (Cambridge, 1998), 175. See also Harrington, "Pseudo-Philo" ("Come and inherit life without limit and time without measure") and Jacobson, *A Commentary on Pseudo-Philo's Liber Antiquitatum Biblicarum* ("Come and inherit a secure life and time without measure").

42 "a human soul worthy for sacrifice": Pseudo-Philo, *L.A.B.* 32.3, as quoted in James L. Kugel, *How to Read the Bible,* 126, and Kugel, *Traditions of the Bible,* 175. See also Jacobson ("The Lord has deemed the soul of a man worthy to be a sacrifice") and Harrington ("The Lord has made the soul of a man worthy to be a sacrifice").

42 Jephthah: Judges 11.

42 "seeing the people freed?": Pseudo-Philo, *L.A.B.* 40:2 (Harrington).

See also Jacobson ("Who is there who would be sad to die, seeing the people freed?").

42 "the one who was offering was rejoicing": Pseudo-Philo, *L.A.B.* 40.2 (Harrington). See also Jacobson: "Or have you forgotten what happened in the days of our fathers when the father placed the son as a burnt offering, and he did not dispute him but gladly gave consent to him, and the one being offered was ready and the one who was offering was rejoicing."

43 Antiochus IV: Martin Goodman, *Rome and Jerusalem: The Clash of Ancient Civilizations* (New York, 2007), 49.

43 hurled from the walls: 2 Maccabees 6:10–18 and 4 Maccabees 4:23–26.

43 burned alive: 2 Maccabees 6:11.

44 Eleazar: See 4 Maccabees 8:1–18:24 and 2 Maccabees 7:1–42.

44 "take my life as a ransom for theirs": 4 Maccabees 6:1–31, in H. Anderson, "4 Maccabees: A New Translation and Introduction," in Charlesworth, *The Old Testament Pseudepigrapha*, 2: 531–564. See also 2 Maccabees 6:18-31.

44 "the same mind as Abraham": 4 Maccabees 14:20 (NRSV).

44 "did not cower": 4 Maccabees 16:20 (NRSV).

44 "sacrificed for piety's sake": 4 Maccabees 13:12 (H. Anderson).

47 They gave her a name, Miriam: *Lamentations Rabbah* 1.16.50, in H. Freedman and Maurice Simon, trans. *Midrash Rabbah*, 10 vols. (New York, 1939, 1983), 7:133.

CHAPTER 8

49 The glory of Jewish literature: Josephus, *Against Apion* 1.37–47 (Thackeray, Loeb Classical Library, 186). Josephus added that every Jew not only abides by those books, but if need be would cheerfully die for them. But the Greek: "Even to save the entire collection of his nation's writings from destruction, he would not face the smallest personal injury."

50 we would be lost: Those who have read anything by James Kugel, or heard one of his engrossing public lectures, will know that I have borrowed and I am employing his "four assumptions," the assumptions about the biblical literature that so many ancient interpreters shared, assumptions with which ancient interpreters not only read sacred texts but, in Kugel's telling, actually created one, by which he means took an anthology of ancient literature and made it, interpreted it, into the Bible. See Kugel, *Traditions of the Bible: A Guide to the Bible as It Was at the Start of the Common Era* (Cambridge, 1998) and

How to Read the Bible: A Guide to Scripture, Then and Now (New York, 2007).

CHAPTER 9

52 whose atoning sacrifice came first: For a relatively recent and relatively concise (considering the extent and complexity of the debate), overview, see Edward Kessler, *Bound by the Bible: Jews, Christians and the Sacrifice of Isaac* (Cambridge, 2004), 8–36. For a deeper immersion I have learned from Geza Vermes, "Redemption and Genesis XXII" in *Scripture and Tradition in Judaism* (Leiden, 1961), 193–227; Philip R. Davies and Bruce D. Chilton, "The Aqedah: A Revised Tradition History," *Catholic Biblical Quarterly* 40 (October 1978): 514–546; Hans Joachim Schoeps, "The Sacrifice of Isaac in Paul's Theology," *Journal of Biblical Literature* 65 (December 1946): 385–392; Robert J. Daly, "Soteriological Significance of the Sacrifice of Isaac," *Catholic Biblical Quarterly* 39 (January 1977): 45–75; Alan F. Segal, " 'He Who Did Not Spare His Own Son': Jesus, Paul, and the Akedah," in *From Jesus to Paul* (Waterloo, Ont., 1984), 169–184; and Segal, "The Akedah: Some Reconsiderations," in *Geschichte—Tradition—Reflexion* (Tubingen, 1996), 99–116. Absolutely essential for understanding the relationship between Jewish and Christian stories and scripture more broadly is Jon D. Levenson, *The Death and Resurrection of the Beloved Son: The Transformation of Child Sacrifice in Judaism and Christianity* (New Haven, Conn., 1993). Levenson's latest book, *Inheriting Abraham: The Legacy of the Patriarch in Judaism, Christianity, and Islam* (Princeton, N.J., 2012), was published just as I was putting this book to bed, but I am certain it will also be essential to our understanding of the similarities and differences between the Abrahams and the "sacrifices" of Judaism, Christianity, and Islam.

52 Targums: See, for example, "Vayera," in J. W. Etheridge, *The Targums of Onkelos and Jonathan Ben Uzziel on the Pentateuch, with the Fragments of the Jerusalem Targum from the Chaldee* (New York, 1968), and Michael L. Klein, *The Fragment-Targums of the Pentateuch: According to Their Extant Sources,* 2 vols. (Rome, 1980), 2: 16–17, 103–104.

53 James Kugel: James L. Kugel, "Exegetical Notes on 4Q225 'Pseudo-Jubilees,' " *Dead Sea Discoveries* 13 (2006): 73–98, and Geza Vermes, "New Light on the Sacrifice of Isaac from 4Q225," *Journal of Jewish Studies* 47 (Spring 1996): 140–146.

55 Epistle to the Hebrews: Hebrews 11:1–39.

CHAPTER 10

58 *pistos:* James L. Kugel, *How to Read the Bible: A Guide to Scripture, Then and Now* (New York, 2007), 122–123, and, in even more depth, Kugel, *Traditions of the Bible: A Guide to the Bible as It Was at the Start of the Common Era* (Cambridge, 1998), 308–311.

58 "Fear not, Abram": Genesis 15:1–6 (Alter).

58 Origen: Origen, *Homily on Genesis* 8.5, in *Homilies on Genesis and Exodus*, vol. 71 in the series The Fathers of the Church (Washington, D.C., 1982), 140.

59 Bishop Succensus: Succensus, *Catena* 1250, quoted in Edward Kessler, *Bound by the Bible: Jews, Christians and the Sacrifice of Isaac* (Cambridge, 2004), 94.

60 no mystery about its meaning: For the typological understanding of the story, the best place to start is with Melito of Sardis. I arrived by way of Kessler, *Bound by the Bible,* and then moved on to Robert L. Wilken, "Melito, the Jewish Community at Sardis, and the Sacrifice of Isaac," *Theological Studies* 37 (1976): 53–69. But cf. Paul R. Trebilco, *Jewish Communities in Asia Minor* (Cambridge, 1991).

62 The Jews were the ass: Cyril of Alexandria, *Glaph. in Genesis,* PG 69 141B-C, quoted in Kessler, *Bound by the Bible,* 93. See also B. Lee Blackburn Jr., "The Mystery of the Synagogue: Cyril of Alexandria on the Law of Moses" (Ph.D. diss., Notre Dame, 2009).

63 the early Christians: Kessler, *Bound by the Bible,* looks at the responses of the church fathers to Genesis 22:1–14, line by line.

63 argued about everything: For a lively and accessible introduction to many of these arguments, see virtually any of Elaine H. Pagels's books, but especially *The Gnostic Gospels* (New York, 1979); *The Origin of Satan* (New York, 1995); and *Beyond Belief: The Secret Gospel of Thomas* (New York, 2003).

65 Augustine: I started with Peter Brown, *Augustine of Hippo* (Berkeley, 1967, 2000) and more recently I have benefited from Paula Fredriksen, *Augustine and the Jews: A Christian Defense of Jews and Judaism* (New York, 2008). Two review essays helped me put Fredriksen's interpretation in the context of the existing literature and history: Jeremy Cohen, "Revisiting Augustine's Doctrine of Jewish Witness," *Journal of Religion* 89 (2009): 564–578, and David Nirenberg, "Slay Them Not," *New Republic* 240 (March 18, 2009): 42–47.

CHAPTER 11

68 midrash: I started with several terrific introductions, most of them written by scholars for general readers, and went from there to trans-

lations of the primary sources, especially H. Freedman and Maurice Simon, eds. and trans. *Midrash Rabbah,* 10 vols. (New York, 1939, 1983) and Menahem Kasher, *Encyclopedia of Biblical Interpretation: A Millennial Anthology (EBI)* (New York, 1953). See Yaakov Elman, "Classical Rabbinic Interpretation" and David Stern, "Midrash and Jewish Interpretation," both in Adele Berlin and Marc Zvi Brettler, eds., *The Jewish Study Bible* (New York, 2007); Lawrence H. Schiffman, *From Text to Tradition: A History of Second Temple and Rabbinic Judaism* (Hoboken, N.J., 1991); Shaye J. D. Cohen, *From the Maccabees to the Mishnah* (Philadelphia, 1987); and Adin Steinsaltz, *The Essential Talmud* (New York, 1976). Also useful, each in its own way, are George Robinson, *Essential Torah: A Complete Guide to the Five Books of Moses* (New York, 2006), and Jacob Neusner and Alan J. Avery-Peck, *Encyclopedia of Midrash: Biblical Interpretation in Formative Judaism,* 2 vols. (Leiden, 2005).

68 the Talmud's midrash: See, for example, b. Sanhedrin 89b.

69 to elevate him, like a banner: *Genesis Rabbah* 55:1,6.

69 tests the righteous: *Genesis Rabbah* 55:2. See also Ramban on Genesis 22:1, in Ramban (Nachmanides), *The Torah with Ramban's Commentary,* translated, annotated, and elucidated by Yaakov Blinder et al. (Brooklyn, 2004).

70 "counteract the sword grasped by Pharaoh": *Genesis Rabbah* 55:8.

70 leave his side to relieve himself: *Leviticus Rabbah* 26:7; *Genesis Rabbah* 55:8; *EBI,* 3:137.

70 "live in his presence": *Genesis Rabbah* 55:6, 56:1.

71 Isaac and Ishmael arguing: For three older versions of this oft-repeated-and-revised midrash, see b. Sanhedrin 89b; *Genesis Rabbah* 55:4; and *Tanhuma, Wayyera,* 4.42, in John T. Townsend, ed. and trans., *Midrash Tanhuma* (Hoboken, N.J., 1989). See also *EBI,* 3:128–129.

72 before anyone tried to stop him: *EBI,* 3:135–137.

72 "Are you crazy?": My paraphrase of *Genesis Rabbah* 56:4.

73 leaving him unfit for sacrifice: *Genesis Rabbah* 56:5; *EBI,* 3:139.

73 "Take your son": b. Sanhedrin 89b; *Genesis Rabbah* 55:7; *EBI,* 3:12–17 and 132–133.

74 "I am not a priest": *Genesis Rabbah* 55:7.

74 that look would have been his last: *Genesis Rabbah* 56:8; *EBI,* 3:143 and 145.

75 God answered his prayers: b. Ta'anit 2. What follows "prevarication" is my paraphrase of Abraham's complaint in *Genesis Rabbah* 56:8.

75 "Now take him down": *Genesis Rabbah* 56:8; *EBI*, 3:132. See also *Tanhuma, Wayyera*, 4.40, in Townsend, ed., *Midrash Tanhuma*.

75 never even entered God's mind: b. Ta'anit 4a; Jeremiah 19:5.

76 "By My own Self I swear": *Tanhuma*, cited in Jacob Culi, *The Torah Anthology*, Me'Am Lo'ez (New York, 1977), 2:336, and Louis Ginzberg, *The Legends of the Jews* (Philadelphia, 1909–1938), 1:282.

76 never test him like that again: *Genesis Rabbah* 56:11.

76 "filled with compassion for them": *Genesis Rabbah* 56:10.

76 "redeemed by the ram's horn": *Genesis Rabbah* 56:9.

77 "Your city, Your land, Your heritage": *ArtScroll Transliterated Linear Siddur* (New York, 1998), 81–87.

CHAPTER 12

78 Exodus! Exodus 32:11–14.

78 Ezekiel: Ezekiel 14 and 18.

79 the promise at the heart of it would be irrevocable: See the notes to Exodus 11–14 in Adele Berlin and Marc Zvi Brettler, eds., *The Jewish Study Bible* (New York, 2004), 184–185.

79 "the will of his creator": *Genesis Rabbah* 56:8.

79 "Nothing. Not a blemish": *Genesis Rabbah* 56:7.

80 "on top of the altar before Thee": See the text and notes in Shalom Spiegel, *The Last Trial: On the Legends and Lore of the Command to Abraham to Offer Isaac as a Sacrifice: The Akedah* (New York, 1967), 60–62 and passim, and *Genesis Rabbah* 56:9.

80 not instead of Isaac: *Genesis Rabbah* 56:9 in H. Freedman and Maurice Simon, eds. and trans. *Midrash Rabbah*, 10 vols. (New York, 1939, 1983).

80 "until a quarter of his blood left him": *Tanhuma, Wa-Yera* 23, quoted in Spiegel, *The Last Trial*, 48.

80 "some other victim in your place": *Yalkut* 101, quoted in Spiegel, *The Last Trial*, 48.

81 "the blood of Isaac's sacrifice": Menahem Kasher, *Encyclopedia of Biblical Interpretation: A Millennial Anthology (EBI)* (New York, 1953) 3:156, and Spiegel, *The Last Trial*, 51–59.

81 " 'Enough! Stay your hand!' ": 1 Chronicles 21:14–15; Spiegel, *The Last Trial*, 51–59; and *EBI*, 3:156.

81 "the ashes of the Akedah of Isaac": Spiegel, *The Last Trial*, 38–44.

81 On Mount Moriah: Ibid.

82 "the foundation of that altar": Ibid., 43–44.

82 "for our sake Isaac's ashes": b. Ta'anit 16a, cited in Spiegel, *The Last Trial,* 42–43.

84 the gathering before the water gate: Nehemiah 8:1–9.

85 Johanan ha-Kohen: Abraham I. Shafir, "'Az Terem'—A Piyyut by Yochanan Hacohen." *Hebrew Studies* 45 (2004): 232–252. See also Abraham Shafir, "Akedat Yitzhak—New Perspectives," Bar-Ilan University's Parashat Hashavua Study Center, Parashat Va-Yera 5767 (November 11, 2006), online at http://www.biu.ac.il/JH/Parasha/eng /vayera/sha.html.

CHAPTER 13

88 "Abraham rose early the next morning": See, for example, Samuel A. Berman, *Midrash Tanhuma-Yelammedenu: An English Translation of Genesis and Exodus from the Printed Version of Tanhuma-Yelammedenu with an Introduction, Notes, and Indexes* (Hoboken, N.J., 1996), 143.

89 Then she died: See, for example, Avivah Gottlieb Zornberg, "Cries and Whispers: The Death of Sarah," in Gail Twersky Reimer and Judith A. Kates, *Beginning Anew: A Woman's Companion to the High Holy Days* (New York, 1997), 174–200; David Goldstein, *Jewish Legends,* rev. ed. (New York, 1987). See and compare to Louis Ginzberg, *The Legends of the Jews* (Philadelphia, 1909–1938).

89 "And Sarah's life": Genesis 23 (Alter).

89 "He came from Mount Moriah": *Genesis Rabbah* 58:5.

89 Basil of Seleucia: *Orat.* 7, quoted in Edward Kessler, *Bound by the Bible: Jews, Christians and the Sacrifice of Isaac* (Cambridge, 2004), 75.

89 Gregory, bishop of Nyssa: Gregory of Nyssa, *De Deitate* PG 46 569A, quoted in Kessler, *Bound by the Bible,* 75–76.

90 fifth- and sixth-century verse homilists: I first encountered references to Romanos and the Syriac homilies in three books, Louis A. Berman, *The Akedah: The Binding of Isaac* (Northvale, N.J., 1997); Burton L. Visotzky, *Reading the Book: Making the Bible a Timeless Text* (New York, 1996); and Kessler, *Bound by the Bible.* From there I found my way to Mikhalis Moshkos, "Romanos' Hymn on the Sacrifice of Abraham: A Discussion of the Sources and a Translation," *Byzantion* 44 (1974): 311–328; R. J. Schork, *Sacred Song from the Byzantine Pulpit: Romanus the Melodist* (Gainesville, Fla., 1995); Sebastian P. Brock, "Genesis 22 in Syriac Tradition," in *Mélanges*

Dominique Barthélemy (Fribourg, 1981), 1–30; Brock, "Genesis 22: Where Was Sarah?," *Expository Times* 96 (October 1984): 14–17; Brock, "Reading Between the Lines: Sarah and the Sacrifice of Isaac (Genesis, Chapter 22)," in *Women in Ancient Societies* (New York, 1994), 169–180; and especially Brock, *From Ephrem to Romanos: Interactions Between Syriac and Greek in Late Antiquity* (Brookfield, Vt., 1999). Also essential is Susan Ashbrook Harvey, "Spoken Words, Voiced Silence: Biblical Women in Syriac Tradition," *Journal of Early Christian Studies* 9 (2001): 105–131.

91 "borne trials along with you?": All my paraphrases and quotations from this homily, which Sebastian Brock refers to as "Memra I," are based on or taken from Brock's translation from the Syriac, in Brock, "Two Syriac Verse Homilies on the Binding of Isaac," in Brock, *From Ephrem to Romanos,* 108–112.

92 and then to God: Memra I, in Brock, "Two Syriac Verse Homilies," 110.

92 Your father won't: All my paraphrases of and quotations from Romanos are based on or taken directly from Moshkos, "Romanos' Hymn on the Sacrifice of Abraham." Cf. R. J. Schork's engaging and enlightening translation and commentary, Schork, *Sacred Song from the Byzantine Pulpit.*

93 "a short time": Romanos, in Moshkos, "Romanos' Hymn," 322–323. Cf. Romanos, in Schork, *Sacred Song from the Byzantine Pulpit,* 153.

93 the world to come: Romanos, in Moshkos, "Romanos' Hymn," 23–24.

93 "Go in peace": Memra II, in Brock, "Two Syriac Verse Homilies," 123.

94 ultimately wouldn't have to: Romanos, in Moshkos, "Romanos' Hymn," 320.

94 "receive my spirit": Ibid., 326–327.

94 "bones in the fire": Memra I, in Brock, "Two Syriac Verse Homilies," 111.

94 "gave you back": Ibid.

95 "her mind and her thoughts": Ibid., 124.

95 "I was wishing I was an eagle": Ibid., 125.

95 "who died and was resurrected": Ibid.

96 no telling what others might do with them: Those interested in Sarah in mid-first-millennium exegesis should also look at the Bodmer Poem. For a recent reading, see Ton Hilhorst, "The Bodmer Poem on

the Sacrifice of Abraham," in Edward Noort and Eibert Tigchelaar, eds., *The Sacrifice of Isaac: The Aqedah (Genesis 22) and Its Interpretations* (Leiden, 2002), 96–108.

CHAPTER 14

98 Islam: This entire chapter takes off from and owes an enormous debt to the scholarship, prodigious as it has been pathbreaking, of Reuven Firestone. See Firestone, *Journeys in Holy Lands: The Evolution of the Abraham-Ishmael Legends in Islamic Exegesis* (Albany, N.Y., 1990); Firestone, "Merit, Mimesis, and Martyrdom: Aspects of Shi'ite Meta-historical Exegesis on Abraham's Sacrifice in Light of Jewish, Christian, and Sunni Muslim Tradition," *Journal of the American Academy of Religion* 66 (Spring 1998): 93–116; Firestone, "Comparative Studies in Bible and Qur'an: A Fresh Look at Genesis 22 in the Light of Sura 37," in *Judaism and Islam: Boundaries, Communications, and Interaction: Essays in Honor of William M. Brinner* (Leiden, Boston, 2000); and Firestone, "The Qūr'ān and the Bible: Some Modern Studies of Their Relationship," in *Bible and Qūr'ān* (Atlanta, 2003), 1–22. Also useful and enlightening are F. Leemhuis, "Ibrahim's Sacrifice of His Son in the Early Post-Koranic Tradition," in Edward Noort and Eibert Tigchelaar, eds., *The Sacrifice of Isaac: The Aqedah (Genesis 22) and Its Interpretations* (Leiden, 2002); F. V. Greifenhagen, "Cooperating Revelations? Qur'an, Bible, and Intertextuality," *ARC* 33 (2005): 302–317; Ayaz Afsar, "A Comparative Study of the Intended Sacrifice of Isaac/Ishmael in the Bible and the Qūr'ān," *Islamic Studies* 46 (2007): 483–498; and Mishael Caspi, *The Binding (Aqedah) and Its Transformations in Judaism and Islam: The Lambs of God* (Lewiston, N.Y., 1995).

99 "This is from God": Qur'an 2:78–79, cited in Firestone, *Journeys in Holy Lands,* 15. See also Arberry, 2:72: "And some there are of them that are common folk not knowing the Book, but only fancies and mere conjectures. So woe to those who write the Book with their hands, then say, 'This is from God.'" A. J. Arberry, *The Koran Interpreted* (New York, 1955).

101 If that's what God wants, let's do it: Firestone, *Journeys in Holy Lands,* 107–115.

101 we do not stray: Ibid., 116–128.

103 "let him into paradise": Ibid., 129–134.

104 "I offered myself up before Thee as a sacrifice!": b. Shabbat 89b. See also Firestone, *Journeys in Holy Lands,* 133.

104 pardon for his descendants through the ages: Firestone, *Journeys in Holy Lands,* 135–151.

105 Their starting point was the Qur'an: Qur'an 37:99–115 (Arberry).

106 Galatians: 4:21–31.

107 polemical and pointed: All three of the quotes that follow come from Firestone, "Merit, Mimesis, and Martyrdom," 99–100.

108 "people disagree about them": Firestone, *Journeys in Holy Lands,* 135. For another view of the debate, especially the chronology, see Leemhuis, "Ibrahim's Sacrifice of His Son in the Early Post-Koranic Tradition." For the place of the conflict between Shiites and Sunnis in the debate about the identity of the nearly sacrificed son, see Firestone, "Merit, Mimesis, and Martyrdom."

CHAPTER 15

110 as good as it got: For the best of times, see Maria Rosa Menocal, *The Ornament of the World: How Muslims, Jews, and Christians Created a Culture of Tolerance in Medieval Spain* (Boston, 2002). For an extraordinarily sophisticated and nuanced view of the complicated relationship between anti-Jewish violence and community, see David Nirenberg, *Communities of Violence: Persecution of Minorities in the Middle Ages* (Princeton, N.J., 1996).

111 *Pirke de Rabbi Eliezer: Pirke de Rabbi Eliezer (The Chapters of Rabbi Eliezer the Great) According to the Text of the Manuscript Belonging to Abraham Epstein of Vienna,* translated and annotated with introduction and indexes by Gerald Friedlander (New York, 1965), 223.

112 nearly sacrificed himself: See *Sifre Deuteronomy* 32.

112 view of the divine presence: See *Fragmentary Targum,* quoted in Geza Vermes, "Redemption and Genesis XXII" in *Scripture and Tradition in Judaism* (Leiden, 1961), 194–195.

112 "nor uttering a sound": Melito, fragment 9, in Melito, *On Pascha and Fragments,* trans. Stuart George Hall (Oxford, 1979).

112 "labors were not equal": Memra I, in Sebastian P. Brock, "Two Syriac Verse Homilies on the Binding of Isaac," in *From Ephrem to Romanos: Interactions Between Syriac and Greek in Late Antiquity* (Brookfield, Vt., 1999), 109.

113 "the Christ who was going to suffer": Melito, fragment 9, in Melito, *On Pascha and Fragments.*

113 "stolen away from death and suffering": Cyril of Alexandria, *Glaphyra in Genesis,* PG 69 144A, quoted in Edward Kessler, *Bound by the Bible: Jews, Christians and the Sacrifice of Isaac* (Cambridge, 2004), 132.

113 Isaac is "a type of the Lord": Clement of Alexandria, *The Paedagogus*

(Christ the Instructor) 1.5, quoted in Kessler, *Bound by the Bible*, 131.

113 "So this is the Torah you talked about": quoted in Shalom Spiegel, *The Last Trial: On the Legends and Lore of the Command to Abraham to Offer Isaac as a Sacrifice: The Akedah* (New York, 1967), 49. Spiegel discusses all of these versions and many more. His essay remains, more than half a century after it was published, the standard work on the *midrashim* in which Isaac dies.

114 "slaughtered according to the rite": Ephraim (of Bonn), "Adekah," in Spiegel, *The Last Trial*, 148.

114 "quickeneth the dead": *Pirke de Rabbi Eliezer* 31, p. 228.

115 would have ended with Isaac's ashes: Spiegel, *The Last Trial*, 36–37.

115 from knife wounds, from the flames: Ibid., 3–8.

116 simply thinking about Abraham and God: *Genesis Rabbah* 56:11; Ibn Ezra to Genesis 22:19, in Abraham Ibn Ezra, *Ibn Ezra's Commentary on the Pentateuch* (New York, 1988), 226–227.

116 "Let our lips compensate for the bulls": See Hosea 14:3: "Instead of bulls we pay [the offering of] our lips."

118 "our Savior alone": Athanasius, *Epistle 6*, in *The Festal Epistles of S. Athanasius, Bishop of Alexandria*, vol. 38 in the series A Library of Fathers of the Holy Catholic Church Anterior to the Division of the East and West (Oxford, 1854). See also Kessler, *Bound by the Bible*, 133.

CHAPTER 16

119 "on account of his blood I chose them": Pseudo-Philo, *L.A.B.* 18:5.

119 difficult when not impossible: The first complete account of Isaac's death and resurrection that can be dated with any precision (though hardly definitively: there is ongoing debate) appears in the *Pirke de-Rabbi Eliezer*, which scholars believe, based on internal evidence (references to contemporary events), to be a late eighth- or early ninth-century text, but it clearly contains material much older than that. See, most recently, Steven Daniel Sacks, *Midrash and Multiplicity: Pirke de-Rabbi Eliezer and the Reinvention of Rabbinic Interpretive Culture* (New York, 2009). See also Edward Kessler, *Bound by the Bible: Jews, Christians and the Sacrifice of Isaac* (Cambridge, 2004), 127–130. I myself, following Shalom Spiegel, *The Last Trial: On the Legends and Lore of the Command to Abraham to Offer Isaac as a Sacrifice: The Akedah* (New York, 1967) and Jon D. Levenson, *The Death and Resurrection of the Beloved Son: The Transformation of Child Sacrifice in Judaism and Christianity* (New Haven, Conn.,

1993), assume that the death-and-resurrection motif was much older than the end of the first millennium.

120 one Rhineland Jewish community after another: For my understanding of the Crusade chronicles and Jewish responses to the First Crusade more generally, I am deeply indebted, in addition to Spiegel, *The Last Trial*, to Robert Chazan, *God, Humanity, and History: The Hebrew First Crusade Narratives* (Berkeley, 2000), and to Jeremy Cohen, *Sanctifying the Name of God: Jewish Martyrs and Jewish Memories of the First Crusade* (Philadelphia, 2004). I would also recommend Alan L. Mintz, *Ḥurban: Responses to Catastrophe in Hebrew Literature* (New York, 1984), and Susan L. Einbinder, *Beautiful Death: Jewish Poetry and Martyrdom in Medieval France* (Princeton, N.J., 2002). On Jewish martyrdom more generally, see Shira Lander, "Martyrdom in Jewish Traditions," *Catholic-Jewish Consultation Committee Meeting* (St. Mary's Seminary, Baltimore, Md., Bishops Committee on Ecumenical and Inter-religious Affairs and the National Council of Synagogues, December 11, 2003), online at http://www.bc.edu/dam/files/research_sites/cjl/texts/cjrelations/resources/articles/Lander_martyrdom/index.html. On Jewish memory and history making more generally, absolutely and always essential is Yosef Hayim Yerushalmi, *Zakhor: Jewish History and Jewish Memory* (Seattle, 1982). For a more deeply contextualized look at memory in general, and memories of the First Crusade in particular, see David Nirenberg, "The Rhineland Massacres of Jews in the First Crusade: Memories Medieval and Modern," in *Imagination, Ritual, Memory, Historiography: Concepts of the Past,* ed. G. Althoff et al. (Cambridge, 2001), 279–310. For consistency, unless otherwise indicated, my quotations from the chronicles come from Shlomo Eidelberg, trans. and ed., *The Jews and the Crusaders: The Hebrew Chronicles of the First and Second Crusades* (Madison, Wis., 1977). You can find nearly identical versions of the same quotations in Spiegel, *The Last Trial*.

120 the killing in Mainz: "Solomon bar Simson Chronicle," in Eidelberg, *The Jews and the Crusaders,* 32–33. See also Spiegel, *The Last Trial,* 18–20.

121 the village of Wevelinghofen: "Chronicle of Eliezer bar Nathan," in Eidelberg, *The Jews and the Crusaders,* 86–87. See also Spiegel, *The Last Trial,* 22–24.

121 a rabbi in Worms: "Narrative of the Old Persecutions (Mainz Anonymous)," in Eidelberg, *The Jews and the Crusaders,* 103–104. See also, Spiegel, *The Last Trial,* 24–25.

122 "Why over the blood of children": Spiegel, *The Last Trial,* 20.

122 "they cannot be counted": Ibid., 20–21.

122 "the Akedah of Isaac son of Abraham?": Ibid., 19–20.

124 "May You avenge the spilt blood": "Chronicle of Solomon bar Simson," in Eidelberg, *The Jews and the Crusaders*, 31, 33, and then also 49: "May the blood of His devoted ones stand us in good stead and be an atonement for us and for our posterity after us, and our children's children eternally, like the Akedah of our Father Isaac when our Father Abraham bound him upon the altar."

125 By his laws, he wants them to live: b. Sanhedrin 74a.

CHAPTER 17

127 others practiced and promoted ways of reading Scripture: My understanding of medieval Jewish interpretation began with and depends throughout on Barry Dov Walfish, "Medieval Jewish Interpretation," in Adele Berlin and Marc Zvi Brettler, eds., *The Jewish Study Bible* (New York, 2004), 1876–1900. From Walfish's terrific essay I went to the available English translations of individual commentators, cited in the notes below.

127 Saadia Gaon: Sa'adia ben Joseph, *Rabbi Saadiah Gaon's Commentary on the Book of Creation* (Northvale, N.J., 2002), 29–34.

127 a "consuming fire": Ibid.

128 more internally consistent: Abraham Ibn Ezra discusses Saadia on Genesis 22:12, in Abraham Ibn Ezra, *Ibn Ezra's Commentary on the Pentateuch* (New York, 1988), 222.

129 Joseph Kara: quoted in Walfish, "Medieval Biblical Interpretation," 1888.

129 Abraham's knife called: Rashi to Genesis 22:6, in *The Torah with Rashi's Commentary,* translated, annotated, and elucidated by Yisrael Isser Zvi Herczeg et al. (Brooklyn, 1994), 234; *Genesis Rabbah* 56:3, in H. Freedman and Maurice Simon, eds. and trans. *Midrash Rabbah,* 10 vols. (New York, 1939, 1983).

129 Rashbam insisted: Rashbam to Deuteronomy 32:42; Rashbam to Genesis 22:6, in *Rabbi Samuel Ben Meir's Commentary on Genesis,* translated and annotated by Martin I. Lockshin (Lewiston, N.Y., 1989), 98.

130 Abraham Ibn Ezra: Ibn Ezra, *Ibn Ezra's Commentary on the Pentateuch,* 1–19.

130 "God tested Abraham": Ibn Ezra to Genesis 22:1, 222–224.

131 "Isaac would quite possibly have fled": Ibn Ezra to Genesis 22:4, 224–225.

131 David Kimhi (Radak): Eliyahu Munk, ed., *Hachut Hameshulash: Commentaries on the Torah by Rabbeinu Chananel, Rabbi Sh'muel Ben Meir (Rash'bam), Rabbi David Kimchi (R'dak), Rabbi Ovadiah Seforno,* 2 vols. (New York, 2003), 2:434–438.

132 Maimonides: Moses Maimonides, *Guide of the Perplexed,* 3:24.

134 Rashbam criticized commentators who spun elaborate yarns: Rashbam to Genesis 22:1, in *Rabbi Samuel Ben Meir's Commentary on Genesis,* 94–96. See also Munk, *Hachut Hameshulash,* 432–434.

134 Martin Luther insisted: Luther to Genesis 22:9, in "Lectures on Genesis, Chapters 21–25" in *Luther's Works,* ed. Jaroslav Pelikan et al., 69 vols. (St. Louis, 1955-), 4:112–113.

135 "Abraham, Abraham": Rashi to Genesis 22:11; Ibn Ezra to Genesis 22:11 (225); Radak to Genesis 22:11 (441); Joseph Ibn Kaspi, *Gevia' Kesef,* chapter 14, in Joseph Kaspi and Basil Herring, *Joseph Ibn Kaspi's Gevia? Kesef: A Study in Medieval Jewish Philosophic Bible Commentary* (New York, 1982), 230.

136 to ensure that he didn't try to run away: Menahem Kasher, *Encyclopedia of Biblical Interpretation: A Millennial Anthology (EBI)* (New York, 1953), 3:145–46.

136 "contradicting Scripture": Ibn Ezra to Genesis 22:19, 226–227.

136 Ibn al-'Arabi: See Sara Sviri, "Dreaming Analyzed and Recorded: Dream in the World of Medieval Islam," in Guy G. Stroumsa and David Dean Shulman, eds., *Dream Cultures: Explorations in the Comparative History of Dreaming* (New York, 1999).

136 an abomination to YHWH: Ibn Kaspi, *Gevia' Kesef,* chapter 14:219. Kaspi also believed that the learned also understood that God didn't ultimately desire animal sacrifice either, but that's another dimension of his interpretation and my story. See Kaspi, *Gevia' Kesef,* chapter 14:225.

136 Isaac, "struck with amazement": Luther to Genesis 22:9, in Luther, "Lectures on Genesis," 4:112–113.

137 Ramban on the word "Moriah": Ramban (Nachmanides) to Genesis 22:2, in *The Torah with Ramban's Commentary,* translated, annotated, and elucidated by Yaakov Blinder et al. (Brooklyn, 2004), 497–501.

CHAPTER 18

139 One obvious place to turn is the walls: The literature on the visual representations of the story is large and growing, but for this chapter, I have looked much more than I have read. For invaluable inventories, see Isabel Speyart van Woerden, "Iconography of the Sacrifice

of Abraham," *Vigiliae Christianae* 15 (December 1961): 214–255, and Princeton University's *Index of Christian Art*. For Augustine, see *Against Faustus* 22.73, quoted in Edward Kessler, *Bound by the Bible: Jews, Christians and the Sacrifice of Isaac* (Cambridge, 2004), 155. For Gregory of Nyssa, see *De deitate,* quoted in Kessler, *Bound by the Bible,* 155. Kessler provides a useful introduction to the early years in *Bound by the Bible,* 153–174. But see also Joseph Gutmann, "The Dura Europos Synagogue Paintings and Their Influence on Later Christian and Jewish Art," *Artibus et historiae* 9 (January 1, 1988): 25–29; Gutmann, "The Sacrifice of Isaac in Medieval Jewish Art," *Artibus et historiae* 8 (January 1, 1987): 67–89; and Gutmann, "The Sacrifice of Isaac: Variations on a Theme in Early Jewish and Christian Art," in *Sacred Images: Studies in Jewish Art from Antiquity to the Middle Ages: Collected Studies* (Northampton, 1989). See also the symposium that begins with Marc Bregman, "Aqedah: Midrash as Visualization," in *The Journal of Textual Reasoning* 2 (June 2003), online at http://etext.lib.virginia.edu/journals/tr/volume2/index.html. Also useful is Jo Milgrom, *The Binding of Isaac: The Akedah, a Primary Symbol in Jewish Thought and Art* (North Richland Hills, Tex., 1988).

140 El Bagawat: Matthew Martin, "Observations on the Paintings of the Exodus Chapel, Bagawat Necropolis, Kharga Oasis, Egypt," in John Burke et al., eds., *Byzantine Narrative: Essays in Honour of Roger Scott,* Australian Byzantine Studies Conference 2004, University of Melbourne (Melbourne, 2006).

140 Consider Abraham's demeanor: Andrea del Sarto: *The Sacrifice of Isaac* (c. 1527–1529); see also del Sarto's *The Sacrifice of Isaac* (1506); Alessandro Allori: *The Sacrifice of Isaac* (1601); for a similar pastoral view, see Domenichino's *Abraham Leading Isaac to Sacrifice* (1602); Domenichino: *The Sacrifice of Isaac* (1627–28); Caravaggio, *The Sacrifice of Isaac* (1603).

141 an anguished Abraham: Donatello, *The Sacrifice of Isaac* (1418); Alonso Berruguete, *The Sacrifice of Isaac* (c.1526–32); Rembrandt, *The Sacrifice of Abraham* (1635) and *The Sacrifice of Abraham* (1655).

143 Then there was Isaac: Cigoli, *The Sacrifice of Isaac* (1605–07); Jacopo da Empoli, *The Sacrifice of Isaac;* Empoli lived from 1554 to 1640, and while some date the painting to the 1590s, others date it to the 1620s; Felice Ficherelli, *The Sacrifice of Isaac,* dated to the early-to-mid-seventeenth century.

144 not every artist imagined him that way: Berruguete, *The Sacrifice of Isaac* (1526–32); del Sarto: *The Sacrifice of Isaac* (c. 1527–1529);

Titian, *The Sacrifice of Isaac* (1542-44); Caravaggio, *The Sacrifice of Isaac* (1603); Pedro Orrente, *The Sacrifice of Isaac* (1616); Rembrandt, *The Sacrifice of Abraham* (1635).

145 mixed feelings in Abraham's pose: See, for example, Jules Lubbock, *Storytelling in Christian Art from Giotto to Donatello* (New Haven, Conn., 2006).

145 the east door of the Baptistery: See Rona Goffen, *Renaissance Rivals: Michelangelo, Leonardo, Raphael, Titian* (New Haven, Conn., 2002), 6-7: "The committee's decision was surely influenced by the fact that Ghiberti's panel weighed 7 kilos [approx. 15½ lbs] less than Brunelleschi's, savings in bronze that signified considerable savings of money." Also engaging and informative is David Drogin and Beth Harris, "Brunelleschi & Ghiberti: The Sacrifice," video, *Smart History* (Khan Academy), online at http://smarthistory.khanacademy.org /brunelleschi-ghiberti-isaac.html. See also "A Peek behind Ghiberti's Florentine Baptistery Doors," *ARTstor Blog,* n.d., online at http:// artstor.wordpress.com/2012/05/29/a-peek-behind-florences-gates-of -paradise/: "The photographs of the backs of the panels clearly show how Ghiberti saved those 7 kilos."

147 Second Nuremberg Haggadah: See Louis A. Berman, *The Akedah: The Binding of Isaac* (Northvale, N.J., 1997), 140. See also the "Nuremberg Haggada II," National Library of Israel, online at http://web.nli.org.il/sites/NLI/English/gallery/jewish/Pages/nuremberg -hagada.aspx.

CHAPTER 19

148 English mystery plays: There are six: Brome, Chester, Coventry (also known as N-Town), Towneley (also known as Wakefield), Dublin (also known as Northampton), and York. See Rosemary Woolf, *The English Mystery Plays* (Berkeley, 1972), and Jerome Taylor, *Medieval English Drama; Essays Critical and Contextual, Patterns of Literary Criticism* (Chicago, 1972). In sorting all this out, I benefited from the brief notes of Gloria J. Betcher, "See How Much Our Understanding of the Middle English Biblical Plays Has Changed Since 1956," in Class Notes on Early Drama in Britain, online at http://www.public.iastate.edu/~gbetcher/373/MEDrama.htm. For consistency, my quotes come from R. T. Davies, ed., *The Corpus Christi Play of the English Middle Ages* (Totowa, N.J., 1972), but I have cross-checked the text of the Dublin play with Osborn Waterhouse and Norman Davis, eds., *Non-cycle Plays and Fragments* (New York, 1970), the text of the Towneley (Wakefield) with Martial Rose, *The Wakefield Mystery Plays* (New York, 1969), and the text of the

Brome play with the version in Waterhouse and Davis as well as with a third version, based on the Beinecke Library manuscript, with help from Waterhouse and Davis, which appears in M. H. Abrams, ed., *The Norton Anthology of English Literature,* 3d ed. (New York, 1974), 395–406.

151 typology: Rosemary Woolf, "The Effect of Typology on the English Mediaeval Plays of Abraham and Isaac," *Speculum* 32 (October 1957): 805–825. Peter Braeger, "Typology as Contrast in the Middle English *Abraham and Isaac* Plays," *Essays in Medieval Studies* 2 (1985): 131–153; Clifford Davidson, "The Sacrifice of Isaac in Medieval English Drama," *Papers on Language & Literature* 35 (Winter 1999): 28–55; Thomas Rendall, "Visual Typology in the Abraham and Isaac Plays," *Modern Philology* 81 (February 1984): 221–232. Also useful, in the context of the broader themes of this book, is Allen J. Frantzen, "Tears for Abraham: The Chester Play of Abraham and Isaac and Antisacrifice in Works by Wilfred Owen, Benjamin Britten, and Derek Jarman," *Journal of Medieval & Early Modern Studies* 31 (Fall 2001): 445–476.

153 added Sarah to the script: The Northampton Abraham and Isaac is the only English mystery in which Sarah has a part.

156 typology works by contrast as well as identity: Braeger, "Typology as Contrast in the Middle English *Abraham and Isaac* Plays," 131–153.

159 "those glorious scars": Charles Wesley, "Lo, He Comes with Clouds Descending."

CHAPTER 20

160 Kierkegaard: My quotes come from Søren Kierkegaard, *Fear and Trembling: Dialectical Lyric by Johannes de Silentio,* trans. Alastair Hannay (London, 2003). But I cross-checked them against and also made much use of Howard V. Hong and Edna H. Hong et al., eds. and trans., *Fear and Trembling; Repetition* (Princeton, N.J., 1983).

163 Augustine: *Against Faustus* 22.73.

163 Kant: Immanuel Kant, *The Conflict of the Faculties,* trans. Mary J. Gregor (New York, 1979), 115.

166 just a test: For a Christian theologian's reading of the word "test" as "just a test," something God never intended to see through, see Gerhard von Rad, *Genesis: A Commentary* (Philadelphia, 1961), 234; for a nearly identical Jewish version, see Nahum M. Sarna, *Understanding Genesis* (New York, 1966), 161–162, or Sarna on Genesis 22, in Sarna, *Genesis: The Traditional Hebrew Text with the New JPS Translation* (Philadelphia, 1989).

166 Abraham arouses Kierkegaard's admiration: Kierkegaard, *Fear and Trembling*, 89–90.

166 "has explained my life": See "Selected Entries from Kierkegaard's Journals and Papers Pertaining to Fear and Trembling," in Hong and Hong, *Fear and Trembling*, 242.

CHAPTER 21

169 the world in which they lived: James L. Kugel, *How to Read the Bible: A Guide to Scripture, Then and Now* (New York, 2007); Richard Elliott Friedman, *Who Wrote the Bible?* (San Francisco, 1997); and Kevin Madigan, "Catholic Interpretation of the Bible," in Donald Senior and John J. Collins, *The Catholic Study Bible* (New York, 2006), 54–67.

171 "on the mount of the Lord there is sight": Genesis 22:14 (Alter).

171 Ibn Ezra suspected that those who read carefully: Friedman, *Who Wrote the Bible?*, 19.

171 origins of the Bible: Kugel, *How to Read the Bible*, 2–46, and from Kugel to his very useful source notes. See also, and most recently, Joanna Weinberg and Anthony Grafton, *"I Have Always Loved the Holy Tongue": Isaac Casaubon, the Jews, and a Forgotten Chapter in Renaissance Scholarship* (Cambridge, 2011).

171 Theories multiplied like Israelites: Friedman, *Who Wrote the Bible?*, 18–21; Kugel, *How to Read the Bible*, 2–46.

172 Spinoza concluded, that the Torah of Moses: Friedman, *Who Wrote the Bible?*, 21.

173 Richard Simon: Ibid., 20–21. See also Kugel, *How to Read the Bible*, 30–33.

173 Wellhausen: Julius Wellhausen, quoted in Kugel, *How to Read the Bible*; Wellhausen, *Prolegomena to the History of Israel*, trans. J. Sutherland Black and Alan Menzies (Edinburgh, 1885).

CHAPTER 22

177 who wrote it: There are good summaries, introductions to arguments, and references to a gigantic literature in Shalom Spiegel, *The Last Trial: On the Legends and Lore of the Command to Abraham to Offer Isaac as a Sacrifice: The Akedah* (New York, 1967), 122–126; John Van Seters, *Abraham in History and Tradition* (New Haven, Conn., 1975), 227-240; E. A. Speiser, *Genesis* (New York, 1964), 166; and in G. W. Coats, "Abraham's Sacrifice of Faith: A Form-Critical Analysis of Genesis 22," *Interpretation* 27 (1973): 395–396. See also Richard Elliott Friedman, *Who Wrote the Bible?* (San

Francisco, 1997), 247, 256–257, and Friedman, *The Bible with the Sources Revealed: A New View into the Five Books of Moses* (San Francisco, 2003), 165, 160. For biblical scholarship on Genesis 22 more generally, there is an invaluable summary and bibliography of the scholarship up to 1980 in Claus Westermann, *Genesis 12–36: A Commentary* (Minneapolis, 1985), 351–365; and a bibliography of work published between 1980 and 2003 in the categories of "human sacrifice, exegesis, and reception history" in Edward Noort and Eibert Tigchelaar, eds., *The Sacrifice of Isaac: The Aqedah (Genesis 22) and Its Interpretations* (Leiden, 2002), 211–223. Also essential are Hermann Gunkel, *Genesis* (Göttingen, 1910, 1977), and Gerhard von Rad, *Genesis: A Commentary* (Philadelphia, 1961).

178 J wrote that story too: See, for example, Van Seters, *Abraham in History and Tradition,* 227–240.

179 turned the chronology upside down: See, for example, ibid. But cf. Ronald S. Hendel, *Remembering Abraham: Culture, Memory, and History in the Hebrew Bible* (Oxford, 2005). See also Noort, "Genesis 22: Human Sacrifice and Theology in the Hebrew Bible," in Noort and Tigchelaar, *The Sacrifice of Isaac,* 14–20.

180 an obvious place in God's plan: R. W. L. Moberly, "The Earliest Commentary on the Akedah," *Vetus Testamentum* 38 (July 1988): 302–323.

180 essential to the rest of the story: See Van Seters, *Abraham in History and Tradition,* 237–240, and Jon D. Levenson, *The Death and Resurrection of the Beloved Son: The Transformation of Child Sacrifices in Judaism and Christianity* (New Haven, Conn., 1993), chapters 11, 12, and 14, especially 138–142 and 173–174.

180 J was a woman: Friedman, *Who Wrote the Bible?,* 85–86, and *The Book of J,* translated by David Rosenberg and interpreted by Harold Bloom (New York, 1990).

180 Something about child sacrifice: For a brief introduction to the literature, I would start with Levenson, *Death and Resurrection,* especially but not only 3–52 and 111–124. Then I would move by way of Levenson's notes to some of the dissertations, books, and essays he cites and wrestles with, including Roland de Vaux, *Studies in Old Testament Sacrifice* (Cardiff, 1964); Paul G. Mosca, "Child Sacrifice in Canaanite and Israelite Religion: A Study in Mulk and [Molech]" (Ph.D. diss., Harvard, 1975); George C. Heider, *The Cult of Molek: A Reassessment* (Sheffield, 1985); and John Day, *Molech: A God of Human Sacrifice in the Old Testament* (Cambridge, 1989). From the monographic literature I moved on to two recent anthologies, Noort and Tigchelaar, *The Sacrifice of Isaac,* and Karin Finsterbusch,

Armin Lange, and Diethard Romheld, eds., *Human Sacrifice in Jewish and Christian Tradition* (Leiden, 2007). Also extremely interesting and useful is John S. Rundin, "Pozo Moro, Child Sacrifice, and the Greek Legendary Tradition," *Journal of Biblical Literature* 123 (Fall 2004): 425–447. For the scholarship that puts ideas of gender and relations among women and men at the center of sacrifice, child sacrifice, and Genesis 22, start with two essential books: Nancy B. Jay, *Throughout Your Generations Forever: Sacrifice, Religion, and Paternity* (Chicago 1992), and Carol L. Delaney, *Abraham on Trial: The Social Legacy of Biblical Myth* (Princeton, N.J., 1998). For two (of a number) of the post-9/11 takes of the legacy of the story and sacrifice in Judaism, Christianity, and Islam, see Yvonne Sherwood, "Binding-Unbinding: Divided Responses of Judaism, Christianity, and Islam to the 'Sacrifice' of Abraham's Beloved Son," *Journal of the American Academy of Religion* 72 (December 2004): 821–861, and Bruce Chilton, *Abraham's Curse: Child Sacrifice in the Legacies of the West* (New York, 2008). For stories of child sacrifice in a Hindu context, see David Dean Shulman, *The Hungry God: Hindu Tales of Filicide and Devotion* (Chicago, 1993). For a very recent, and also very lucid and persuasive, essay on sacrifice, focusing on the differences between sacrifice *to* and sacrifice *for,* see Moshe Halbertal, *On Sacrifice* (Princeton, N.J., 2012).

181 old and essential element of Israelite theology: Jon Levenson has a clear and concise overview of the existing scholarship alongside his own views in *Death and Resurrection,* especially but not only 3–17 and 111–124.

182 "to substitute an animal for the firstborn son": See, for example, Van Seters, *Abraham in History and Tradition,* 227–240, and also Westermann, *Genesis,* 351–365.

182 But what place?: Levenson, *Death and Resurrection,* 114–124. See also Gunkel, *Genesis.*

183 Israel would be redeemed: Among the scholars who see the story as about something or some things in addition to or other than child sacrifice, see von Rad, *Genesis: A Commentary;* Noort, "Genesis 22: Human Sacrifice and Theology in the Hebrew Bible," 1–20; Moberly, "The Earliest Commentary on the Akedah"; and Delaney, *Abraham on Trial.*

185 literary critics of the Bible: I started with Robert Alter and Frank Kermode, *The Literary Guide to the Bible* (Cambridge, 1987); Alter, *The Art of Biblical Narrative* (New York, 1981); and Alter's introductions and commentary in Alter, *The Five Books of Moses: A Translation with Commentary* (New York, 2004).

186 Auerbach: Erich Auerbach, *Mimesis: The Representation of Reality in Western Literature* (Princeton, N.J., 1953).

CHAPTER 23

190 *The Last Trial:* In addition to Goldin's introduction, I have learned from Arnold J. Band, "Scholarship as Lamentation: Shalom Spiegel on 'The Binding of Isaac,'" in Band, *Studies in Modern Jewish Literature* (Philadelphia, 2003); Yael Feldman, "'The Most Exalted Symbol for Our Time'?: Rewriting 'Isaac' in Tel Aviv," *Hebrew Studies Journal* 47 (2006): 253–273; and Feldman, *Glory and Agony: Isaac's Sacrifice and National Narrative* (Stanford, 2010).

192 "which in Judaism remained peripheral": Shalom Spiegel, *The Last Trial: On the Legends and Lore of the Command to Abraham to Offer Isaac as a Sacrifice: The Akedah* (New York, 1967), 116–117.

193 "The ancient pagan demand": Ibid., 129.

CHAPTER 24

197 Auschwitz, a father there with his son: Irving J. Rosenbaum, *The Holocaust and Halakhah* (New York, 1976), 3–5.

198 Simhah Elberg: "The *Akedah* of Treblinka," in Steven T. Katz, Shlomo Biderman, and Gershon Greenberg, eds., *Wrestling with God: Jewish Theological Responses during and after the Holocaust* (New York, 2007), 192–197. This useful volume includes biographical sketches of each author, illuminating introductions, and a bibliography.

198 Reuven Katz: "Torah Portion *Behukotai:* Israel's Misery and Israel's Redemption," in Katz et al., *Wrestling with God,* 107.

199 "the bitterest punishment of all": Elberg, "The *Akedah* of Treblinka," 192.

199 Kalonymus Kalman Shapira: See Nehemia Polen, *The Holy Fire: The Teachings of Rabbi Kalonymus Kalman Shapira, the Rebbe of the Warsaw Ghetto* (Northvale, N.J., 1994), and Kalonimus Kalmish ben Elimelekh (Kalonymus Kalman Shapira), *Sacred Fire: Torah from the Years of Fury, 1939–1942,* trans. J. Hershy Worch, ed. Deborah Miller (Northvale, N.J., 2000). My quotes here come from Shapira, *Sacred Fire,* 140.

200 nowhere more than in Palestine: Yael Feldman's *Glory and Agony: Isaac's Sacrifice and National Narrative* (Stanford, 2010) is absolutely essential for anyone interested in the complicated place, uses, and power (especially the psychological and psychoanalytical place and power) of Genesis 22 (and ideas of sacrifice more generally) among Jews in Palestine and the state of Israel in the twenti-

eth century. I have also benefited enormously from Mishael Caspi, *Take Now Thy Son: The Motif of the Aqedah (Binding) in Literature* (North Richland Hills, Tex., 2001); Yoseph Milman, "The Sacrifice of Isaac and Its Subversive Variations in Contemporary Hebrew Protest Poetry," *Religion & Literature* 23 (Summer 1991): 61–83; Stanley Nash, "Israeli Fathers and Sons Revisited," *Conservative Judaism* 38 (Summer 1986): 28–37; and Abraham (Avi) Sagi, "The Meaning of the *Akedah* in Israeli Culture and Jewish Tradition," *Israel Studies* 3 (1998): 45–60.

201 "silently stretch out our necks over the altar": Isaac Lamdan, "Upon the Altar." I have used the translation of Ruth Kartun-Blum, in Kartun-Blum, " 'Where Does This Wood in My Hand Come From?': The Binding of Isaac in Modern Hebrew Poetry," *Prooftexts* 8 (1988): 296. Compare to Mishael Caspi's translation, reprinted in Caspi and John T. Greene, eds., *Unbinding the Binding of Isaac* (Lanham, Md., 2007), 137. For the Hebrew original, see Isaac Lamdan, *Kol Shire Yitshak Lamdan* (Jerusalem, 1973).

201 "I didn't ask for a ram": Isaac Lamdan, trans. and quoted in Kartun-Blum, " 'Where Does This Wood in My Hand Come From?,' " 296. For the Hebrew, see Lamdan, *Kol Shire Yitshak Lamdan.*

201 Natan Alterman: This is the translation of Vivian London, which appears along with the Hebrew in Ruth Kartun-Blum, *Profane Scriptures: Reflections on the Dialogue with the Bible in Modern Hebrew Poetry* (Cincinnati, 1999), 28–29.

202 *Days of Ziklag,* S. Yizhar: I've relied on two translations (and fascinating discussions): Yael Feldman's, in *Glory and Agony,* 171–176, and Avi Sagi's, in "The Meaning of the Akedah in Israeli Culture and Jewish Tradition," 46–47. For the Hebrew, see S. Yizhar, *Yeme Tsiklag* (Tel Aviv, 1958). For another example of the same take, see the Polish-born American poet Jacob Glatstein's "Isaac," in David Curzon, *Modern Poems on the Bible: An Anthology* (Philadelphia, 1994).

202 Zalman Shazar: quoted and discussed in Feldman, *Glory and Agony,* 100–104.

203 wholly the work of men: There are endless examples. For one, see Emil L. Fackenheim, *God's Presence in History: Jewish Affirmations and Philosophical Reflections* (New York, 1970).

204 Pinchas Peli: "Borderline: Searching for a Religious Language of the Shoah," in Katz et al., *Wrestling with God,* 244–262, quote on 258.

204 in an attempt to exterminate "a race": Fackenheim, *God's Presence in History,* 69–79.

205 Elie Wiesel: *Messengers of God: Biblical Portraits and Legends* (New York, 1976), 76. For one more example, of countless possible examples, of Jewish writers drawing the sharpest possible distinction between Jewish and Christian foundation stories, see Ignaz Maybaum, "The Face of God after Auschwitz," in Katz et al., *Wrestling with God*, 402–408.

206 "built on Moriah, not Sinai": Wiesel, *Messengers of God*, 97.

CHAPTER 25

207 biblical scholarship out into the wider world: Abraham Geiger, *Judaism and Its History* (New York, 1865, 1911), 64; Hirsch to Genesis 22, in *Hirsch Commentary on the Torah*, 2nd ed., revised and corrected (Gateshead, 1966), and *The Hirsch Chumash: The Five Books of Torah* (New York, 2000); and Harry Gersh, *The Story of the Jew* (New York, 1964), 16. Gersh's book is a rewriting of Lee J. and Elma Ehrlich Levinger's 1928 volume, which has next to nothing to say about the patriarchal age. James Carroll, unlike Gersh and Geiger, understands that some ancient Israelites, like some "pagans," probably practiced child sacrifice. Otherwise Carroll's understanding of the story (Abraham's willingness to sacrifice and God's merciful rejection of the practice) is identical. See James Carroll, *Jerusalem, Jerusalem: How the Ancient City Ignited Our Modern World* (Boston, 2011), 15, 69–72.

208 Bob Dylan: *Highway 61 Revisited*, 1965.

208 G. Henton Davies: Gwynne Henton Davies, "Genesis, Introduction and Commentary on the Text," in *The Broadman Bible Commentary* (Nashville, 1969), 196–199. For an Islamic version of the idea that God would never ask such a thing, would neither command a Muslim to sin nor test a Muslim by commanding him to break one of his laws), see "Abraham and the Sacrifice: God Never Ordered Abraham to Sacrifice His Son," *Submitters Perspective* 15 (April 1999), online at http://www.masjidtucson.org/publications/books/SP/index.html.

209 Woody Allen's God: Allen, *Without Feathers* (New York, 1975), 26–27. Allen's God, by contrast, tells Abraham to get some rest and check back in the morning. For one of myriad recent midrash in which Abraham fails God's test, see Avraham Burg, *Very Near to You* (Jerusalem; New Jersey, 2012), 30–32.

209 Jean-Paul Sartre and Martin Buber: Sartre, "Existentialism Is a Humanism" (1945–46), in John Kulka et al., *Existentialism Is a Humanism* (New Haven, Conn., 2007), 26, and Buber, "On the Suspension of the Ethical," in Buber, *Eclipse of God: Studies in the Relation Between Religion and Philosophy* (New York, 1952, 1999).

210 Lévinas: Emmanuel Lévinas, *Proper Names* (Stanford, 1996), 77, quoted and discussed in Claire Elise Katz, "The Voice of God and the Face of the Other," *The Journal of Textual Reasoning* 2 (June 2003), online at http://etext.lib.virginia.edu/journals/tr/volume2/index.html.

210 a tried-and-true "weapon of the weak": a concept many commentators borrowed from the political scientist James Scott, or imagined in one form or another for themselves. For the former, see Ron Krebs, "Rosh Hashana 5768," *Divrei Torah*, Congregation Darchei Noam, online at http://darcheinoammn.org/Learning/Learning.htm. For the latter, see all five essays in the first part of Lippman Bodoff, *The Binding of Isaac, Religious Murders, & Kabbalah: Seeds of Jewish Extremism and Alienation?* (Jerusalem, 2005), 27–92.

211 Claire Elise Katz: "The Voice of God and the Face of the Other." See also Joan Baez, "Isaac and Abraham" (1992). Baez's Abraham doesn't stop the sacrifice himself but wishes he had: "Said 'My darlin' son, I wish I was the one / Who spared you, spared your precious life.'"

211 Omri Boehm: Boehm, *The Binding of Isaac: A Religious Model of Disobedience* (New York, 2007). See also Boehm, "The Binding of Isaac: An Inner-Biblical Polemic on the Question of 'Disobeying' a Manifestly Illegal Order," *Vetus Testamentum* 52 (January 2002): 1–12; and Boehm, "Child Sacrifice, Ethical Responsibility and the Existence of the People of Israel," *Vetus Testamentum* 54 (April 2004): 145–156. For a complementary interpretation, forcefully argued, though lacking most of Boehm's evidence, see Harold Bloom's commentary in *The Book of J*, translated by David Rosenberg and interpreted by Harold Bloom (New York, 1990).

211 Jack Miles: Miles, *God: A Biography* (New York, 1995), 47–66.

CHAPTER 26

213 "The Way of the Wind": in Amos Oz, *Where the Jackals Howl, and Other Stories* (London, 1981). The story is reprinted in Nitza Ben-Dov, ed., *The Amos Oz Reader* (Boston, 2009).

215 "before his ideals are realized": Aharon, *The Battle,* quoted in Avi Sagi, "The Meaning of the Akedah in Israeli Culture and Jewish Tradition," *Israeli Studies* 3 (1998): 47. For the Hebrew, see Yariv Ben-Aharon, *ha-Kerav, Sifriyah La-'am,* 102 (Tel Aviv, 1966).

215 Eli Alon: quoted in Ruth Kartun-Blum, *Profane Scriptures: Reflections on the Dialogue with the Bible in Modern Hebrew Poetry* (Cincinnati, 1999), 58, and quoted and discussed at length in Yael Feldman, *Glory*

and Agony: Isaac's Sacrifice and National Narrative (Stanford, 2010), 229–31: "I would not want Abraham to be the father of my nation and such a God to be my God. God in this story is a Moloch and Abraham is simply an idol-worshipper."

215 *The Queen of the Bath*: On Levin and the play, see Hanoch Levin, *The Labor of Life: Selected Plays,* trans. and ed. Barbara Harshav (Stanford, 2003), xiii–xx; Feldman, *Glory and Agony,* 235–240; Kartun-Blum, *Profane Scriptures,* 55–58; and Sagi, "The Meaning of the Akedah in Israeli Culture and Jewish Tradition," 49–50.

216 "Father dear": Levin, *The Labor of Life,* xix–xx.

217 Yitzhak Laor: "This Idiot, Isaac." I've used the translation of Avi Sagi, in Sagi, "The Meaning of the Akedah in Israeli Culture and Jewish Tradition," 50. For a second English translation and discussion, see Feldman, *Glory and Agony,* 278–281. For the Hebrew, see Yitzhak Laor, *Rak ha-guf zokher* (Tel Aviv, 1985).

218 "the real hero of the sacrifice was the ram": Yehuda Amichai, *A Life of Poetry, 1948–1994,* trans. Benjamin Harshav and Barbara Harshav (New York, 1994), 345. See also Yehuda Amichai, *The Selected Poetry of Yehuda Amichai,* ed. and trans. Stephen Mitchell and Chana Bloch (New York, 1986), 151.

219 "Let God Cry": Amichai, "Abraham Had Three Sons." This is the "free translation" of Tova Forti, in Forti, "The Topos of the Binding of Isaac in Modern Hebrew Poetry," in Mishael Caspi and John T. Greene, eds., *Unbinding the Binding of Isaac* (Lanham, Md., 2007), 144. For the Hebrew, see Yehuda Amichai, *Patuah Sagur Patuah* (Jerusalem, 1998).

220 he owed his life to God: Abraham B. Yehoshua, "Mr. Mani and the Akedah," *Judaism* 50 (2001): 61–65.

220 *Early in the Summer of 1970*: Abraham B. Yehoshua, *Early in the Summer of 1970* (Garden City, N.Y., 1977).

221 *Mr. Mani*: Abraham B. Yehoshua, *Mr. Mani* (New York, 1992). In addition to Yehoshua's own commentary on his writing, I have found invaluable Yael Feldman's writing on *Mr. Mani* and many other twentieth-century Israeli novels. See Feldman, *Glory and Agony.*

CHAPTER 27

222 Eleanor Wilner's Sarah: "Sarah's Choice," in *Sarah's Choice* (Chicago, 1989).

224 she and God must have cried out together: Marek Halter, *Sarah: A Heroine of the Old Testament* (London, 2004), 290–293.

224 Rashi's sister: Dvora Yanow, "Sarah's Silence: A Newly Discovered

Commentary on Genesis 22 by Rashi's Sister," *Judaism* 43 (Fall 1994): 398–408.

224 a Colorado rabbi: David J. Zucker, "The Mysterious Disappearance of Sarah," *Judaism* 55 (Fall–Winter 2006): 30–39.

224 Carol Ochs: *Behind the Sex of God* (Boston, 1977), 45–46.

225 Carol Delaney: *Abraham on Trial: The Social Legacy of Biblical Myth* (Princeton, N.J., 1998). For an earlier, and overlapping, interpretation of the relationship between gender and sacrifice, see Nancy B. Jay, *Throughout Your Generations Forever: Sacrifice, Religion, and Paternity* (Chicago, 1992).

226 Alicia Ostriker's poem: "The Story of Abraham," reprinted in *Invisible Light: Poems about God* (New York, 2000), 23–24, and also in Delaney, *Abraham on Trial,* 132–133.

227 "bury my dead out of my sight": Alicia Ostriker, *Feminist Revision and the Bible* (Oxford, 1993), 38–50.

227 Phyllis Trible: Trible, "Genesis 22: The Sacrifice of Sarah," in Alice Bach, ed., *Women in the Hebrew Bible: A Reader* (New York, 1999), 285.

227 Wendy Zierler: Deuteronomy 6:5 (Alter); Zierler, "In Search of a Feminist Reading of the Akedah," *Nashim* (June 2005): 10–26. This translation of Genesis 24:67 is Robert Alter's.

228 Benjamin Galai: "The Life of Sarah," translated by Ruth Kartun-Blum and reprinted along with the Hebrew in *Profane Scriptures,* 44–45. For a second translation, see Bernhard Frank, ed. and trans., *Modern Hebrew Poetry* (Iowa City, 1980), 71. For the original collection, see Benjamin Galai, *Mas'a Tsafonah: Shirim* (Tel Aviv, 1968).

229 Shin Shifrah's "Hagar": translated by Irit Aharony, in "The Outcry, Question, and the Silence—Sarah and the Akedah in the Midrash and in Contemporary Israeli Literature," in Mishael Caspi and John T. Greene, eds., *Unbinding the Binding of Isaac* (Lanham, Md., 2007), 174. For the Hebrew, see Shin Shifrah, "Hagar," *Sipurei Bereshit* (Stories of Our Beginnings), ed. Zion Tanyah (Tel Aviv, 2003).

229 Yehudit Kafri: "In the Beginnings," translated by Irit Aharony, in "The Outcry, Question, and the Silence," in Caspi and Greene, *Unbinding the Binding of Isaac,* 177. For a second translation, and the Hebrew, see David C. Jacobson, *Does David Still Play Before You?: Israeli Poetry and the Bible* (Detroit, 1997), 216–217. For the volume in which the poem originally appeared, see Yehudit Kafri, *Mal'an shel layits: shirim* (Tel Aviv, 1988).

230 "whether all of me or part of me is killed?": Kalonimus Kalmish ben Elimelekh (Kalonymus Kalmish Shapira), *Sacred Fire: Torah from the*

Years of Fury, 1939–1942, trans. J. Hershy Worch and ed. Deborah Miller (Northvale, N.J., 2000), 14.

230 Eli Alon: "*Beresheit*," translated by Jonathan Mohrer, with the generous assistance of Naomi Danis. For another English translation and discussion, see Yael Feldman, *Glory and Agony: Isaac's Sacrifice and National Narrative* (Stanford, 2010), 277–278. For the Hebrew, see A. Eli, *Ba-derekh la-arets ha-muvtahat* (Tel Aviv, 1989).

231 Haim Gouri, whose poem, "Heritage": in T. Carmi, trans. and ed., *The Penguin Book of Hebrew Verse* (New York, 1981), 565. For a second translation, see Haim Gouri, *Words in My Lovesick Blood: Poems*, trans. and ed. Stanley F. Chyet (Detroit, 1996), 27.

232 "if we had only listened to her voice": the final lines of Gouri's "Eyval," translated by Jonathan Mohrer, with the generous assistance of Naomi Danis and Noah Horowitz. For another English translation, see Feldman, *Glory and Agony*, 318. For the Hebrew, see Haim Gouri, *Eyval: shirim* (Tel Aviv, 2009), 52.

CHAPTER 28

235 the command had come from God: Clyde T. Francisco, "Genesis, Introduction and Commentary on the Text," in *The Broadman Bible Commentary*, vol. 1 rev. (Nashville, 1973), 187–189. For the controversy, see Jerry Faught, "Round Two, Volume One: The Broadman Commentary Controversy," *Baptist History and Heritage* 38 (Winter 2003): 94–114; Carl L. Kell, *Against the Wind: The Moderate Voice in Baptist Life* (Knoxville, 2009), 27–45; and Jeff Rogers, "Genesis 22—'The Sacrifice of Isaac' or 'Finding the Way Out,'" *PulpitBytes*, online at http://pulpitbytes.blogspot.com/2006/09/genesis-22-sacrific-of-isaac-or.html.

235 Kalonymus Shapira: Kalonimus Kalmish ben Elimelekh (Kalonymus Kalmish Shapira), *Sacred Fire: Torah from the Years of Fury, 1939–1942*, trans. J. Hershy Worch and ed. Deborah Miller (Northvale, N.J., 2000), 131–132.

235 Seyyed Hossein Nasr: in Bill D. Moyers, *Genesis: A Living Conversation* (New York, 1996), 233.

236 a beloved pet dog or cat: Dr. Gene Scott, "Heroes of Faithing: Abraham," n.d., online at http://asis.com/users/stag/heroes/abraham.html.

236 "because you said no to God": "Abraham and Isaac," *Mr. Kent's Devotional and Sunday School Lessons*, n.d., online at http://www.mrkent.com/devotionals/sschool/abe_isaac.htm.

236 diagnose Abraham as depressed or accuse him of abuse: See, for example, Joanne Carlson Brown and Rebecca Parker, "For God So

Loved the World?" in Joanne Carlson Brown and Carole R. Bohn, *Christianity, Patriarchy, and Abuse: A Feminist Critique* (New York, 1989), 26; Michael Lerner, *Jewish Renewal: Path to Healing and Transformation* (New York, 1994), 39–46; and Burton L. Visotzky, *The Genesis of Ethics* (New York, 1996), 104. See also Alice Miller, *The Untouched Key: Tracing Childhood Trauma in Creativity and Destructiveness* (New York, 1990).

236 Levenson: Jon D. Levenson, "Abusing Abraham: Traditions, Religious Histories, and Modern Misinterpretations," *Judaism* 47 (Summer 1998): 259–277. See also Terence E. Fretheim, "God, Abraham, and the Abuse of Isaac," *Word and World* 15 (1995), 49–57, and Andrew S. Yang, "Abraham and Isaac, Child Abuse and Martin Luther," *Lutheran Quarterly* 19 (Summer 2005): 153–166.

237 Yitzhak Laor: "This Idiot, Isaac (Late Version)." This translation is my own. For Gabriel Levin's, together with the Hebrew, see David C. Jacobson, *Does David Still Play Before You?: Israeli Poetry and the Bible* (Detroit, 1997),129–130. Levin's translation originally appeared in *Modern Hebrew Literature* 11 (Autumn–Winter 1993): 32.

237 Abraham killed Isaac: Shalom Spiegel, *The Last Trial: On the Legends and Lore of the Command to Abraham to Offer Isaac as a Sacrifice: The Akedah* (New York, 1967), 122–126, and Richard Elliott Friedman, *Who Wrote the Bible?* (San Francisco, 1997), 247, 256–257. See also Richard Elliott Friedman, *The Bible with Sources Revealed: A New View into the Five Books of Moses* (San Francisco, 2003), 65.

238 Anthony Shadid: *Night Draws Near* (New York, 2005), 260–291.

239 Yeshayahu Leibowitz: *Judaism, Human Values, and the Jewish State,* ed. and trans. Eliezer Goldman et al. (Cambridge, 1992), 14 and passim. On Sodom and Gomorrah, see also Levenson, "Abusing Abraham," 272 and 277n53. Also provocative in pondering Leibowitz's way of thinking about the story is Richard S. Ellis, "Human Logic, God's Logic, and the Akedah," *Conservative Judaism* 52 (Fall 1999): 28–32. In sermons, essays, and Bible commentary on the World Wide Web, there are countless other examples of this perspective (and every other). One that echoes Leibowitz and Ellis that has stuck with me over the years is Hillel Goldberg, "What Did Abraham Hear?," *Genesis Project,* 1999, online at http://www.torah.org/features/genesis/topic7.html.

240 "this free gift of love": Marcellino D'Ambrosio, "The Sacrifice of Isaac," The Crossroads Initiative, online at http://www.crossroads initiative.com/library_article/907/sacrifice_of_isaac.html.

240 Muslim parents: Orhan Pamuk dramatizes each of these responses

and explanations and several more in a just few pages of *The Museum of Innocence* (New York, 2009), 34–42.

240 Joseph B. Soloveitchik: The Rav (or Rov), quoted in Harold Schulweis, "The Sculpture of George Segal: Skirball Museum Lecture—May, 1997," online at http://www.vbs.org/page.cfm?p=870&newsid=187, posted January 28, 2011; in Schulweis, "Obedience and Conscience, Rosh Hashanah 1999," online at http://www.vbs.org/page.cfm?p=870&newsid=233, posted February 11, 2011; and in Chaim Navon, Lecture #24: The *Akeida, Theological Issues in Sefer Bereishit,* The Israel Koschitzky Virtual Beit Midrash, Yeshivat Har Etzion, online at http://vbm-torah.org/archive/bereishit/24bereishit.htm.

241 Chava Cohen-Pinchas's poem: "A Request," translated by Irit Aharony and reprinted in Aharony, "The Outcry, Question, and the Silence," in Mishael Caspi and John T. Greene, eds., *Unbinding the Binding of Isaac* (Lanham, Md., 2007), 178. For the Hebrew, see Chava Cohen-Pinchas, *Masa' Ayalah* (Tel Aviv, 1994).

241 Shin Shifrah's "Isaac": "Isaac," translated by Irit Aharony and reprinted in Aharony, "The Outcry, Question, and the Silence," in Caspi and Greene, *Unbinding the Binding of Isaac,* 178–179. For the Hebrew, see Shin Shifrah, *Shir Ishah: Shirim* (Tel Aviv, 1962).

242 "Abraham knew it was his turn": Jon D. Levenson, *The Death and Resurrection of the Beloved Son: The Transformation of Child Sacrifice in Judaism and Christianity* (New Haven, Conn., 1993), 17.

243 Levenson demurs: See Spiegel, *The Last Trial,* especially 63–64, and Jon D. Levenson, *The Death and Resurrection of the Beloved Son: The Transformation of Child Sacrifice in Judaism and Christianity* (New Haven, Conn., 1993), 3–17 and 111–142.

245 Uri Zvi Greenberg: "On a Night of Rain in Jerusalem," in T. Carmi, ed., *The Penguin Book of Hebrew Verse* (New York, 1981), 530–531.

246 Ra'yah Harnik: translated by Ruth Kartun-Blum and reprinted along with the Hebrew in Ruth Kartun-Blum, *Profane Scriptures: Reflections on the Dialogue with the Bible in Modern Hebrew Poetry* (Cincinnati, 1999), 5. For the original Hebrew collection, see Ra'yah Harnik *Shirim le-Guni* (Tel Aviv, 1983).

CHAPTER 29

251 Micah paid homage: Jon D. Levenson, *The Death and Resurrection of the Beloved Son: The Transformation of Child Sacrifice in Judaism and Christianity* (New Haven, Conn., 1993), 10–11.

Index

PERMISSIONS ACKNOWLEDGMENTS

Grateful acknowledgment is made to the following for permission to reprint previously published material:

Alfred A. Knopf: Excerpt from "Of Mere Being" from *The Collected Poems of Wallace Stevens* by Wallace Stevens, copyright © 1954 by Wallace Stevens and renewed 1982 by Holly Stevens. Reprinted by permission of Alfred A. Knopf, a division of Random House, Inc.

Alicia Ostriker: Excerpt from "Story of Abraham" by Alicia Ostriker. Reprinted by permission of the author.

Bob Dylan Music Company: Excerpt from "Highway 61 Revisited" by Bob Dylan. Copyright © 1965 by Warner Bros. Inc.; renewed 1993 by Special Rider Music. Reprinted by permission of Bob Dylan Music Company.

Hana Amichai: Excerpt from "The Real Hero" from *Yehuda Amichai: A Life or Poetry, 1948–1994* by Yehuda Amichai, translated by Benjamin Harshav and Barbara Harshav. Reprinted by permission of the Estate of Yehuda Amichai, as administered by Hana Amichai.

Hebrew Union College Press: Excerpt from the poem "The Life of Sarah" by Benjamin Galai, and the poem "I Will Not Offer" by Ra'aya Harnik, translated by Ruth Kartun-Blum from *Profane Scriptures: Reflections on the Dialogue with the Bible in Modern Hebrew Poetry* by Ruth Kartun-Blum. Reprinted by permission of Hebrew Union College Press.

Indiana University Press: Excerpt from "Where Does This Wood in My Hand Come From?" by Isaac Lamdan, translated by Ruth Kartun-Blum in *Prooftexts* Vol. 8, No. 3. Excerpt from the poem "This Idiot, Issac" by Yitzhak Laor, translated by Sagi, from the essay "The Meaning of the Akedah in Israeli Culture and Jewish Tradition" in *Israel Studies* Vol. 3, No. 1. Reprinted by permission of Indiana University Press as administered by Copyright Clearance Center.

National Association of Professors of Hebrew: Excerpt from "'Az Terem'— A Piyyut" by Yohanan ha-Cohen, translated by Abraham I. Shafir. This translation originally published in *Hebrew Studies* 45 (2004). Reprinted by permission of the National Association of Professors of Hebrew.

Stanford University Press: Excerpt from *The Labor of Life: Selected Plays* by Hanoch Levin, translated and edited by Barbara Harshav. Copyright © 2003 by the Board of Trustees of the Leland Stanford Jr. University. All rights reserved. Reprinted by permission of Stanford University Press, www.sup.org.

University Press of America: Excerpt from the poem "Abraham Had Three Sons" by Yehuda Amichai, translated by Tova Forti, from the essay "The Topos of the Binding of Isaac in Modern Hebrew Poetry" by Tova Forti. Excerpt from the poem "A Request" by Chava Cohen-Pinchas; excerpt from the poem "In the Beginnings" by Yehudit Kafri; and excerpts from the poems "Hagar" and "Isaac" by Shin Shifrah, all translated by Irit Aharony and from the essay "The Outcry, Question, and the Silence" by Irit Aharony. These two essays published in *Unbinding the Binding of Isaac,* edited by Mishael M. Caspi and John T. Greene. Reprinted by permission of the University Press of America.

W. W. Norton & Company, Inc.: Excerpt from *The Five Books of Moses: A Translation with Commentary,* translated by Robert Alter. Copyright © 2004 by Robert Alter. Reprinted by permission of W. W. Norton & Company, Inc.

Yitzhak Laor: Excerpt from "This Idiot, Isaac" (Late Version) by Yitzhak Laor, translated from the Hebrew by James E. Goodman. Reprinted by permission of the author.

ABOUT THE AUTHOR

JAMES GOODMAN IS a professor at Rutgers University, Newark, where he teaches history and creative writing. He is the author of two previous books, including *Stories of Scottsboro,* which was a finalist for the Pulitzer Prize. He lives in New York.